Principles of Data Management

Facilitating Information Sharing

The British Computer Society

BCS is the leading professional body for the IT industry. With members in over 100 countries, BCS is the professional and learned society in the field of computers and information systems.

BCS is responsible for setting standards for the IT profession. It is also leading the change in public perception and appreciation of the economic and social importance of professionally managed IT projects and programmes. In this capacity, the society advises, informs and persuades industry and government on successful IT implementation.

IT is affecting every part of our lives and that is why BCS is determined to promote IT as the profession of the 21st century.

Joining BCS

BCS qualifications, products and services are designed with your career plans in mind. We not only provide essential recognition through professional qualifications but also offer many other useful benefits to our members at every level.

BCS membership demonstrates your commitment to professional development. It helps to set you apart from other IT practitioners and provides industry recognition of your skills and experience. Employers and customers increasingly require proof of professional qualifications and competence. Professional membership confirms your competence and integrity and sets an independent standard that people can trust. Professional Membership (MBCS) is the pathway to Chartered IT Professional (CITP) Status.

www.bcs.org/membership

Further Information

Further information about BCS can be obtained from: BCS, First Floor, Block D, North Star House, North Star Avenue, Swindon SN2 1FA, UK.

Telephone: 0845 300 4417 (UK only) or + 44 (0)1793 417 424 (overseas)

Email: customerservice@hq.bcs.org.uk

Web: www.bcs.org

Principles of Data Management

Facilitating Information Sharing

Keith Gordon

BCS

The British Computer Society
Publishing and Information Products
First Floor, Block D
North Star House
North Star Avenue
Swindon
SN2 1FA
UK

www.bcs.org

ISBN 978-1-902505-84-8

British Cataloguing in Publication Data.
A CIP catalogue record for this book is available at the British Library.

All trademarks, registered names etc. acknowledged in this publication are to be the property of their respective owners.

Disclaimer:
The views expressed in this book are those of the author and do not necessarily reflect the views of the British Computer Society except where explicitly stated as such.
Although every care has been taken by the authors and the British Computer Society in the preparation of the publication, no warranty is given by the authors or the British Computer Society as publisher as to the accuracy or completeness of the information contained within it and neither the authors nor the British Computer Society shall be responsible or liable for any loss or damage whatsoever arising by virtue of such information or any instructions or advice contained within this publication or by any of the aforementioned.

 captured, authored, published, delivered and managed in XML
CAPDM Limited, Edinburgh, Scotland   **www.capdm.com**

Printed and bound in England by Antony Rowe Ltd, Chippenham, Wiltshire

100507098X

There is nothing more difficult to take in hand, more perilous to conduct, or more uncertain in its success, than to take the lead in the introduction of a new order of things.

Niccolo Machiavelli (1469–1527)

The beginning of wisdom is the definition of terms.

Socrates (470–399 BC)

Data analysis is a very useful tool for efficient database design. It is much less useful as a means of identifying information requirements (especially where these are 'fuzzy' and unstructured), or in allowing different viewpoints to be taken into consideration. Too often based on an analysis of current situations, data analysis - in the extreme case - is a great way of encapsulating organisational ineffectiveness in the resultant database!

Professor Robert Galliers (1947–)

Contents

Figures and tables

About the author

Keith Gordon was a professional soldier for 38 years, joining the Army straight from school at 16 and retiring on his 55th birthday. During his service he had a number of technical, educational and managerial appointments and gained a Higher National Certificate in Electrical and Electronic Engineering, a Certificate in Education from the University of London Institute of Education, a BA from the Open University and an MSc from Cranfield Institute of Technology. From 1992 until his retirement in 1998, he was first a member of and then head of the Army's data management team.

He is now an independent consultant and lecturer specialising in data management and business analysis. As well as developing and teaching commercial courses, he is also a tutor for the Open University.

He is a Chartered Member of the British Computer Society and a Member of the Chartered Institute of Personnel and Development.

He holds the Diploma in Business Systems Development specialising in Data Management from the Information Systems Examination Board (ISEB) and he is now a member of their Business Systems Development Examination Panel.

He is the secretary of the Data Management Specialist Group of the British Computer Society and is both a founder member and current committee member of the UK chapter of DAMA International, the worldwide association of data management professionals.

Foreword

The author of this book is a soldier through and through – but he also has a comprehensive understanding of the principles of data management and is a highly skilled professional educator. This rather unusual blend of experience makes this book very special.

Data management can be seen as a chore best left to people with no imagination but Keith Gordon taught me that it can be a matter of life and death.

We all know that any collective enterprise must have records that are both reasonably accurate and readily accessible. In a commercial operation, failures in data management can lead to bankruptcy. In a public service it can put the lives of thousands of people at risk and waste public money on a grand scale. For a soldier in the heat of battle, any weakness in the availability, quality or timeliness of information can lead to a poor decision that may result in disaster.

So what has this to do with the 'principles of data management'? It serves as a reminder that a computer application is only as good as the data on which it depends.

It is common for the development of computer systems to start from the desired facilities and work backwards to identify the objects involved and so to the data by which these objects are described. One bad result of this approach is that the data resource gets skewed by the design of specific facilities that it is required to support.

When the business decides that these facilities have to be changed, the data resource must be modified. Does this matter? Some people would say 'Oh, it's easy enough to add another column to a table – no problem.' But these are the same people that get bogged down in the soul-destroying tasks of data fill and the mapping of one database onto another.

There is another way. We don't have to treat data design as a minor detail understood only by the programmers of a single system. An enterprise can choose to treat its data as a vital corporate asset and take appropriate steps to ensure that it is fit for purpose. To do this it must draw on the body of practical wisdom that has been built up by those large organisations that have already taken this message to heart. The British Army is one such organisation and it was Keith Gordon that made this happen.

The big issue here is how to ensure that the records on which an enterprise depends remain valid and useful beyond the life of individual systems and facilities. This requires good design resting on sound principles validated through extensive practical experience. We live in a changing world where new demands for information are arising all the time. Whether this is due to new technology, new social problems or the pressures of competition, these new demands cannot be met by creating yet more stove-pipe systems.

The goal we should aim at is for all data to be captured in digital form once only, as close as possible to the time and place of the observations, decisions and results that it is required to reflect. Once captured it should then be stored and distributed in such a manner that it can be made readily available to any person or system with a legitimate 'need to know' while remaining safe from loss, damage or theft.

The tricks of the trade through which the best practitioners contrive to bring this about are well documented in this book. I commend it to all people who seek to understand what is involved as well as those who aspire to develop the necessary skills.

Harry Ellis FBCS CITP
Independent consultant and member of W3C
Little Twitchen
Devon, UK

Glossary

Access control The ability to manage which users or groups of users have the privilege to create, read, update or delete data that is held in a database.

Attribute Any detail that serves to qualify, identify, classify, quantify or express the state of a relation or an entity.

Boyce–Codd normal form (BCNF) In relational data analysis, a relation is in Boyce–Codd normal form if every determinant is a candidate key.

CASE Acronym for Computer Aided Software Engineering – a combination of software tools that assist computer development staff to engineer and maintain software systems, normally within the framework of a structured method.

Column The logical structure within a table of a relational database management system (RDBMS) that corresponds to the attribute in the relational model of data.

Conceptual data model A detailed model that captures the overall structure of organisational data while being independent of any database management system or other implementation consideration – it is normally represented using entities, relationships and attributes with additional business rules and constraints that define how the data is to be used.

Corporate data model A conceptual data model whose scope extends beyond one application system.

Data A re-interpretable representation of information in a formalised manner suitable for communication, interpretation or processing.

Data administration A role in data management concerned with mechanisms for the definition, quality control and accessibility of an organisation's data.

Data dictionary Software in which metadata is stored, manipulated and defined – a data dictionary is normally associated with a tool used to support software engineering.

Data management A corporate service which helps with the provision of information services by controlling or co-ordinating the definitions and usage of reliable and relevant data.

Data mining The process of finding significant, previously unknown, and potentially valuable knowledge hidden in data.

Data model (i) An abstract, self-contained logical definition of the data structures and associated operators that make up the abstract machine with which users interact (such as the relational model of data). (ii) A model of the persistent data of some enterprise (such as an entity–relationship model of data required to support the human resources department of Jameson Wholesale Limited – the example used in Chapter 2).

Data modelling The task of developing a data model that represents the persistent data of some enterprise.

Data owner (i) The owner of a data definition is the person in the organisation who has the authority to say that this data should be held and that this definition is the appropriate definition for the data. (ii) The owner of a data value is the person or organisation that has authority to change that value.

Data profiling A set of techniques for searching through data looking for potential errors and anomalies, such as similar data with different spellings, data outside boundaries and missing values.

Data quality The state of completeness, validity, consistency, timeliness and accuracy that makes data appropriate for a specific use.

Data recovery Restoring a database to a state that is known to be correct after a failure.

Data security Protecting the database against unauthorised users.

Data steward The person who maintains a data definition on behalf of the owner of the data definition.

Data warehouse A specialised database containing consolidated historical data drawn from a number of existing databases to support strategic decision making.

Database (i) An organised way of keeping records in a computer system. (ii) A collection of data files under the control of a database management system.

Database administration A role in data management concerned with the management and control of the software used to access physical data.

Database management system (DBMS) A software application that is used to create, maintain and provide controlled access to databases.

Datatype   A constraint on a data value that specifies its intrinsic nature, such as numeric, alphanumeric, date.

Discretionary access control (DAC)   Access control where the users who are granted access rights are allowed to propagate those rights to other users.

Domain   A pool of values from which an attribute must take its value – a domain provides a set of business validation rules, format constraints and other properties for one or more attributes that may exist as a list of specific values, as a range of values, as a set of qualifications, or any combination of these.

Enterprise architecture   A process of understanding the different elements that make up the enterprise, such as the people, the information, the processes and the communications, and how those elements interrelate.

Enterprise resource planning (ERP) software   A software package that provides a single integrated database that is planned to meet an organisation's entire data needs for the management of its resources.

Entity   In a conceptual data model, a named thing of significance about which information needs to be held in support of business operations.

First normal form (1NF)   In relational data analysis, a relation is in first normal form if all the values taken by the attributes of that relation are atomic or scalar values – the attributes are single-valued or, alternatively, there are no repeating groups of attributes.

Foreign key   One or more attributes in a relation (or columns in a table) that implement a many-to-one relationship that the relation (or table) has with another relation (or table) or with itself.

HTML   Acronym for HyperText Markup Language – the markup language used to convey the way that a document is presented by a web browser.

IEC   Acronym for the International Electrotechnical Commission – collaborates with ISO in the development of international standards for information systems.

Information   (i) Something communicated to a person. (ii) Knowledge concerning objects, such as facts, events, things, processes, or ideas, including concepts, that have a particular meaning within a certain context.

Information management   The function of managing information as an enterprise resource, including planning, organising and staffing, and leading, directing, and controlling information.

Information resource management   The concept that information is a major corporate resource and must be managed using the same basic principles used to manage other assets.

Information system   A collection of manual and automated components that manages a specific information resource.

ISO   Acronym for the International Organization for Standardization – collaborates with IEC in the development of international standards for information systems.

Mandatory access control (MAC)   Access control where access rights cannot be changed by the users.

Metadata   Data about data – that is, data describing the structure, content or use of some other data.

Multi-level security   The ability of a computer system to process information with different security levels, to permit access by users with different security clearances, and to prevent users from obtaining access to information for which they do not have authorised access.

Multimedia data   Data representing documents, audio (sound), still images (pictures) and moving images (video).

Normal form   A state of a relation that can be determined by applying simple rules regarding dependencies to that relation.

Normalisation   Another name for relational data analysis.

Object orientation   A software-development strategy based on the concept that systems should be built from a collection of reusable components called objects that encompass both data and functionality.

ODMG   Acronym for the Object Data Management Group, a body that has produced a specification for object-oriented databases.

OLAP   Acronym for online analytical processing – a set of techniques that can be applied to data to support strategic decision making.

OLTP   Acronym for online transactional processing – data processing that supports operational procedures.

Primary key   The set of mandatory attributes in a relation (or mandatory columns in a table) that is used to enforce uniqueness of tuples (or rows).

RDBMS   Acronym for relational database management system – a database management system whose logical constructs are derived from the relational model of data. Most relational database management systems available are based on the SQL database language and have the table as their principal logical construct.

Relation   The basic structure in the relational model of data – formally a set of tuples, but informally visualised as a table with rows and columns.

Relational data analysis   A technique of transforming complex data structures into simple, stable data structures that obey the rules of relational data design, leading to increased flexibility and reduced data duplication and redundancy – also known as normalisation.

Relational model of data   A model of data that has the relation as its main logical construct.

Relationship   In a conceptual data model, an association between two entities, or between one entity and itself.

Repository   Software in which metadata is stored, manipulated and defined – a repository is normally associated with a corporate data management initiative.

Repository administration   A role in data management concerned with the management and control of the software in which 'information about information' is stored, manipulated and defined.

Schema   A description of the overall logical structure of a database expressed in a data definition language (such as the data definition component of SQL).

Second normal form (2NF)   In relational data analysis, a relation is in second normal form if it is in first normal form and every non-key attribute is fully functionally dependent on the primary key – there are no part-key dependencies.

SQL   Originally, SQL stood for structured query language. Now, the letters SQL have no meaning attributed to them. SQL is the database language defined in the ISO/IEC 9075 set of international standards, the latest edition of which was published in 2003. The language contains the constructs necessary for data definition, data querying and data manipulation. Most vendors of relational database management systems use a version of SQL that approximates to that specified in the standards.

Structured data   Data that has enforced composition to specified datatypes and relationships and is managed by technology that allows for querying and reporting.

Table   The logical structure used by a relational database management system (RDBMS) that corresponds to the relation in the relational model of data – the table is the main structure in SQL.

Third normal form (3NF)   In relational data analysis, a relation is in third normal form if it is in second normal form and no transitive dependencies exist.

Tuple   In the relational model of data, the construct that is equivalent to a row in a table – it contains all the attribute values for each instance represented by the relation.

Unified Modeling Language (UML)   A set of diagramming notations for systems analysis and design based on object-oriented concepts.

Unstructured data   Computerised information which does not have a data structure that is easily readable by a machine, including audio, video and unstructured text such as the body of a word-processed document – effectively this is the same as multimedia data.

XML   Acronym for eXtensible Markup Language – the markup language used to convey the definition, structure and meaning of the information contained in a document.

Preface

I think I first decided that I wanted to be a soldier when I was about three years of age. In 1960, aged 16 and with a slack handful of GCE 'O' Levels, I joined the Royal Armoured Corps as a junior soldier. I suppose I thought that driving tanks would be fun, but my time with the Royal Armoured Corps was short-lived and, in 1962, I joined the Royal Corps of Signals and trained as an electronics technician. I learned to repair and maintain a range of electronics equipment that used logic AND, OR, NAND and NOR gates, multivibrators, registers and MOD-2 adders, all of which are the building blocks of the central processing units at the heart of computers. Nine years later, I attended a course that turned me into a technical supervisor. This course extended my knowledge to include the whole range of telecommunications equipment. I now knew about radio and telephony as well as being the proud owner of a Higher National Certificate in Electrical and Electronic Engineering. On this course we also met a computer, an early Elliot mainframe, and learned to program it. After this course I found myself in Germany with a brilliant job, responsible for the 'system engineering' of the communications for an armoured brigade headquarters. Not only was I ensuring that my technicians kept the equipment on the road, but I was also designing and having my staff build the internal communications of the headquarters – which involved the interconnection of about a dozen vehicles.

A career change happened in 1978 when, following a year's teacher training, I was commissioned into the Royal Army Educational Corps. I spent the next nine years in classrooms in Aberdeen, London, the Falkland Islands (not sure that some of the places where I taught when there could be called classrooms, but...) and Beaconsfield. In Beaconsfield, I taught maths, electronics and science; in the other jobs, I taught a mixture of literacy, numeracy, current affairs and management. It was these teaching jobs that gave me my greatest sense of personal satisfaction. I also extended my knowledge of computing by studying for a BA with the Open University. 1987 saw me getting deeper into computing by studying for an MSc in the Design of Information Systems, where I was introduced to databases and structured methods. I left the course thinking I knew about data and data modelling. I now know that I had hardly scraped the surface.

In 1992, after two more educational jobs, I was offered a job in 'data management'. Well, I knew about 'data' and I had taught 'management' so, despite never having before heard the two words used together, I thought it sounded like my thing. I may have been influenced by the belief that the job would involve an office in London which was close enough to home to commute daily. It came as shock to find that the office was in Blandford, where I had already served for over seven years during my time in the Signals, and it severely disrupted my home life. But this was nothing unusual; disruption of home life is a substantial part of the lot of a soldier.

The Army had commissioned one of the large consultancy companies to conduct a major study into its information systems. This study had recommended that the Army should have a data management team and this team came together in 1992. There were five of us: four officers and a civil servant. All we knew was that data management was to be good for the Army. Nowhere was there a description of what data management was. So we were in a highly desirable position: we had to work out what we had to do. I think this period provided me with the greatest technical challenge of my Army career. What I was aware of was that the Army had a large number of information systems, all independently designed, and it was virtually impossible to share information between them. And the Army was also undertaking a large programme of information systems procurement, in some important cases into areas that had not previously had information systems support. To make the Army more effective on the battlefield and, at the same time, to reduce our casualties, it was vital that the information systems could share information. The Army had a vision of a single, fully integrated information system. This would not, of course, be a single system, but a federation of systems that appeared to the user as a single system. This could not be achieved without data management.

Thus began my interest in data management. Three years later I was promoted and became the head of the team until I retired from the Army in 1998. I now work as an independent consultant and lecturer. As well as teaching commercial courses in data management and business analysis, I have also been a tutor with the Open University since 1999, tutoring database and general computing courses in the undergraduate and postgraduate programmes. My data management journey continues.

I believe that all medium to large organisations, commercial and government, need a corporate data management service. I see many instances where the inability to share information between information systems leads to mistakes and misunderstanding, which in turn leads to poor customer service (even government departments have customers) and extra expenditure. These organisations cannot really afford to be without data management, yet very few recognise the problems, let alone that data management is the solution. Regrettably, this ignorance exists not only amongst business managers; it is rare to find an IT or IS manager who sees the need for data management. In fact most, like me 14 years ago, have never heard the two words 'data' and 'management' used together. I hope that this book goes some way to bring data management to the attention of those who really ought to know about it.

This book, therefore, represents the knowledge I have gained over the last 14 years. Some of this knowledge came from doing the job, some from the people I have taught and some from the many books sitting on my bookshelves, most of which are listed either as specific references or as suggestions for further reading.

I owe a debt of gratitude to a number of people who have helped me on my data management journey. Ian Nielsen, Martin Richley, Duncan Broad and Tim Scarlett were my colleagues in that original Army data management team who shared those many hours around a whiteboard trying to work out what it was all about. There were others involved as well. David Gradwell and Ken Allen were our first consultants, introducing us to the mysteries of metadata models and naming standards. Later on when we started data modelling in earnest we had the benefit of the experience of Harry Ellis and Ron Segal (who is now in New Zealand). I learnt masses from working with all of these people and I think we were all (including our experienced consultants) on a learning curve. At the start of my data management journey, I attended a Principles of Data Administration course run by Chris Newton for Stehle Associates. This course set data management and data administration in context. It is Chris's Principles of Data Administration course that is the skeleton on which I have built my own Principles of Data Management course which I now deliver for Stehle Associates. Dave Beaumont, the principal of Stehle Associates, has encouraged me to develop data management courses and he and I have spent many hours discussing data management issues. He has also kindly reviewed early drafts of some of the chapters of this book. Thanks too to Ian Sinclair, one of my colleagues on the committee of the UK chapter of DAMA International, who reviewed the chapter on data quality; to Matthew West, who reviewed the appendix on generic data models; and to Tony Jenkins who has reviewed the whole book and provided many useful recommendations for its improvement. I would also like to thank the many people I have not mentioned but whom I have either worked with or discussed data management issues with over the last 14 years. I have learnt from you all.

Particular thanks are due to Matthew Flynn, Suzanna Marsh and Florence Leroy of the British Computer Society who have been instrumental in getting this book into print.

Finally, a massive thank you to my wife, Vivienne, for her unstinting support over the last 40 years. Being a soldier's wife for 32 years was never going to be a picnic and she had a right to expect things to be more relaxed and easier when I retired. Instead, with consulting, teaching and, now, the writing of this book, I have neglected her far more than I should have done and still she is there looking after me.

Keith Gordon
High Wycombe
January 2007

Introduction

This book is called *Principles of Data Management* but it is really about having the policies and procedures in place within an organisation so that the various information systems that the organisation uses to support its activities can provide high-quality information to their users, even if that information did not originate in the information system with which the user is currently interacting. For this to happen, the organisation's information systems must be able to share information. If there is no automatic sharing of information between the information systems, some departments may be kept in the dark about what is going on in other departments and information may have to be keyed into more than one system. Neither of these situations helps the organisation's effectiveness or efficiency.

The key to the provision of high-quality information and the sharing of information between information systems is to have an effective corporate data management policy in place. Yet very few senior business and IT or IS managers have heard of data management, let alone have an effective data management policy in place.

This book is aimed at three audiences. First, there are the data management practitioners themselves. They are presumably already committed to data management but may be struggling to find all the information that they need to set their role in the wider business context or to perform the myriad tasks that fall within the scope of data management.

This book will not have all the answers, but it may provide an indication of what the answer should be and, perhaps, where to go and look for the answer. Secondly, there are the IT or IS managers who have heard of data management, are probably aware that it might be a good idea, but are not sure what it involves or what the implications of having a corporate data management function will be. Maybe they already have a data management team working within their department but are not sure what that team does or what it should do. The third group who should read this book – or, at least, the sections that are not too technical – are the business managers who want to understand why they are being asked to pay for a team of data managers who do not look as if they are going to deliver the much-sought-after return on investment within the current budgetary cycle.

For the data management practitioners, I commend the data management qualifications offered by the Information Systems Examination Board of the British Computer Society. At the time of writing, two qualifications are provided, a Certificate in Data Management Essentials and a Diploma in Data Management, but it is anticipated that additional certificates will become available. The certificate level is examined by a short written examination and the diploma level is examined by an oral examination. This book covers the existing syllabus for the Certificate in Data Management Essentials as well as providing additional material for anyone proposing to take the Diploma in Data Management examination.

So, to meet the requirements of practitioners, IT or IS managers and business managers, this book covers the whole range of data management activities. There are 12 chapters and eight appendices:

- Chapter 1 – Data and the Enterprise – introduces the idea that information is a key business resource. It starts by exploring the relationship between information and data. We then move on to a discussion of the importance of the quality of the data that underlies the information. If the quality of data is important what are the common problems with data? Why must we take an enterprise-wide view of data? The chapter concludes by highlighting that the management of data is a business issue and not a technical issue.

- Chapter 2 – Database Development – is a long, largely technical, chapter that provides an explanation of how the databases at the heart of all information systems are designed. It introduces the concepts of database architecture and then provides examples of two analysis techniques – conceptual data modelling and relational data analysis – and how these lead to a physical database design.

- Chapter 3 – What is Data Management? – first considers the problems encountered without data management then introduces the scope of the responsibilities of data management. We then look at the three separate roles within data management – data administration, database administration and repository administration. We end this chapter by summarising the benefits of data management.

- Chapter 4 – Corporate Data Modelling – looks at data modelling when applied to an enterprise's total data requirements as opposed to being applied to the smaller set of requirements that are to be met by a single information system. We explain why corporate data models are required and then introduce some more data modelling concepts. We discuss where corporate data models should lie on the continuum from abstract to detailed. We then suggest how the development of a corporate data model may be approached and introduce six principles to be applied to the development of corporate data models.

- Chapter 5 – Data Definition and Naming Conventions – introduces the key data definition and naming 'standards' used by data managers. We discuss the principles underlying these standards and provide some examples.

- Chapter 6 – Metadata – introduces the concept of 'data about data' and the way that it is used.

- Chapter 7 – Data Quality – provides an overview of this important area. We define the term 'data quality', we look at how poor-quality data can affect a business, we consider what causes poor-quality data and we look at techniques for improving data quality. The fact that the achievement of data quality requires an ongoing procedural and cultural change, and not just a one-off project, is stressed.

- Chapter 8 – Data Accessibility – brings together in one chapter the related issues of data security, protecting the database against unauthorised users, data integrity, protecting the database against authorised users, and data recovery, bringing the database to a usable consistent state after a failure.

- Chapter 9 – Database Administration – provides an overview of the roles and responsibilities of database administrators, particularly the monitoring and tuning of the performance of a database.

- Chapter 10 – Repository Administration – looks at the management and control of the software in which 'information about information' is stored, manipulated and defined.

- Chapter 11 – The Management of Data Management – describes the knowledge and skills required for each of the three data management roles: data administration, database administration and repository administration. We then discuss where in the organisational hierarchy the data management function and its subordinate elements should be placed.

- Chapter 12 – Industry Trends and their Effects on Data Management – covers a number of fads, advances and developments, including the recent developments in SQL. Data management practitioners should not only be aware of these trends, but should ensure that their organisations have policies in place to take account of these developments. The trends considered are:

    + the use of software application packages, such as accounting packages;

    + distributed data and databases;

    + data warehousing and data mining;

    + object orientation and databases;

+ multimedia databases;

+ data and web technology.

- Appendix A – Comparison of Data Modelling Notations – looks at some alternatives to the data modelling notation used throughout the book.

- Appendix B – Hierarchical and Network Databases – looks at two popular pre-relational database models and their implementations.

- Appendix C – Generic Data Models – looks at why data models become generic (or abstract) and the advantages and disadvantages of using generic data models as the basis for database design.

- Appendix D – An Example of a Data Naming Convention – provides a complete example of a data naming convention.

- Appendix E – Metadata Models – looks at the data models that underpin data dictionaries and repositories.

- Appendix F – A Data Mining Example – provides a worked example of just one of the many data-mining techniques that are available.

- Appendix G – HTML and XML – looks in more detail at these two key 'technologies' used with web technology.

- Appendix H – XML and Relational Databases – looks at the support for XML provided in the SQL standard.

1 Data and the Enterprise

This chapter introduces the concepts of information and data and discusses why they are important business resources within the enterprise. The problems caused by data which is of poor quality or is inconsistent are introduced.

INFORMATION IS A KEY BUSINESS RESOURCE

When asked to identify the key resources in any business, most business people will readily name money, people, buildings and equipment. This is because these are the resources that senior business managers spend most time managing. This means that in most businesses there is a clear investment by the business in the management of these resources. The fact that these resources are easy to manage and that the management processes applied to these resources can be readily understood by the layman means that it is seen to be worthwhile investing in their management. It is usually easy to assess how much the business spends on managing these resources and the return that is expected from that investment.

But there is a key resource missing from that list. That missing resource is 'information'. Without information, the business cannot function. Indeed, the only resource that is readily available to senior management is information. All important decisions made within an enterprise are based on the information that is available to the managers.

Despite its importance, most business people do not recognise information as a key business resource. Because of its association with technology (with 'information technology' having become in effect one word, generally with more emphasis on the 'technology' than on the 'information'), information is seen as something mystical that is managed on behalf of the business by the specialist Information Technology or Information Systems department. The management of information is seen, therefore, as something requiring special skills beyond the grasp of the layman. It is very difficult to determine how much the business spends on managing information or, indeed, the return it can expect from that expenditure.

Information is a business resource that is used in every aspect of a business: it supports the day-to-day operational tasks and activities; it enables the routine administration and management of the business; and it supports strategic decision making and future planning.

For a supermarket chain, the operational tasks and activities include the processing of customers' purchases through the electronic point-of-sale system and the ordering of goods from suppliers; for a high street bank, they include the handling of customers' cash and cheques by the cashiers, the processing of transactions through ATMs and the assessment of the credit status of a customer who is requesting a loan; for an online book 'store', they include the collection of customers' orders, the selection and dispatch of the books and the production of a customer profile enabling the 'store' to make recommendations to customers as they log on to the website.

For all types of business, information in various forms is routinely used by managers to monitor the efficiency and effectiveness of the business. Some of this information comes in the form of standard reports. Other information may come to the managers as a result of their ad-hoc questions, maybe directed to their subordinates but, increasingly, directed to the information systems that support the business.

All businesses need to plan for their future and take high-level, strategic decisions. In some cases the consequence of making an incorrect strategic decision could be the ultimate collapse of the business. To carry out this future planning and strategic decision making, the senior management of the business relies on information about the historic performance of the business, the projected future performance of the business (and this, to a large extent will be based on an extrapolation of the historic information into the future), their customers' present and future needs, and the performance of their competitors. Information relating to the external environment, particularly the economy, is also important. For a supermarket chain, these decisions may include whether to diversify into, say, clothing; for a high street bank, they may include the closure of a large number of branches; and for an online book 'store' whether to open new operations overseas.

Information is important, therefore, at every level in the business. It is important that the information is managed and presented in a consistent, accurate, timely and easily understood way.

THE RELATIONSHIP BETWEEN INFORMATION AND DATA

Wisdom, knowledge, information and data are all closely related through being on the same continuum – from wisdom, to knowledge, then to information and, finally, to data. This book is about managing data to provide useful information, so we will concentrate on the relationship between information and data.

An often-heard definition of information is that it is 'data placed in context'. This implies that some information is the result of the translation of some data using some processing activity, and some communication protocol, into an agreed format that is identifiable to the user. In other words, if data has some meaning attributed to it, it becomes information.

For example, what do the figures '190267' represent? Presented as '19/02/67', it would probably make sense to assume that they represent a date. Presented on a screen with other details of an employee of a company, such as name and address, in a field that is labelled 'Date of Birth' the meaning becomes obvious. Similarly, presented as '190267 metres', it immediately becomes obvious that this is a long distance between two places but, for this to really make sense, the start point and the end point have to be specified as well as, maybe, a number of intermediate points specifying the route.

Whilst these examples demonstrate the relationship between data and information, they do not provide a clear definition of either data or information.

There are many definitions of data available in dictionaries and textbooks but, in essence, most of these definitions basically say that data is 'facts, events, transactions and similar that have been recorded'. Furthermore, as I pointed out earlier, the definition of information is usually based on this definition of data. Information is seen as data in context or data that has been processed and communicated so that it can be used by its recipient.

The idea that data is a set of recorded facts is found in many books on computing. However, this concept of data as recorded facts is used beyond the computing and information systems communities. It is, for example, also the concept used by statisticians. Indeed, the definition of data given in Webster's 1828 Dictionary – published well before the introduction of computers – is:

> Things given, or admitted; quantities, principles or facts given, known, or admitted, by which to find things or results unknown.

However, starting the development of our definitions by looking at data first appears to be starting at the wrong point. It is information that is important to the business, and it is there that our definitions, and our discussion about the relationship between information and data, should really start.

We start by considering the everyday usage of information – something communicated to a person – and, with that, we can have a definition of data that is relevant to the theme of this book. Data is 'a re-interpretable representation of information in a formalised manner suitable for communication, interpretation or processing' (ISO/IEC 2382-1, 1993). There is a note attached to this definition in the ISO/IEC standard which states that data can be processed by human or automatic means; so this definition covers all forms of data but, importantly, includes data held in information systems used to support the activities of an organisation at all levels: operational, managerial and strategic.

Figure 1.1 provides an overview of the relationship between data and information in the context of a computerised information system. The user of the system extracts the required information from their overall knowledge and inputs the information into the system. As it enters the system, it is converted into data so that it can be stored and processed. When another system user requires that information, the data is interpreted – that is, it has meaning applied to it – so that can be of use to the user.

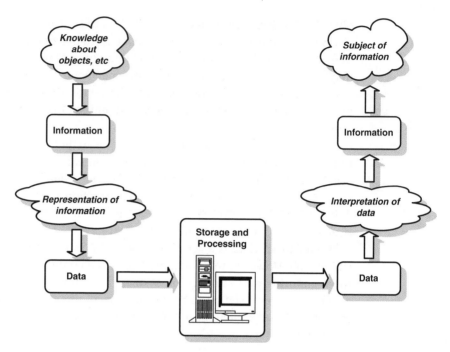

FIGURE 1.1   *The relationship between data and information*

For most of this book, we consider data stored in a database. This is often called 'structured data'. However, it must be understood that a considerable proportion of an organisation's information may be held in information systems as 'unstructured data' – in word-processed documents, drawings, etc.

THE IMPORTANCE OF THE QUALITY OF DATA

Since information is an important resource for any organisation, information presented to users must be of high quality. The information must be up to date, complete, sufficiently accurate for the purpose it is required, unambiguously understood, consistent and available when it is required.

It is essential that information is up to date. When customers buy their shopping at the supermarket they need to be charged the current price for the items they have bought, not the price that was current yesterday before the start of today's cut-price promotion. Similarly, managers reordering stock need to be aware of the current, not last week's, stock levels in order to ensure that they are not over or under-stocked.

Only when the information available is complete can appropriate decisions be made. When a bank is considering a request for a loan from a customer, it is important that full details of the customer's financial position is known to safeguard both the bank's and the customer's interests.

Information on which important decisions are made must be accurate; any errors in the potential loan customer's financial information could lead to losses for the bank, for example. Whilst it is important that information is accurate, it is possible for the information to be 'too accurate', leading to the information being misinterpreted. Earlier I quoted '190267 metres' as the distance between two points, say London and Birmingham. But the figure '190267' implies that this distance has been measured to the nearest metre. Is this realistic? Would it not be more appropriate to quote this figure as '190 kilometres (to the nearest 10 kilometres)'? I cannot answer that question without knowing why I need to know the distance between London and Birmingham. Information should be accurate, but only sufficiently accurate for the purpose for which it is required.

To be accurate from a user perspective, information must also be unambiguously understood. There should be no doubt as to whether the distance the user is being given is the straight-line distance or the distance by road. The data should also be consistent. A query asking for the distance between London and Birmingham via a specified route should always come up with the same answer.

Information has to be readily available when and where it is required to be used. When it is time to reorder stock for the supermarket then the information required to decide the amount of replacement stock to be ordered has to be available on the desk of the manager making those decisions.

Information is derived from the processing of data. It is vital, therefore, that the data we process to provide the information is of good quality. Only with good-quality data can we guarantee the quality of the information. Good-quality data is data that is accurate, correct, consistent, complete and up to date. The meaning of the data must also be unambiguous.

THE COMMON PROBLEMS WITH DATA

Unfortunately, in many organisations there are some major, yet unrecognised or misunderstood, data problems. These problems are generally caused by a combination of the proliferation of duplicate, and often inconsistent, occurrences of data and the misinterpretation and misunderstanding of the data caused by the lack of a cohesive, enterprise-wide data definition regime.

Whenever it is possible for any item of information to be held as data more than once, there is a possibility of inconsistency. For example, if the addresses of customers are held in more than one place – or, more specifically, in more than one information system – and a customer informs the company that they have changed their address, there is always the danger that only one instance of the address is amended, leaving the other instances showing the old, incorrect address for that customer. This is quite a common scenario. The marketing department and the finance department may have separate information systems: the marketing department has a system to help it track customers and potential customers whilst the finance department has a completely separate system to support its invoicing and payments received accounting functions. With information systems independently designed and developed to support individual business areas or specific business processes, the duplication of data, and the consequent likelihood of inconsistency, is commonplace. Unfortunately, in most organisations, the potential for inconsistency through the duplication of data is getting worse because of the move away from centralised mainframe systems, the proliferation of separate departmental information systems and the availability of personal desktop computing power, including the provision of spreadsheet and database software.

Even where it is understood that it would be to the advantage of the organisation for information to be shared between these separate systems, this is often impossible without there being the possibility of misinterpretation or misunderstanding of the information that is shared.

In its 1994 publication 'Corporate Data Modelling', the Central Computer and Telecommunications Agency – now part of the Office of Government and Commerce – recognised that there are a number of possible reasons for sharing information. These are:

- when central reference data is used by independent operational units, such as product codes and product prices;
- when public domain datatypes are used and exchanged, for example, when publicly available statistical data sets are to be used;
- when operational results need to be collated across several profit centres, for example, to collate or compare the sales figures from stores within a supermarket chain;
- when the output from one system forms the input to another, for example, the output of a forecasting system is used by another system to determine resource and budget implications;
- when application systems performing a similar function for distinct autonomous units are required to harmonise their data to permit close collaboration, for example, the command and control systems for the police, fire and ambulance services need to 'work together' in the event of an emergency.

The sharing of information between independently designed and developed information systems is technically straightforward. It is a relatively simple matter to electronically connect two or more information systems together using a network and then to transfer data between them. The difficulties come after the data has been transferred and the receiving information system cannot interpret the data or, worse still, interprets the received data according to its understanding of the meaning of the data, but this interpretation differs from that used in the originating system. This possibility of the misinterpretation of transferred data is very common in organisations and the situation is getting worse.

This is also a consequence of the proliferation of independently designed and developed departmental or single-function information systems. At the heart of an information system is a database whose purpose is to provide persistent storage of the data. Each of these databases is designed to ensure that the data is available when required by the applications supported by that information system and, possibly, to maintain the integrity of the data within that particular database. A database is designed to provide effective and efficient support to the business area or function that the information system is being designed to support by meeting the immediate data requirements for that business area or function as they are understood by the database designer. It is very rare for a wider view of current or future data requirements to be taken.

The proliferation of departmental or function-specific information systems, each with its own database designed without recognition of wider data requirements, has led to widespread problems of data: inconsistency caused by duplication across different information systems and misinterpretation when data is shared between information systems.

AN ENTERPRISE-WIDE VIEW OF DATA

In order to improve the quality of information across an organisation, we must first understand the data that provides that information and the problems that are associated with that data. We must also look at business information needs and move the organisation to a position where the required data is made available to support the current information needs in a cost-effective manner whilst providing the flexibility to cope with future needs in a reasonable time scale. We need to consider the information needs of the whole organisation and then manage the data in such a way that it supports the organisation's total information needs.

In order to manage the organisation's data resources effectively we must first understand it. This requires more than just recognising data as being the raw material in the production of information. It implies knowledge of what data is important to the business, and where and how it is used. What functions and processes use the data? When is it created, processed and destroyed? Who is responsible for that data in all stages of its life?

It is also essential that we produce a clear and unambiguous definition of all data that the organisation uses. Such a definition must be a common view, accepted and agreed by all business areas.

Effective management of data also requires an understanding of the problems that relate to data. These problems often cross departmental boundaries and their solutions consist of both technical and organisational aspects.

Organisations vary tremendously in size and nature. A large multinational organisation tends to have different data-related problems from a small company although, even in a small company, the problems can be quite complex. The type of business may also affect the nature of the problems. A large proportion of the information systems in a finance or insurance company relate to customers or potential customers. In a manufacturing environment, however, dealing with customers is only one part of the overall business processes.

7

At the more technical level, data-related problems are affected by the types of computer system in place. Are the systems networked or distributed? Is extensive use made of personal computers? Are there multiple computer sites? And so on.

Individual departments do not necessarily perceive a given problem as having a potential impact across the whole organisation. One of the difficulties often faced by a central team responsible for managing the data for the whole organisation is bridging the gap between different departmental views. This requires patience and tact. It certainly requires authority, or access to appropriate authority, as the implementation of a solution may well involve co-operation with several managers within the organisation. Most importantly, it demands an understanding both of the information needs of the whole business and of the nature of the associated technical and organisational problems.

In reality, the problems relating to data are often very complex and affect many different areas within an organisation. Data is used in different ways by different business functions. Data can take many forms and the technologies for handling and storing data are constantly changing. Data problems do not appear in a form that enables a neatly packaged, stand-alone solution for the handling and management of data.

Recently a number of vendors have been supplying enterprise resource planning (ERP) software, which is supposed to provide a single integrated database that meets an organisation's entire data needs for the management of its resources. In general, these products do not appear to be providing the advantages claimed. Unless the organisation is prepared to replace all of its information systems in one go there will still be a need for the data held by the enterprise resource planning system to be integrated with the data held by the existing information systems that are still in use. Also, to really take advantage of enterprise resource planning software the organisation probably needs to change its business processes to conform to the processes supported by the software, and many businesses are not prepared to make these changes.

MANAGING DATA IS A BUSINESS ISSUE

We identified money, people, buildings and equipment as the key resources in any business and we added information to that list.

For all of these resources some special responsibilities exist within the organisation:

- The finance department has special responsibilities for managing the organisation's money, including the allocation of budgets, managing investments and accounting.
- The personnel department has special responsibilities for managing the organisation's employee base, including the provision of advice on legislation affecting personnel issues and the recruitment of staff.

- The estates department has special responsibilities for managing the buildings used by the organisation, including ensuring that the buildings meet legal requirements in respect of health and safety and discrimination issues, buying, selling and leasing of buildings and ensuring that the estate is adequately insured.
- The stores and maintenance department has special responsibilities for managing the organisation's equipment, including the provision of a central purchasing function, the accounting for equipment in use and the storage of equipment until it is required for use.
- The IT or IS department has special responsibility for data and information, including the physical storage, distribution, security, backup and archiving of data.

In most organisations, it is now common practice for line management to have responsibility for the day-to-day administration and management of these resources, with the specialist departments only providing specialist advice to the line management. People have to be managed on a day-to-day basis; money is allocated to budget holders to use and manage according to specific rules; buildings are run and administered; equipment is used and maintained.

Additionally, information is collected, validated and used. This is very much the responsibility of the business. All the decisions about what is collected and how it is validated are business decisions. So are the decisions about how information is to be handled and stored as data. Any data management function must, therefore, support the business. Data management is not purely a technical issue; the definition of the data to be stored should be the responsibility of the business. Most organisations are counting the cost of ineffective data management. Real business opportunities may be lost as a result of the inability to respond quickly to changing requirements. There are many situations where information exists but is not accessible in the right time frame.

In many cases the only way that information may be shared between information systems is by reading information from one screen and keying it into another system or, worse still, systems. The cost of continually rekeying information in this way is significant both in terms of the resource required to carry out this task and in potential errors through misinterpretation of the information that is to be rekeyed. Such costs impact on the business as well as on the IT or IS department, although the greater impact is on the business. Surprisingly, this approach to information sharing is still in use in some organisations in 2007.

There are many claimed benefits for having a data management function within the organisation. These benefits nearly all make sound business sense and can be recognised as such. However, not all of them can be related to direct cost savings. Consequently, it requires a degree of faith on the part of management that the end result, the benefits, will justify the costs.

The benefits split into two areas: those which are business-oriented and those which are systems-oriented. The former include cost savings through, for example, the reduction in duplicated marketing mailings and improved customer service, whilst the latter include reduced time to develop new applications, which also translates into financial savings. I firmly believe, however, that the systems-oriented benefits are a natural by-product of a business-oriented data management initiative. The reverse is not necessarily true. There may be no additional benefits to business effectiveness and efficiency if the IT or IS function implements data management in order to save on development costs.

It is relatively easy to quantify the costs of today's problems, both in financial terms and as lost business opportunities. Thus, it is possible to demonstrate relatively easily the potential benefits of reducing or even eradicating such problems and enabling the business to exploit the huge investment it has already made in data for optimum returns. It is possible to make the business case for the establishment of a data management function.

SUMMARY

In this chapter we have seen that information, an often neglected key business resource that needs to be shared across an enterprise, is developed from data. To provide quality information, data has to be properly managed. There has to be an enterprise-wide view of data, and the business, not the IT or IS function, has to take the lead in the management of data.

2 Database Development

This is a long chapter that takes a look at the complex subject of the development of databases. Some concepts are only briefly explained, whilst others are discussed in more detail. The intention is not to teach the reader how to develop a database – that would take a complete book many times the size of this one, and even then the reader would probably need help and guidance from an experienced practitioner before they could put the ideas into practice.

This chapter is here to help those who have not been involved in the development of databases to put the other material in this book in context; because of the complex nature of the subjects being discussed it may need to be read more than once. The experienced database developer can safely miss out this chapter, although they may discover some new insights by reading it.

THE DATABASE ARCHITECTURE OF AN INFORMATION SYSTEM

This section introduces the concept of a database and the software used to manage it – a database management system, commonly called a DBMS.

File systems

Before the advent of databases, any data that was required by an application program was stored in specially constructed files designed for and associated with the application programs. These file-based approaches to the storage of data presented many problems, and it was to overcome these problems that databases were developed.

Each of these files would contain many records, with each record being a collection of data values held in fields within the record. There are a number of ways of organising records within files, leading to many different methods of data access. These include sequential access, where data is accessed by searching through the file from the beginning until the data is found, and direct access, where there is a mechanism that knows the 'location' in the file of the required data and knows how to go directly to that location. Any application program has to be written for a specific file structure with a specific access method. This means that each application program becomes closely coupled to its data structure. The application program is both logically and physically dependent on the data structure; any change to the data structure of the file requires a corresponding change to the application program and, probably, any change to the application program requires a corresponding change to the data file.

The database approach

A database is an organised way of keeping records in a computer system. Databases provide a means of overcoming the problems caused by storing data in files coupled with application programs. If properly applied, the database approach manages data as a shared resource, providing both logical and physical data independence. The data still has to be stored (usually on disks these days) and that storage is in a file physically similar to those used in the old file-based approaches. The difference is that between the file and the application programs there is a suite of software called a database management system, as shown in Figure 2.1.

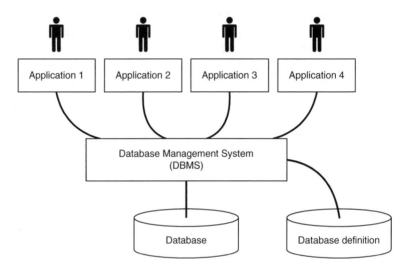

FIGURE 2.1   *A model of a database system*

This model shows a number of user processes interacting with the general-purpose database management system. It also shows that the database management system interacts with two 'datastores', physical storage areas for data in files. One datastore is the database itself, providing persistent storage of the data required by the various user processes. The other datastore contains the data definitions. The set of data definitions is generally known as a schema. The schema contains the specification of the properties of all the data in the associated database. It is used by the database management system to determine how the data in the associated database is to be processed. The schema is independent of the database management system and the user processes, and is normally expressed in terms of easily understood conceptual constructs. The data definitions are, therefore, not embedded in the application programs. This overcomes one of the main problems of the file-based approach to the storage of data.

There are a number of claimed advantages of the database approach over the file-based approaches. Assuming that databases are properly designed and used, these advantages include:

- *Data independence* – there is a layer of software, the database management system, between the users and their applications and the stored data; this layer of software insulates the users from changes to the way that data is physically stored.

- *Integration and sharing of data* – a database can store all the data needed by many different business areas so that many users from different business areas can access the same database.

- *Consistency of data* – with the data being integrated in a database, the data inconsistency problems associated with separate application-specific data files are prevented.

- *Minimal data redundancy* – with many applications sharing an integrated set of data, the redundancy of data caused by duplication is avoided; there may, however, be some planned and controlled data duplication to meet specific requirements.

- *Uniform security and integrity controls* – since the controls necessary to maintain the security and integrity of the data is handled by the database management system software, these controls are applied uniformly to all users of the database. Security and integrity are explained in more detail in Chapter 8.

- *Data accessibility and responsiveness* – within the database there may be many different ways to access any required set of data; it is even possible to answer ad-hoc queries in addition to the pre-planned queries encoded in the application programs.

- *Ease of application development and reduced program maintenance* – the application developers and those responsible for the future maintenance of those applications do not need to know and understand the way that the data is physically stored; instead, they only need to understand the conceptual constructs used in the schema.

Database management systems may be specifically developed for particular purposes, but most databases in use today are built on general-purpose database management systems. Most general-purpose database management systems on the market are based on the standard SQL database language (ISO/IEC 9075, 2003), which is itself based on the relational model of data, although it is possible to purchase database management system software based on other models of data.

Irrespective of whether the database management system software is specifically developed or general purpose, there are a number of common functions that should be provided by all database management systems. These are:

- *Data definition* – the ability to use easily understood conceptual constructs to define the way that the data is to be organised and structured within the database.

- *Constraint definition and enforcement* – the ability to define semantic constraints on the data (for example, restrictions that are to be applied to data values) and then to enforce those constraints universally.

- *Access control* – the ability to define the rights of users to access all or some of the data and to prevent access by users without the appropriate rights.
- *Data manipulation* – the ability to retrieve and update data as well as the ability to perform calculations and structuring for presentation purposes.
- *Restructuring and reorganisation* – the ability to change a database in some way, either to logically restructure – that is, to change, add or delete some element of the data structure – or to physically reorganise how the data is stored – for example, to add an index.
- *Transaction support* – the ability to ensure that a database is in a consistent state both before and after a transaction has been completed.
- *Concurrency support* – the ability to allow many user processes – and, therefore, many users – to access a database at the same time without conflict or interference.
- *Recovery* – the ability to return the database to a usable state after a hardware or software failure, including the return of the database to a consistent state if a transaction fails to complete.

The first of these functions of a database management system is the ability to define the way that the data is to be conceptually organised and structured within the database. This is the ability to define the database schema.

There are a number of ways to think of the organisation of data. In the pre-database file-based approach, the conceptual view of the data taken by the application program had to match exactly the physical structure of the file. This was often complex and the understanding was complicated by the requirement to fully understand any coding used in the file structure. These complex structures are difficult for people to visualise and understand. With a database management system, the data can be conceptually organised in a more convenient form, with the database management software taking care of the translation to and from the file format in which the data is actually stored.

If the database management system is based on the SQL database language, this conceptual view of the data is based on interrelated tables, which are a representation of the mathematical relations at the heart of the relational model of data. Each table comprises a number of columns with each column holding data of a common type. For example, an Employee table may well have columns called Staff Number and Name, amongst others. Each row of such a table holds data about a single employee.

For an object-oriented database management system, the conceptual view of the data is a series of object classes whose instances interact through the passing of messages. The Employee class may be able to respond to messages asking questions such as 'What is your staff number?' and 'What is your name?'

The three level schema architecture

In attempting to understand how a database management system works, it is useful to think in terms of a layered approach with three separate levels of schema. These are the logical (or conceptual) level, the internal (or storage) level and the external level, as shown in Figure 2.2.

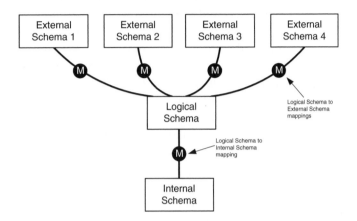

FIGURE 2.2   *The three level schema architecture*

This three level schema architecture was originally proposed by the American National Standards Institute (ANSI) Standards Planning and Requirements Committee (SPARC) in 1975. It is a theoretical concept only, but it provides a valuable insight into the way that the use of a database avoids data dependence.

The schema at the logical level is the central, and main, component of the architecture. It defines the properties of all the data. It includes the data definitions and the associated constraints, using the appropriate conceptual constructs – tables, object classes, etc. – appropriate to the database management system being used.

The schema at the internal level defines how the database is physically stored in files and how these files are accessed. The addition of indexes to speed retrieval may be viewed as an addition to the internal or storage schema.

Each schema at the external level defines the data required to support one or, occasionally, more user processes. Each schema at the external level may be viewed as a subset or an abstraction of the schema at the logical level, although it is not necessary for the same conceptual constructs to be used at both the logical and external levels. For example, the logical schema may have the relational table as its main construct, whilst one or more of the external schemas may have the object class as its main construct.

The separation between the schema at the logical level, where the data is conceptually visualised – tables and columns, object classes, etc. – and the schema at the internal level – where the way that the data is actually stored is known – provides a level of data independence that we call 'physical data independence'. It is necessary to be able to translate the conceptual constructs at the logical level to the physical file definitions at the internal level, and this translation is handled by the mapping from the schema at the logical level to the schema at the internal level. We generally say that the mapping provides the physical data independence. This separation of the two levels and the mapping between them means that the schema at the logical level is immune to changes in the schema at the internal level. Changes affecting the way that the data is physically stored (such as the addition of new indexes to speed up querying of the data or a restructuring of the file) should not require any changes to the schemas at the logical and external levels. The only additional changes required are to the mapping. The only effect, if any, seen by the users is a change in performance. Indeed, changes to the internal schema are often made in response to a need to improve the performance of the database.

Similarly, the mappings from the schema at the logical level to the schemas at the external level provide logical data independence. These mappings specify how the conceptual constructs used at the logical level correspond to the conceptual constructs used at the external level. A schema at the external level is immune to changes in the schema at the logical level that are outside the scope of the external schema. Changes in the schema at the logical level, such as the addition of a new table or the addition of a new column in an existing table, are possible without having to change any of the schemas at the external level or to amend any of the application programs, except of course for the external schema and the associated application program for the users for whom the changes have been made. It is only the external schema and application program associated with those users that are affected; the rest are not.

AN OVERVIEW OF THE DATABASE DEVELOPMENT PROCESS

All information systems are developed to meet a set of information needs or requirements that belong to a set of users. An important part of the overall development process is to understand and document those requirements so that the information system that is developed and eventually delivered does in fact help the users by meeting their requirements.

There are a number of different approaches to the development of information systems, with a number of formalised methods available to the development team. All of these methods use diagramming techniques to record the results of the analysis of the information requirements.

All systems, whether supported by information technology or not, help to improve business processes – those specific activities that are designed to achieve defined goals or objectives. All systems also have to record information as data in order to provide their processes with something to work on.

The use of recorded data by specific processes is likely to be sequenced in the business; there are liable to be restrictions or constraints in the business that limit the application of processes to recorded data. Thus it may be that certain processes must precede others, or, once a particular process has been applied, certain other processes are prohibited.

So, for each system there are three facets that need to be considered: the information (or its associated data), the processes and the timing or sequencing. The diagramming techniques of information systems development methods provide ways to document these three facets of the system. Depending on the method, the diagrams may provide views of the data, processes and timing from the perspective of the business system that the information system needs to support; they may provide views of the data, processes and timing as they will be implemented in the information system; or they may provide both.

Our focus is on data management and, therefore, we concentrate on how information requirements are documented and understood to lead to the development of a database. However, anyone involved in data management will find it helpful to also understand the techniques used to document processes and timing.

Any database at the heart of an information system has to be designed so that it meets the information requirements of the user community. The relationship between the information requirements and the implemented database is shown in Figure 2.3. It can be seen that there is a defined process that delivers the final implemented database based on the set of information requirements.

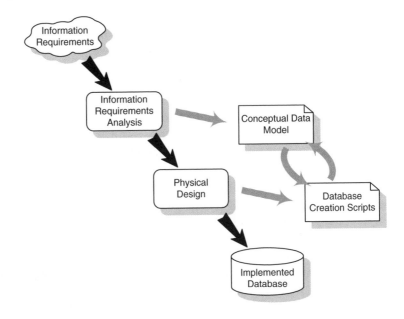

FIGURE 2.3   *A simplified view of the database development process*

Figure 2.3 shows that to get from the stated requirements to the final implemented database there are two main stages in the process: the information requirements analysis phase and the physical database design phase. The results of the information requirements analysis phase are recorded in a conceptual data model. Such a model probably consists of a diagram and a set of supporting documentation. An example of a conceptual data model diagram is shown in Figure 2.4.

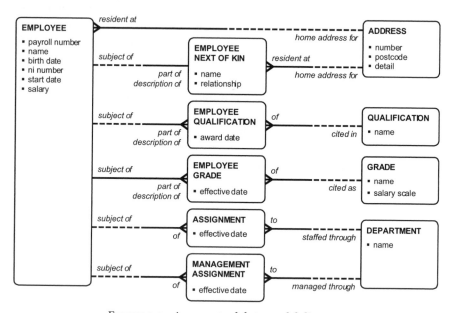

FIGURE 2.4   *A conceptual data model diagram*

This conceptual data model is for a small subset of the information normally used by a human resources function. It shows personal details of the employees, their addresses, their qualifications and their next of kin, and, additionally, some company-related information, such as the employees' grades and their assignments to departments. This conceptual data model may have been arrived at as a result of discussions with the staff of the human resources department or through an analysis of the information in the manual records currently held by the department, or by a combination of both.

There are a number of different data modelling notations in use, and some analysts even use object class models from object-oriented analysis and design methods such as the Unified Modeling Language (UML) in place of data models. Some of these notations are easier to use and to understand than others. The Ellis–Barker notation used in Figure 2.4 is my preferred notation. I have found it very easy to discuss models drawn using this notation with non-modellers, such as business representatives. Appendix A provides a discussion of the capabilities of some other data modelling notations.

There are also a number of different approaches to the development of data models and it is not the intention of this book to teach you how to model data. There are many excellent data modelling books already on the market. The one I would recommend to anyone new to data modelling is *CASE*METHOD: Entity Relationship Modelling* by Richard Barker (1990). One approach to the development of the data model in Figure 2.4 will be used in the 'Conceptual Data Modelling (from a Project-Level Perspective)' section later in this Chapter to demonstrate some of the ideas behind data modelling.

Having finalised the requirements analysis phase and produced an appropriate conceptual data model, the next step is to design the database. In many methods, this stage is (mistakenly) called 'physical design', but what we are doing at this stage is developing a schema using the appropriate conceptual constructs for the proposed database management system. This schema may be considered as the equivalent of the schema at the logical level in the three level database architecture we discussed earlier.

If the database is to be implemented using a database management system based on the SQL database language then the schema is defined in terms of tables and columns. The most convenient method of achieving this is to document the schema in a 'script' – a listing in plain text of the commands needed by the database management system to build the database (see Figure 2.5 for a small portion of the script needed to create the database developed from the conceptual data model in Figure 2.4). This script can then be executed by the database management system to create the database.

```
CREATE TABLE employee
(
        payroll_number    CHAR(5)      NOT NULL,
        name              CHAR(30)     NOT NULL,
        number            CHAR(25)     NOT NULL,
        post_code         CHAR(8)      NOT NULL,
        birth_date        DATE,
        ni_number         CHAR(9),
        start_date        DATE         NOT NULL,
        salary            INTEGER,
        PRIMARY KEY payroll_number,
        FOREIGN KEY (number, post_code) REFERENCES address
);
```

FIGURE 2.5 *A portion of an SQL create script*

Figure 2.5 shows the command to create a table called **employee**. This table has eight columns: **payroll_number, name,** etc. The data held in the **payroll_number** column is made up of five characters. This is shown by the declaration of the datatype for that column as **CHAR(5)**. There must also always be a value in the **payroll_number** column. This is shown by the **NOT NULL** constraint declaration for the column. **NULL** is an indicator in SQL that a value is missing. A column is said to be **NULL** at a row and column intersection if no value is specified for that column for that row. The constraint declaration **NOT NULL** says that missing values are not allowed. Each employee, therefore, must have a payroll number recorded in the database.

The data held in the **birth_date** column will be a date (the datatype is **DATE**) and it is possible that, for some employees, the birth date is not recorded – **NOT NULL** is not specified for the **birth_date** column. Note that database management systems from different vendors handle dates in different ways despite the fact that SQL is supposed to be an international standard.

The declaration of a primary key identifies a column (or a number of columns) that uniquely identify each row in the table. In this case, each employee's payroll number is unique and can be used to identify an employee.

The declaration of a foreign key identifies a column or columns that represent a relationship between this table and another table. In this case, the combination of the values in the **number** and **post_code** columns should match corresponding values in the **address** table; the **number** and **post_code** columns in the **address** table are declared as the primary key of that table.

The script includes a comparable **CREATE TABLE** command for each table in the database. There may also a number of other commands within this script, or in another script, to implement any constraints that may need to be placed on the data. It is not included in Figure 2.5, but there may, for instance, be a constraint that an employee must be between the ages of 16 and 75 when they start employment. If such a constraint were implemented, it would be impossible to insert data about an employee who did not meet these age restrictions.

Figure 2.3 shows that there is a possibility of iteration between the conceptual data model and the database creation scripts. It could well be that the conceptual data model contains a constraint that it is not possible to implement in the chosen database management system. Or it could be that, on testing of the database, it is found that there is an error in the logic of the database (maybe some important data is missing) and the creation script has to be amended and the database created afresh. In many cases, these later amendments to the creation scripts are not reflected back into the conceptual data model and the documentation for the database becomes inconsistent and unreliable.

CONCEPTUAL DATA MODELLING (FROM A PROJECT-LEVEL PERSPECTIVE)

Figure 2.4 showed a conceptual data model diagram for the data required to support part of a human resources function. It is a very small data model and represents only a small part of the business of a commercial enterprise. Any information system built using this data model would probably end up as what is known as a 'small system' – a system to support a small, clearly defined community of users. It is a data model developed purely from the perspective of the small part of the business that the information system will be developed to support. It takes no account of any corporate need to share information across the enterprise. The problems associated with developing data models that do take account of the corporate need are discussed in Chapter 4.

Although it is not my intention to teach data modelling I am going to show, using just one of the many approaches available, the development of the model in Figure 2.4. The main purpose of this is to demonstrate the concepts used in data modelling. An understanding of these concepts will help you to 'read' a new conceptual data model that you come upon in the future.

Introducing the entity concept

Figure 2.6 shows the first of our data modelling concepts. The single box, labelled **EMPLOYEE**, represents the concept known as an entity. In fact the box represents all the employees of the company; it represents all the instances of the type or class of 'things' called employees. The concept should more properly be known as an entity type but, regrettably, the word 'type' has been almost universally dropped by data modellers. Entities are always named with singular nouns despite representing all instances of the concept represented by the entity (type).

FIGURE 2.6   *The EMPLOYEE entity*

An entity is usually defined as 'something of significance to the business about which information is to be recorded'. The 'something' may be physical, such as an employee or an item of equipment, or it may be conceptual, such as an order (although there may be a physical representation of the order on a piece of paper). It may even be details of the specification of something else about which information is to be recorded. An example of this latter situation may be found in the airline industry. An airline may wish to record details about the individual aircraft in its fleet, such as their current location and the date they were last serviced. But all aircraft come off a production line where they are built to a specification, and all aircraft of a particular type have a number of common characteristics that the airline may wish to record, such as maximum range and average speed. The conceptual data model would, therefore, have two entities: the first would probably be called AIRCRAFT and would record the location and date last serviced whilst the other would probably be called AIRCRAFT MODEL and would record maximum range and average speed.

Introducing the attribute concept

In Figure 2.7, I have added details of the information that we wish to record about our employees. You may or may not agree with this particular list of information, but it is a list that was developed interactively by a group of students on a course I ran. In real life, the information required would be determined from the actual requirements of the human resources department.

EMPLOYEE

- payroll number
- name
- address
- birth date
- next of kin
- ni number
- start date
- qualifications
- grade
- department
- salary

FIGURE 2.7   *The attributes of the EMPLOYEE entity*

Each of these items of information is known as an attribute, a 'detail that serves to qualify, identify, classify, quantify or express the state of an entity'. Each of the attributes of EMPLOYEE listed in Figure 2.7 does one or more of these. The value of *payroll number* identifies the employee. It could be argued that the value of *name* also identifies the employee, but it is unlikely that names are guaranteed to be unique within the organisation and, therefore, it would be inappropriate to say that the value of *name* identifies the employee. It does, however, help to qualify the employee, in that it helps to distinguish one employee from another. An employee's *grade* helps to classify the employee.

Each of these attributes is then investigated to see if it is truly an attribute of the EMPLOYEE entity or whether it should be represented by another data modelling construct. Consider the *address* attribute. What if more than one employee lives at the same address? It may be important for the company to know that, and then addresses become significant to the business. Because it is now considered to be significant to the business, **ADDRESS** becomes an entity in its own right (as shown in Figure 2.8).

EMPLOYEE
• payroll number
• name
• address
• birth date
• next of kin
• ni number
• start date
• qualifications
• grade
• department
• salary

ADDRESS
• number
• postcode
• detail

FIGURE 2.8 *The ADDRESS entity*

ADDRESS now appears as an entity with three attributes, *number*, *postcode* and *detail*. The attributes *number* and *postcode* are there because, in the UK at least, house number (or name if there is no house number) and post code are sufficient to uniquely identify any address. The attribute *detail* is there to hold the rest of the address. (For the purposes of this exercise I am deliberately hiding details, such as how addresses are structured, to make the explanation of the key concepts easier.) Note that the *address* attribute in the **EMPLOYEE** entity has now been deleted.

Introducing the relationship concept

We now have two entities, **EMPLOYEE** and **ADDRESS**, but we still need to represent that employees live at addresses. For this we need our third (and final, for now) data modelling concept, the relationship. This is shown in Figure 2.9.

The fact that there is a relationship between the **EMPLOYEE** and **ADDRESS** entities is represented by a line on the diagram joining the two entities together. This line has a specific set of notation which I will describe soon. But first the definition.

A relationship is simply defined as 'an association between two entities'. In fact a relationship may exist between instances of the same entity. A relationship such as this is known as arecursive relationship. The possibility of a recursive relationship leads to a fuller definition of relationship as 'an association between two entities, or between one entity and itself'. For example, we may have a relationship to represent the fact that some employees manage subordinate employees: Joe Smith manages Phil Jones and Jenny Rogers; Jenny Rogers manages Barbara Watson, Roger Harrison and Henry Phillips.

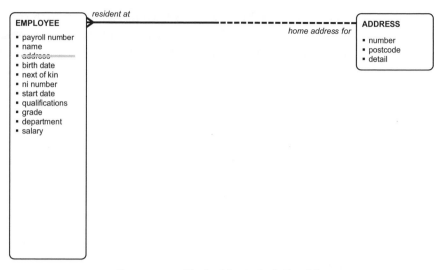

FIGURE 2.9   *The 'resident at' relationship*

Joe Smith, Phil Jones, Jenny Rogers, Barbara Watson, Roger Harrison and Henry Phillips are all instances of the entity **EMPLOYEE**.

Data models need to be interpreted both by business people, who are required to negotiate or approve the data requirements to be met by the system, and by technical people, who have to implement the system. It is important that the models are interpreted unambiguously and an important contribution to this unambiguous understanding is to have a formal method of 'reading' these relationships.

For example, consider the relationship between **ADDRESS** and **EMPLOYEE** that is introduced in Figure 2.9. Reading this relationship from right to left we have the sentence:

Each **ADDRESS** <u>may be</u> *home address for* <u>one or more</u> **EMPLOYEES**

I have used text formatting, **BOLD SMALL CAPITALS**, <u>underlining</u> and *italics*, to indicate the different elements of the sentence, which is constructed using the following rules:

- The word 'Each' is used because the box with the word 'ADDRESS' inside it is an entity type (that is, it represents all instances of the type – all the addresses) but we want to refer to a single instance of the type.
- 'Each' is followed by the name of the entity at the end from which we are starting the sentence – in this case, **ADDRESS**.
- The term '<u>may be</u>' is used because not every address has to be associated with an employee – this is represented on the diagram by a dotted line at the **ADDRESS** end of the relationship; a dotted line is always read as '<u>may be</u>'.
- '*home address for*' comes from the name of the relationship at the **ADDRESS** end of the relationship.

- The term 'one or more' is used because there is an inverted three-pronged arrow head (known as a crow's foot) at the EMPLOYEE end of the relationship – a crow's foot is always read as 'one or more'.
- The sentence ends with the name of the entity type at the end of the line; we make it plural so that the sentence reads easily, in this case, EMPLOYEES.

Each relationship can also be read in the opposite direction. Reading the relationship from left to right – from EMPLOYEE to ADDRESS – we have the sentence:

✳   Each EMPLOYEE must be *resident at* one and only one ADDRESS

This sentence is constructed as follows:
- 'Each' because we want to refer to a single instance of the type.
- EMPLOYEE from the name of the left-hand entity.
- 'must be' because every employee has to be associated with an address (their home address) – this is represented on the diagram by the solid line at the EMPLOYEE end of the relationship and a solid line is always read as 'must be'.
- '*resident at*' comes from the name of the relationship at the EMPLOYEE end of the relationship.
- The term 'one and only one' is used because there is no crow's foot at the far end, the ADDRESS end, of the relationship – the absence of a crow's foot is always read as 'one and only one'.
- 'ADDRESS' comes from the name of the right-hand entity type.

In data modelling parlance, this relationship is known as a one-to-many relationship. An address can be associated with many employees (Each ADDRESS may be *home address for* one or more EMPLOYEES) but an employee can only be associated with one address (Each EMPLOYEE must be *resident at* one and only one ADDRESS) through this relationship There could be other legitimate relationships between EMPLOYEE and ADDRESS which may mean that an employee can be associated with more than one address overall, but an employee can only be resident at one address.

Further development of the model

We now turn our attention back to the attributes of EMPLOYEE. One of these attributes is *qualifications*. Since this is plural we can deduce that each employee may have more than one qualification and, of course, some employees may have no qualifications at all. For those employees who do have qualifications, we may need to know when these qualifications were awarded.

We can now enhance our data model to show this. These enhancements are shown in Figure 2.10.

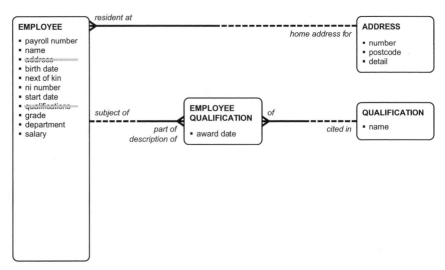

FIGURE 2.10   *The QUALIFICATION and EMPLOYEE QUALIFICATION entities*

We have introduced two new entities: **QUALIFICATION** with a *name* attribute and **EMPLOYEE QUALIFICATION** with an *award date* attribute.

The new relationships are read from left to right as follows:

✱   Each **EMPLOYEE** <u>may be</u>
        subject of <u>one or more</u> **EMPLOYEE QUALIFICATIONS**

✱   Each **EMPLOYEE QUALIFICATION** <u>must be</u>
        of <u>one and only one</u> **QUALIFICATION**

And from right to left as follows:

✱   Each **QUALIFICATION** <u>may be</u>
        cited in <u>one or more</u> **EMPLOYEE QUALIFICATIONS**

✱   Each **EMPLOYEE QUALIFICATION** <u>must be</u>
        part of description of <u>one and only one</u> **EMPLOYEE**

As with the *address* attribute, the *qualifications* attribute of **EMPLOYEE** has been deleted.

One of the other attributes of **EMPLOYEE** is *grade*. Every employee must have a grade but this grade probably changes over time and the human resources department may need to know the history of how an employee's grade has changed. This leads to further enhancements to the model, as shown in Figure 2.11.

As before, we have deleted the *grade* attribute of **EMPLOYEE** and introduced two new entities: **GRADE**, with *name* and *salary scale* attributes, and **EMPLOYEE GRADE**, with an *effective date* attribute.

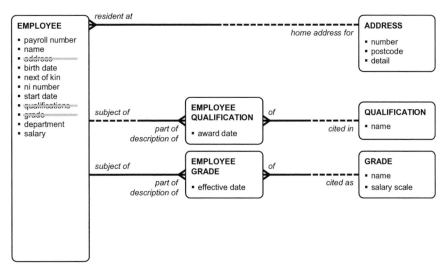

FIGURE 2.11   *The GRADE and EMPLOYEE GRADE entities*

The relationships are read from left to right as follows:

✳   Each **EMPLOYEE** must be *subject of* one or more **EMPLOYEE GRADES**

✳   Each **EMPLOYEE GRADE** must be *of* one and only one **GRADE**

And from right to left as follows:

✳   Each **GRADE** may be *cited as* one or more **EMPLOYEE GRADES**

✳   Each **EMPLOYEE GRADE** must be
       part of description of one and only one **EMPLOYEE**

The **EMPLOYEE GRADE** entity records both the current and past grades for the employee. The ***effective date*** attribute of **EMPLOYEE GRADE** records the date that an employee is appointed to a new grade. There is no record of the date that an employee ceases to hold a particular grade because it is assumed that this is the date of the next appointment to a new grade and so could be determined from other data in the database. In companies or organisations where there is a more complex grade structure with, for example, the concept of temporary grades, this simple model would not be sufficient to record all of the data.

The entity **EMPLOYEE** has a ***department*** attribute. The human resources department needs to record information about employees from the time that they are first given a contract but they are not formally assigned to a department until they arrive for their first day's work. This means that not every employee has a department recorded for them, but most do. Employees may move between departments and the human resources department may need to know the history of which departments an employee has worked in. This leads to further enhancements to the model, as shown in Figure 2.12.

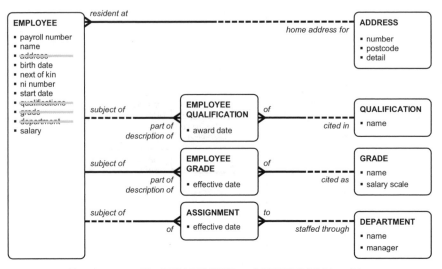

FIGURE 2.12   *The DEPARTMENT and ASSIGNMENT entities*

We have deleted the ***department*** attribute of EMPLOYEE and introduced another two new entities: DEPARTMENT, with ***name*** and ***manager*** attributes, and ASSIGNMENT, with an ***effective date*** attribute.

The relationships are read from left to right as follows:

Each EMPLOYEE may be *subject of* one or more ASSIGNMENTS

Each ASSIGNMENT must be *to* one and only one DEPARTMENT

And from right to left as follows:

Each DEPARTMENT may be *staffed through* one or more ASSIGNMENTS

Each ASSIGNMENT must be *of* one and only one EMPLOYEE

All assignments of employees to departments can, therefore, be recorded and the human resources department can determine all the departments to which an employee has been assigned. They can also determine the start date of each current assignment and the start and end dates of each completed assignment. The human resources department can also produce a listing of all the employees who are or have been assigned to a particular department, with the appropriate dates of the assignments.

The new DEPARTMENT entity has a ***manager*** attribute, with which we can record who manages the department. But a manager of a department is also an employee, and we have already provided, with the EMPLOYEE entity, the means to record details of employees. The ***manager*** attribute in DEPARTMENT should, therefore, be replaced by a relationship between DEPARTMENT and EMPLOYEE, as shown in Figure 2.13.

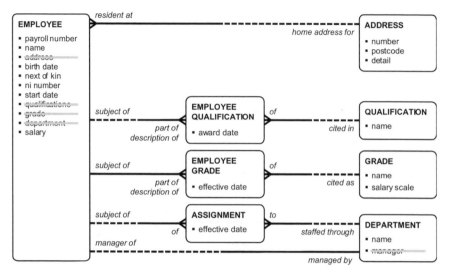

FIGURE 2.13   *The one-to-one 'managed by' relationship*

This new relationship is a one-to-one relationship and can be read as follows:

Each **DEPARTMENT** must be *managed by* one and only one **EMPLOYEE**

Each **EMPLOYEE** may be *manager of* one and only one **DEPARTMENT**

Using this relationship the human resources department can determine which employee currently manages each department, but they cannot determine who managed a department in the past or which departments were managed by a particular employee in the past. To achieve this would require a relationship such as:

Each **DEPARTMENT** must be *managed by* one or more **EMPLOYEES**

Each **EMPLOYEE** may be *manager of* one or more **DEPARTMENTS**

This is known as a many-to-many relationship and is shown in Figure 2.14.

But with this relationship, although the human resources department can determine who managed a department in the past and which departments were managed by a particular employee in the past, they cannot put any dates to these management assignments.

To achieve this requires a new entity and associated relationships to replace this many-to-many relationship, as shown in Figure 2.15. This replacement of a many-to-many relationship by a new entity and relationships is known by data modellers as 'resolving the many-to-many relationship'.

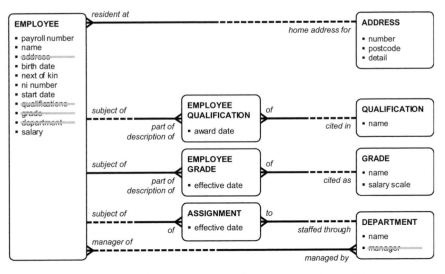

FIGURE 2.14   *The many-to-many 'managed by' relationship*

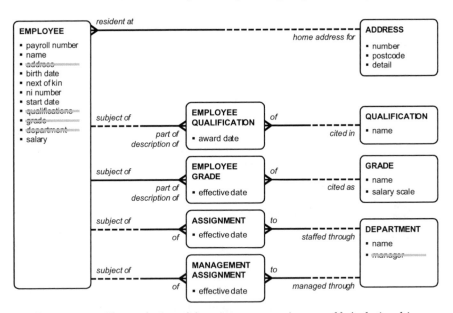

FIGURE 2.15   *The resolution of the many-to-many 'managed by' relationship*

This new entity, **MANAGEMENT ASSIGNMENT**, has an ***effective date*** attribute and relationships such that:

✱ Each **EMPLOYEE** <u>may be</u>
   subject of <u>one or more</u> **MANAGEMENT ASSIGNMENTS**

✱ Each **MANAGEMENT ASSIGNMENT** <u>must be</u>
   to <u>one and only one</u> **DEPARTMENT**

✱ Each **DEPARTMENT** <u>may be</u>
 managed through <u>one or more</u> **MANAGEMENT ASSIGNMENTS**

✱ Each **MANAGEMENT ASSIGNMENT** <u>must be</u> *of* <u>one and only one</u> **EMPLOYEE**

This simple model clearly allows all assignments to departments to be recorded and also allows details of who manages a department at any one time to be recorded but there are a number of issues that must be considered.

Jenny Rogers manages the Finance Department and, therefore, has an instance of the **MANAGEMENT ASSIGNMENT** entity associated with her instance of the **EMPLOYEE** entity, but it is not clear whether she should also have an instance of the **ASSIGNMENT** entity associated with her instance of the **EMPLOYEE** entity. That is, it is not clear whether a department manager is also recorded as an employee working within that department or not. This is not a big issue provided a decision one way or the other is made and then this rule is applied consistently. If it is not and the database is queried to list all the current employees of each department, the following inconsistencies could occur:

- If only the **ASSIGNMENT** records are queried, those managers who are only recorded through instances of **MANAGEMENT ASSIGNMENT** do not appear.
- If both the **ASSIGNMENT** and the **MANAGEMENT ASSIGNMENT** records are queried, those managers who are recorded through instances of **ASSIGNMENT** as well as through instances of **MANAGEMENT ASSIGNMENT** appear twice in the lists produced as a result of the query.

Furthermore the fact that each **DEPARTMENT** <u>may be</u> *managed through* <u>one or more</u> **MANAGEMENT ASSIGNMENTS** means that the business requirement that there can only be one current manager for each department could be compromised. It could be possible to record two overlapping instances of **MANAGEMENT ASSIGNMENT** for any one instance of **DEPARTMENT**.

There are a number of modelling conventions that can be used to overcome these problems but, as it is not the intention to teach data modelling, they are not discussed further here.

Our final enhancement to the data model comes through further consideration of the ***next of kin*** attribute of the **EMPLOYEE** entity. A next of kin must live somewhere and it would be useful to know the address of the next of kin and their relationship to the employee as well as their name. This requires an **EMPLOYEE NEXT OF KIN** entity with relationships such that:

✱ Each **EMPLOYEE** <u>may be</u>
 subject of <u>one and only one</u> **EMPLOYEE NEXT OF KIN**

✱ Each **EMPLOYEE NEXT OF KIN** <u>must be</u>
 resident at <u>one and only one</u> **ADDRESS**

✱ Each **ADDRESS** <u>may be</u>
  home address for <u>one or more</u> **EMPLOYEE NEXT OF KIN**

✱ Each **EMPLOYEE NEXT OF KIN** <u>must be</u>
  part of description of <u>one and only one</u> **EMPLOYEE**

These enhancements are shown in Figure 2.16.

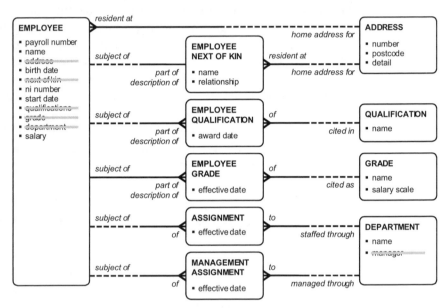

FIGURE 2.16   *The EMPLOYEE NEXT OF KIN entity*

Since an individual employee can only have one next of kin this could have been modelled with two attributes in the **EMPLOYEE** entity (***next of kin name*** and ***next of kin relationship***) and a relationship between **EMPLOYEE** and **ADDRESS** such that:

✱ Each **EMPLOYEE** <u>must be</u>
  related to next of kin resident at <u>one and only one</u> **ADDRESS**

✱ Each **ADDRESS** <u>may be</u>
  home address for next of kin of <u>one or more</u> **EMPLOYEES**

However, the construct in Figure 2.16 is preferred for two reasons. First, it more clearly represents the semantics that there are two separate 'things' of interest to the business – the employee and the next of kin of an employee. Secondly, should there be a later decision to allow an employee to record more than one 'next of kin' the changes required are relatively simple – the addition of a crow's foot at the **EMPLOYEE NEXT OF KIN** end of the relationship between **EMPLOYEE** and **EMPLOYEE NEXT OF KIN** and, possibly, a means of identifying (through an additional attribute in **EMPLOYEE NEXT OF KIN**) the principal next of kin of an employee where more than one is recorded.

This is now the final model as seen in Figure 2.4. Whilst the intention was not to teach you how to data model, I hope that by working through this example you now understand the concepts embodied in a data model and the way in which it can represent the data requirements of a business, or business area, to be supported by an information system.

Our conceptual data model only covers some of the data requirements of our business area – the human resources function. It is restricted to the perspective of a single project. In Chapter 4, we look at data modelling from a corporate perspective. We then need to look at some more advanced data modelling concepts.

RELATIONAL DATA ANALYSIS

In the previous section, we saw one approach to the development of a conceptual data model. This was typical of the approach that might be taken when there is no formal documentation of the requirements that are to be met. The model is developed by the analyst as a result of information about the business data requirements gathered through interviews, workshops or observation of working practices.

There is another, much more formal approach to the analysis of data requirements that relies on there being some document or other existing record (such as a program file) that lists the items of data that are to be recorded. This set of data items is then analysed using this process, which is known as relational data analysis. The result is a set of relations in third normal form (more about these terms in a short while) and this set of relations can be shown diagrammatically in a form that looks remarkably similar to our previous conceptual data model, although there are some significant differences.

Although relational data analysis is based upon the relational model of data proposed by Edgar F Codd (1970), there is no presumption that relational data analysis is followed by an implementation using a relational database. The implemented database could be object oriented or follow some other model of database implementation.

As with our look at the development of a conceptual data model, the easiest way to explain relational data analysis is to work through an example. Before we can do that, however, it is necessary to explain the relational model of data, which is founded on well-established mathematical set theory.

The relational model of data

In the relational model of data, the data is recorded in a set of linked relations. The relation used as the main concept of the model is not the same as the relationship in a conceptual data model and it is inappropriate to use these two terms interchangeably in the data/database community despite the fact that they are used interchangeably in general usage.

A relation has two parts – a heading and a body. The heading consists of a set of attributes; the attribute in the relational model of data is a similar concept to the attribute we saw in the conceptual data model, although there are some differences. The body is a set of elements that are called tuples (which rhymes with 'couples'). Each tuple is, in turn, a set of data values, one value for each of the attributes defined in the relation heading. More formally, a tuple is a set of attribute-name:attribute-value pairs. The set of values from which the individual values of an attribute may be taken is known as a domain. More than one attribute can take its values from any one domain. The domain is a very important concept in relational theory, but it plays no part in the relational data analysis process described later in this chapter.

The easiest way to visualise a relation is as a table (although in some important respects a table is an inappropriate representation of a relation). The representation of a relation as a table is shown in Figure 2.17. The relational concepts are highlighted in the diagram.

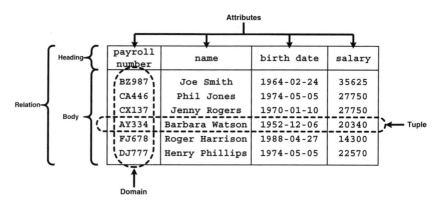

FIGURE 2.17 *A relation shown as a table*

The heading of the relation comprises four attributes called **Payroll Number, Name, Birth Date** and **Salary.** The body of the relation comprises six tuples, one for each of the employees Joe Smith, Phil Jones, Jenny Rogers, Barbara Watson, Roger Harrison and Henry Phillips. The set of values for each of these four attributes for each employee forms a tuple. The tuple for Barbara Watson is highlighted. The domain for the attribute **Payroll Number** is also highlighted. We can see that this has at least six values, but there may be more values in the domain that are not used by the **Payroll Number** attribute in this particular relation.

There are a number of rules associated with relations. Without going into too much technical detail these are:

- There is no significance to the order of the attributes within the relation heading; this is because the relation heading is a set of attributes and one of the properties of a mathematical set is that the elements of the set are unordered. The fact that in Figure 2.17 the attributes are arranged in a particular order from left to right is purely for presentational purposes; that order has no significance to the relation that Figure 2.17 is representing.

- Similarly, since the body of the relation is a set of tuples, there is no significance to the order of the tuples within the body of the relation. Again, the fact that in Figure 2.17 the tuples are arranged in a particular order from top to bottom is purely for presentational purposes.

- Attributes within the relation heading should be unique; that is, there should be no duplication of attribute names.

- There should be no attributes whose values can be derived from the values taken by other attributes whether those attributes are in the same relation or in another relation.

- Relations have unique identifiers, known as primary keys; the primary key comprises the attribute, or combination of attributes, whose values are the minimum required to uniquely identify each instance of the relation. The primary key of the relation represented in Figure 2.17 is the `Payroll Number` attribute; each employee has a unique payroll number.

- No two tuples in a relation may have the same value of primary key. If the `Payroll Number` attribute is the primary key of the relation representing employees, no two employees can have the same payroll number.

- In each tuple, each part of the primary key must have a value. Every employee must have a payroll number.

- The attributes of a relation represent characteristics that are determined by the primary key; that is, they describe the 'thing' defined by the primary key. The name of the employee with payroll number AY334 is Barbara Watson, her date of birth is 6 December 1952 and her salary is £20,340 per annum.

- In any tuple, no attribute may take more than one value; that is, each attribute is single-valued – there are no multiple-valued attributes within a relation.

Normalisation

We use the process of relational data analysis – the development of a set of relations in third normal form – to develop a conceptual database design in which there will be no update anomalies when data is input into the database or later updated. In general terms, this means that for any piece of information there is only one place in the database where the data representing the information can be stored and that place is unambiguously recognised. This process of relational data analysis allows us to confirm that we are associating attributes that are all about one thing (person, product, account, etc.) or concept (promotion, order, transaction, etc.) of interest to the business.

This is exactly what we were trying to achieve when we earlier developed the conceptual data model using the entity–relationship notation.

The example we use to demonstrate relational data analysis is also based on the human resources department that we saw earlier, although now our starting point is the existing paper records in use within that department. An example of one of these paper records is shown in Figure 2.18.

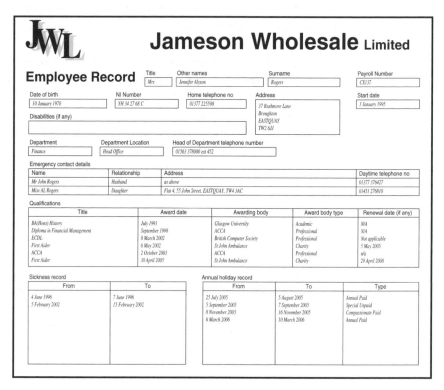

FIGURE 2.18　*The human resources paper record*

The first stage in the process is to list all the 'data items' on the form. The result of doing this is shown in Figure 2.19, which is laid out as a form that can be used for the whole relational data analysis process. Beside each entry is a level indication – 1 or 2. All entries for which there are groups of data items that can be repeated, for example, the emergency contact details and the qualifications held by the employee, are indicated with a 2. We call these 'repeating groups'. The remainder are indicated with a 1.

This listing is known as the un-normalised form (UNF). One of the data items, **Payroll Number**, has been underlined. This is because the payroll number of an employee uniquely identifies that employee within the company. When we start the normalisation process, **Payroll Number** will become the primary key of the main relation, in this case the EMPLOYEE relation.

UNF	Level	1NF	2NF	3NF	Relation
Title	1				
Other Names	1				
Surname	1				
Payroll Number	1				
Date of Birth	1				
NI Number	1				
Home Tel No	1				
Address	1				
Disabilities	1				
Start Date	1				
Department Name	1				
Department Location	1				
Head of Department Tel No	1				
Emergency Contact Name	2				
Emergency Contact Relationship	2				
Emergency Contact Address	2				
Emergency Contact Day Tel No	2				
Qualification Title	2				
Qualification Award Date	2				
Qualification Awarding Body	2				
Qualification Award Body Type	2				
Qualification Renewal Date	2				
Sickness From	2				
Sickness To	2				
Annual Holiday From	2				
Annual Holiday To	2				
Annual Holiday Type	2				

FIGURE 2.19   *The un-normalised EMPLOYEE 'relation'*

First normal form

The first stage in our normalisation process is to move from this un-normalised form to produce a set of relations that are in first normal form (often abbreviated as 1NF). A relation is in first normal form if all the values taken by the attributes of that relation are atomic or scalar values – we say that the attributes are single-valued. This is to comply with the rule that there must not be any multiple-valued attributes in a relation. To move to first normal form we need to remove the repeating groups from the initial 'relation' (in quotes because in the un-normalised form this does not comply with the rules of relations).

Each of the repeating groups then becomes a relation in its own right. In our example, we have four new relations: one for the emergency contact details; one for the qualifications held by the employee; one for the periods that the employee has been absent through sickness; and one for the periods that the employee has been on holiday. From the information on the form in Figure 2.18, we can see that the form records sickness absences since the employee started with the company, whereas holiday periods are only recorded for the current holiday year. This is not something that we need to take into consideration in our relational data analysis. We are only interested in the data that needs to be recorded; we are not interested, in this process, of when that data is recorded and for how long it is recorded.

For each of these new relations we need to identify a primary key. For the employee's emergency contacts, the name is sufficient to uniquely identify one amongst the contacts recorded for a single employee. But we need to uniquely identify an emergency contact amongst all the emergency contacts recorded in the company. In any but the smallest company it is possible for two employees to have an emergency contact called John Rogers, and for them to be two different people. The name of the emergency contact is, therefore, insufficient to uniquely identify an emergency contact within the company. What we really need to uniquely identify an emergency contact is both the name of the contact and an indication, such as the payroll number, of the employee for whom this person is an emergency contact. The primary key of this relation is, therefore, the combination of `Payroll Number` and `Emergency Contact Name`.

Our first normal form relations are shown in Figure 2.20. These are now relations as they comply with all the rules we listed earlier. Each of the data items listed is now an attribute.

UNF	Level	1NF	2NF	3NF	Relation
Title	1	Payroll Number			
Other Names	1	Title			
Surname	1	Other Names			
Payroll Number	1	Surname			
Date of Birth	1	Date of Birth			
NI Number	1	NI Number			
Home Tel No	1	Home Tel No			
Address	1	Address			
Disabilities	1	Disabilities			
Start Date	1	Start Date			
Department Name	1	Department Name			
Department Location	1	Department Location			
Head of Department Tel No	1	Head of Department Tel No			
Emergency Contact Name	2				
Emergency Contact Address	2	Payroll Number			
Emergency Contact Relationship	2	Emergency Contact Name			
Emergency Contact Day Tel No	2	Emergency Contact Relationship			
Qualification Title	2	Emergency Contact Address			
Qualification Award Date	2	Emergency Contact Day Tel No			
Qualification Awarding Body	2				
Qualification Award Body Type	2	Payroll Number			
Qualification Renewal Date	2	Qualification Title			
Sickness From	2	Qualification Award Date			
Sickness To	2	Qualification Awarding Body			
Annual Holiday From	2	Qualification Award Body Type			
Annual Holiday To	2	Qualification Renewal Date			
Annual Holiday Type	2				
		Payroll Number			
		Sickness From			
		Sickness To			
		Payroll Number			
		Annual Holiday From			
		Annual Holiday To			
		Annual Holiday Type			

FIGURE 2.20   *The first normal form relations*

All our new relations have a primary key identified (in this case by underlining the relevant attributes). All of these primary keys comprise at least two attributes, the primary key of the main relation and sufficient extra attributes to uniquely identify each instance of the real world thing that the relation represents. As explained above, for the emergency contacts relation, this is the combination of the employee's payroll number, the `Payroll Number` attribute, and the name of the emergency contact, the `Emergency Contact Name` attribute. For the relations representing sickness absence periods and holiday periods, it is the combination of the employee's payroll number and the start date for the relevant period. For the relation representing the employee's qualifications there are three elements to the primary key since three items of data are required to uniquely identify each employee's qualification. One of these is the employee's payroll number, as before. There is also the title (or name) of the qualification. But the combination of the employee's payroll number and the title of the qualification is insufficient to uniquely identify a qualification held by an employee. Inspection of the form shows that Jenny Rogers holds two first aid qualifications, one of which is now out of date. So, to uniquely identify a qualification held by an employee we also need another item of information, the date that the qualification was awarded. Hence the primary key of the relation representing the qualifications held by employees is the combination of `Payroll Number`, `Qualification Title` and `Qualification Award Date`.

When the primary key of a relation appears as an attribute in another relation it is known as a foreign key in the other relation. In this case, `Payroll Number` is a foreign key in our four new relations.

These first normal form relations can be depicted in the form of a diagram approximating to the notation of our previous conceptual data model (see Figure 2.21). Every relation that has a foreign key amongst its attributes has a relationship line drawn to the relation with the corresponding primary key. This relationship line has a crow's foot at the end of the relationship with the relation with the foreign key. At the other end of the relationship, the end with the relation with the primary key that corresponds to the foreign key, there is a plain end (i.e. there is no crow's foot). This diagram is less expressive than our conceptual data model because we cannot show the 'may be' or 'must be' nature of the relationships and we do not have any names for the relationships. The diagram does, however, help to demonstrate our progress through the relational data analysis process.

Second normal form

The next stage of our relational data analysis process is to move our relations to second normal form (2NF). For a relation to be in second normal form, it has to be in first normal form and, in addition, it must meet the condition that every attribute that is not part of the primary key is dependent on the whole of the primary key. More formally, a relation is in second normal form if

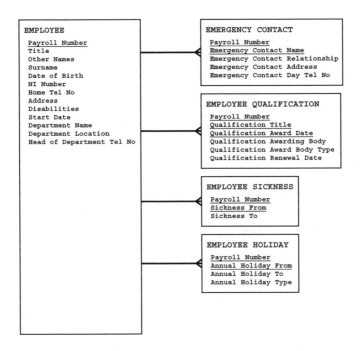

FIGURE 2.21   *Diagram of the first normal form relations*

and only if it is in first normal form and every non-key attribute is irreducibly dependent on the primary key.

In this context, 'dependence' means that if we have two attributes, **Payroll Number** and **Employee Surname**, and we know the value of the attribute **Payroll Number**, we can determine the value of the attribute **Employee Surname** (for example, given the payroll number CX137, we know that the surname of that employee is Rogers). We say that **Employee Surname** is dependent on **Payroll Number**. The reverse is not true. If we know that an employee's surname is Rogers, we cannot determine that employee's payroll number – there may be more than one Rogers working for the company. So **Payroll Number** is not dependent on **Employee Surname**.

We achieve second normal form by reviewing every attribute that is not part of the primary key in the first normal form relations to see if any of those attributes are dependent on one or more parts of a multiple-part primary key. If so, then those attributes need to be removed.

Our main first normal form relation (labelled **EMPLOYEE** in Figure 2.21) has **Payroll Number** as its primary key. This is a single-part primary key and, therefore, each of the attributes in that relation must be dependent on the whole of the primary key. This first normal form relation is, therefore, also in second normal form.

Let us now consider the **EMERGENCY CONTACT** relation shown in Figure 2.21. This relation has a multiple-part primary key of two attributes – **Payroll Number** and **Emergency Contact Name** – and three non-key attributes – **Emergency Contact Relationship**, **Emergency Contact Address** and

Emergency Contact Day Tel No. If we know the combined values of **Payroll Number** and **Emergency Contact Name** we can determine the values of the non-key attributes. The test is to take each non-key attribute in turn and see if it is possible to determine its value using only a part of the primary key. For **Emergency Contact Relationship** we need to know the values of both **Payroll Number** and **Emergency Contact Name** to know its value. Knowing just the value of **Payroll Number** is insufficient. The employee with payroll number CX137 has both a husband and a daughter as emergency contacts.

Similarly knowing just the value of **Emergency Contact Name** is insufficient; it is possible that more than one employee has an emergency contact called Mr John Rogers. The same is true for both **Emergency Contact Address** and **Emergency Contact Day Tel No**. This **EMERGENCY CONTACT** relation is, therefore, also in second normal form.

Similar inspection also indicates that the relations **EMPLOYEE SICKNESS** and **EMPLOYEE HOLIDAY** are also already in second normal form.

Let us now consider the **EMPLOYEE QUALIFICATION** relation. This has a multiple-part primary key of three attributes – **Payroll Number**, **Qualification Title** and **Qualification Award Date** – and three non-key attributes – **Qualification Awarding Body**, **Qualification Award Body Type** and **Qualification Renewal Date**. We need to know the values of all three elements of the primary key to determine the value of **Qualification Renewal Date**. The same is not true for **Qualification Awarding Body** and **Qualification Award Body Type**. The values of these two attributes are not dependent on the value of **Payroll Number** or on the value of **Qualification Award Date**. They are only dependent on the value of **Qualification Title** (assuming that only one body issues any qualification of a given name or title; this may not be true in the real world but we make that assumption for the purposes of this exercise).

To create our second normal form relations we need, therefore, to remove **Qualification Awarding Body** and **Qualification Award Body Type** to another relation, which I call **QUALIFICATION**. But this new relation also needs **Qualification Title** as its primary key since we know that the values of **Qualification Awarding Body** and **Qualification Award Body Type** are dependent on **Qualification Title**.

The second normal form relations are now shown on the form (Figure 2.22) and in a diagram (Figure 2.23).

FIGURE 2.22 *The second normal form relations*

UNF	Level	1NF	2NF	3NF	Relation
Title	1	Payroll Number	Payroll Number		
Other Names	1	Title	Title		
Surname	1	Other Names	Other Names		
Payroll Number	1	Surname	Surname		
Date of Birth	1	Date of Birth	Date of Birth		
NI Number	1	NI Number	NI Number		
Home Tel No	1	Home Tel No	Home Tel No		
Address	1	Address	Address		
Disabilities	1	Disabilities	Disabilities		
Start Date	1	Start Date	Start Date		
Department Name	1	Department Name	Department Name		
Department Location	1	Department Location	Department Location		
Head of Department Tel No	1	Head of Department Tel No	Head of Department Tel No		
Emergency Contact Name	2				
Emergency Contact Relationship	2	Payroll Number	Payroll Number		
Emergency Contact Address	2	Emergency Contact Name	Emergency Contact Name		
Emergency Contact Day Tel No	2	Emergency Contact Relationship	Emergency Contact Relationship		
Qualification Title	2	Emergency Contact Address	Emergency Contact Address		
Qualification Award Date	2	Emergency Contact Day Tel No	Emergency Contact Day Tel No		
Qualification Awarding Body	2				
Qualification Award Body Type	2	Payroll Number	Payroll Number		
Qualification Renewal Date		Qualification Title	Qualification Title		
Sickness From		Qualification Award Date	Qualification Award Date		
Sickness To		Qualification Awarding Body	Qualification Renewal Date		
Annual Holiday From		Qualification Award Body Type			
Annual Holiday To		Qualification Renewal Date	Qualification Title		
Annual Holiday Type			Qualification Awarding Body		
			Qualification Award Body Type		
		Payroll Number			
		Sickness From	Payroll Number		
		Sickness To	Sickness From		
			Sickness To		
		Payroll Number			
		Annual Holiday From	Payroll Number		
		Annual Holiday To	Annual Holiday From		
		Annual Holiday Type	Annual Holiday To		
			Annual Holiday Type		

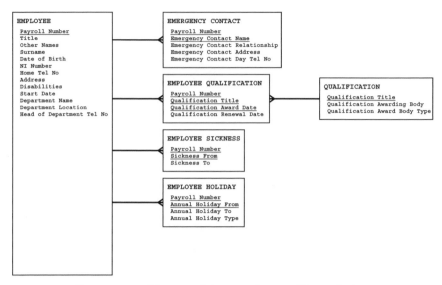

FIGURE 2.23   *Diagram of the second normal form relations*

Third normal form

We now need to move our relations from second normal form to third normal form (3NF). For a relation to be in third normal form it has to be in second normal form and also has to meet the condition that every attribute that is not part of the primary key is not dependent on an attribute that is also not part of the primary key. More formally, a relation is in third normal form if and only if it is in second normal form and every non-key attribute is nontransitively dependent on the primary key.

We achieve third normal form by reviewing every attribute that is not part of the primary key in the second normal form relations to see if any of those attributes are dependent on another attribute that is not part of the primary key. If so, then those attributes need to be removed.

In the second normal form **EMPLOYEE** relation, the value of **Title** is dependent on the value of **Payroll Number**, the primary key. If I know that the value of the **Payroll Number** attribute is CX137, I can determine that the value of the **Title** attribute is Mrs. The same is true of the **Other Names**, **Surname**, **Date of Birth**, **NI Number**, **Home Tel No**, **Address**, **Disabilities**, **Start Date** and **Department Name** attributes. However, if I know the value of the **Department Name** attribute then I can determine the values of both the **Department Location** and **Head of Department Tel No** attributes. The attributes **Department Location** and **Head of Department Tel No** are not, therefore, directly dependent on the primary key, the **Payroll Number** attribute. We say that **Department Location** and **Head of Department Tel No** are transitively dependent (that is, indirectly dependent) on **Payroll Number** through **Department Name**.

The attributes Department Location and Head of Department Tel No are, therefore, removed from the EMPLOYEE relation to form a new relation, called DEPARTMENT. This new relation also needs Department Name as its primary key since both Department Location and Head of Department Tel No are dependent on Department Name.

The attribute Department Name remains in EMPLOYEE as a foreign key, but it is not part of the primary key. So that it can be identified as a foreign key that is not part of the primary key it is marked with an asterisk (*).

In the second normal form EMERGENCY CONTACT relation, all the non-key attributes are directly dependent on the primary key. The relation EMERGENCY CONTACT is, therefore, also in third normal form.

In the second normal form QUALIFICATION relation, the value of the attribute Qualification Award Body Type is determined by the value of the attribute Qualification Awarding Body. This means that we need a new third normal form relation, say called QUALIFICATION BODY, with Qualification Awarding Body as its primary key and Qualification Award Body Type as its only non-key attribute. The relation QUALIFICATION retains the attribute Qualification Awarding Body as a foreign key.

Inspection shows that both the EMPLOYEE SICKNESS and EMPLOYEE HOLIDAY relations are already in third normal form.

The third normal form relations are shown on the form (Figure 2.24) and in a diagram (Figure 2.25). The form also has the final names for the relations completed.

UNF	Level	1NF	2NF	3NF	Relation
Title	1	**Payroll Number**	**Payroll Number**	**Payroll Number**	EMPLOYEE
Other Names	1	Title	Title	Title	
Surname	1	Other Names	Other Names	Other Names	
Payroll Number	1	Surname	Surname	Surname	
Date of Birth	1	Date of Birth	Date of Birth	Date of Birth	
NI Number	1	NI Number	NI Number	NI Number	
Home Tel No	1	Home Tel No	Home Tel No	Home Tel No	
Address	1	Address	Address	Address	
Disabilities	1	Disabilities	Disabilities	Disabilities	
Start Date	1	Start Date	Start Date	Start Date	
Department Name	1	Department Name	Department Name	*Department Name	
Department Location	1	Department Location	Department Location		
Head of Department Tel No	1	Head of Department Tel No	Head of Department Tel No	**Department Name**	DEPARTMENT
Emergency Contact Name	2			Department Location	
Emergency Contact Relationship	2	**Emergency Contact Name**	**Payroll Number**	Head of Department Tel No	
Emergency Contact Address	2	Emergency Contact Relationship	Emergency Contact Name		
Emergency Contact Day Tel No	2	Emergency Contact Address	Emergency Contact Relationship	**Payroll Number**	EMERGENCY CONTACT
Qualification Title	2	Emergency Contact Day Tel No	Emergency Contact Address	Emergency Contact Name	
Qualification Award Date	2		Emergency Contact Day Tel No	Emergency Contact Relationship	
Qualification Awarding Body	2	**Payroll Number**		Emergency Contact Address	
Qualification Award Body Type	2	**Qualification Title**	**Payroll Number**	Emergency Contact Day Tel No	
Qualification Renewal Date	2	Qualification Award Date	**Qualification Title**		
Sickness From	2	Qualification Awarding Body	Qualification Award Date	**Payroll Number**	EMPLOYEE QUALIFICATION
Sickness To	2	Qualification Award Body Type	Qualification Renewal Date	**Qualification Title**	
Annual Holiday From	2	Qualification Renewal Date		Qualification Award Date	
Annual Holiday To	2		**Qualification Title**	Qualification Renewal Date	
Annual Holiday Type	2		Qualification Awarding Body		
			Qualification Award Body Type	**Qualification Title**	QUALIFICATION
				*Qualification Awarding Body	
				Qualification Awarding Body	QUALIFICATION BODY
				Qualification Award Body Type	
		Payroll Number	**Payroll Number**	**Payroll Number**	EMPLOYEE SICKNESS
		Sickness From	**Sickness From**	**Sickness From**	
		Sickness To	Sickness To	Sickness To	
		Payroll Number	**Payroll Number**	**Payroll Number**	EMPLOYEE HOLIDAY
		Annual Holiday From	**Annual Holiday From**	**Annual Holiday From**	
		Annual Holiday To	Annual Holiday To	Annual Holiday To	
		Annual Holiday Type	Annual Holiday Type	Annual Holiday Type	

FIGURE 2.24 *The third normal form relations*

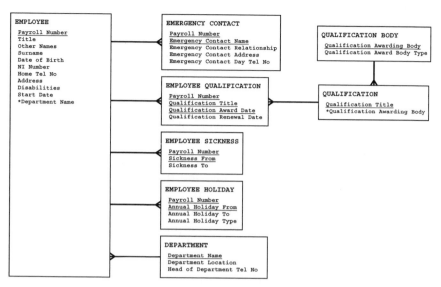

FIGURE 2.25   *Diagram of the third normal form relations*

Our relations are now in third normal form and this is as far as we can go with the process of relational data analysis.

Further normal forms

There are, however, a number of higher normal forms, the most significant of which is known as Boyce–Codd normal form (BCNF).

Until now we have been talking about the primary key for a relation as if there is only one possible primary key. Sometimes there is more than one possible primary key. Consider our human resources department. For our **EMPLOYEE** relation, we almost intuitively selected the attribute **Payroll Number** as the primary key. If the company issues unique payroll numbers to its employees then we know that the payroll number can be used to uniquely identify an employee and it makes sense to use the **Payroll Number** attribute as the primary key. There may, however, be other possible combinations of attributes that could have been used as a primary key. It could well be that, for all except very large organisations, the combination of the values of **Other Names**, **Surname** and **Date of Birth** is sufficient to uniquely identify any employee. These three attributes could have been chosen as the primary key. All possible primary keys are known as candidate keys. So, our **EMPLOYEE** relation has two candidate keys: **Payroll Number** on its own and the combination of **Other Names**, **Surname** and **Date of Birth**. One of the candidate keys, in this case **Payroll Number**, is chosen as the primary key. The choice of which candidate key to use as a primary key is sometimes quite arbitrary, although there is often a clear preferred option. Candidate keys not selected to be the primary key are sometimes referred to as alternate keys.

With our discussion of first, second and third normal forms we have been focusing on the dependencies of the non-key attributes to the primary keys.

With Boyce–Codd normal form, the emphasis has shifted from the primary key to all the candidate keys. For most practical purposes, Boyce–Codd normal form and third normal form are equivalent. The only exceptions occur when there are two or more candidate keys, where those candidate keys are composed of more than one attribute and where the multi-attribute keys overlap (that is, they share a common attribute). In this situation, it is possible for update anomalies to occur at third normal form, but not if the relations are restructured to be in Boyce–Codd normal form. Boyce–Codd normal form is really just a stricter form of third normal form.

Further normal forms – fourth-normal form, fifth-normal form and, most recently, sixth-normal form – have been proposed. They are beyond the scope of this book and are not discussed further.

Many database developers prefer to use a meaningless primary key (sometimes called a surrogate key) instead of constructing a primary key from real-world attributes such as **Payroll Number**, **Surname**, **Other Names** and **Date of Birth**. There are many advantages to taking this approach, not the least being that any values for real world attributes may be subject to change (for example, following real-world change, a change in company policy, or the need to correct errors). If surrogate keys are to be used, it is still sensible to use relational data analysis to check normalisation using candidate keys involving appropriate real-world attributes.

Relational data analysis and conceptual data modelling

The application of relational data analysis, essentially a 'bottom-up' approach, to the employee record in Figure 2.18 has produced the diagram in Figure 2.25. This is notationally very similar to the conceptual data model in Figure 2.16 which we developed using a less formal, 'top-down', approach. The model in Figure 2.16 is in Boyce–Codd normal form although we did not apply the relational data process. An experienced data modeller intuitively produces a model that is in Boyce–Codd normal form without applying the rigour of relational data analysis.

Inspection of the two models developed using the two approaches reveals that there are similarities in content between them. This is to be expected as they are models of the same business area – the human resources department. There are also some differences in the content of the models. This is also to be expected. When discussing requirements with management and staff who are very familiar with their job, some significant details are often missed. On the other hand, the documentation used for relational data analysis may be out of date. It is by no means clear which of these two models is more correct than the other. The discrepancies need to be resolved by further discussion with the experts in the business and a consolidated data model produced.

THE ROLES OF A DATA MODEL

Conceptual data models can be developed to understand the information requirements of a business and to form the basis for a physical database design to support the business.

Understanding information requirements

In the first case, the data model is used to document the information that is used by the business and the way that that information is grouped and related. The aim here is either to highlight inconsistencies in the information used by the business or, if the conceptual data model is being developed as a prelude to the development of an information system, to enable an expert in the business to agree that all the information requirements have been completely and faithfully documented. Business experts could even be involved in the development of the model. Irrespective of whether the analyst developing the model is primarily a business person or an experienced data modeller, it is the duty of the analyst to develop a model that can be meaningfully discussed with the business. All the information that is needed by the business must be explicitly included in the model. All the names of entities, attributes and relationships in the model must be meaningful to the business. The analyst who is an experienced data modeller must resist the temptation to include constructs in the model that hide or distort the business relevance of the information. The model must be easy to read and interpret.

A conceptual data model that is to be used to understand the information requirements of a business, or a business area, should be the result of the analysis of those information requirements alone. No design considerations should be included in the model. The model should be the result of pure analysis, untainted by design.

The basis for physical database design

A conceptual data model, that is, a data model that has been developed to understand the information requirements of the business, could also be used as the basis for the design of a database that is to be at the heart of an information system which supports that business. However, such a design may be inappropriate. It may not meet some future information requirement without some significant restructuring of the logical schema for the database. It could be that the data modeller has identified that some of the information requirements are similar to those of a previous project for which a good data modelling solution is already known or for which there is a published 'data model pattern'.

When the modeller has used his or her experience to create a data model that creates an effective logical schema design, the conceptual data model may well use data modelling constructs and names that are alien to the business. Although such a model provides a well-considered and robust input to the 'physical design' of the database, it is no longer correct to claim that the model completely and faithfully documents the information requirements of the business. These information requirements may be hidden by a data modelling construct that has been introduced into the model for sound reasons. For example, a business that buys and sells products would expect to see CUSTOMER and SUPPLIER entities in their conceptual data model but these two concepts may be wrapped up in a single entity, often called PARTY, to recognise the fact that a company that is the supplier of some products may also be the customer for other products. It is not unknown for the PARTY entity to also include the employee concept, as sometimes employees can also be customers. In this case, it is incorrect to call the data modelling activity 'analysis'. It has gone beyond analysis; it is the start of design.

PHYSICAL DATABASE DESIGN

Once the conceptual data model is complete it provides the start point for the design of the physical database.

> *Aside*: When new to data modelling some 15 years ago (before the wide-spread use of drawing packages and tools to support data modelling), I naively asked a consultant when I would know that a data model was complete. The answer I got was 'When the correction fluid on the model is so thick that it is able to stand on its edge'. The implication is that even an experienced data modeller has to rework the model many times.

The conceptual data model, with its entities, attributes and relationships, does not presuppose the form of the implemented database. Because the model is in Boyce–Codd normal form, it is very easily translated into a design for a relational database (a database managed by a database management system based on SQL). The model could, however, be translated into a design for a database managed by some other form of database management system, such as an object-oriented database management system. We assume, however, that the database is to be implemented using an SQL-based relational database management system, where the main construct at the logical level is the database table.

This 'physical database design' process has two stages:

(i)   first-cut database design;
(ii) optimised database design.

First-cut database design stage

In the first-cut database design stage, the aim is to use the conceptual constructs of the logical-level schema of the target database management system to develop a design that matches the conceptual data model as closely as possible.

Each entity in the conceptual data model becomes a table, with each of the attributes of the entity becoming a column of that table. If the foreign keys needed to implement the relationships are not already identified as attributes they need to be identified and become additional columns of the table.

There should be a consistent approach to the naming of tables and columns. It should be possible to relate the schema design back to the conceptual data model from which it is derived, so the names of the tables and columns should be as close to the names in the conceptual data model as possible within the limitations that all database management systems place on the lengths of names. Ideally, each table name should be identical to the entity name, and this is normally possible within the naming length restrictions. The table corresponding to the **EMPLOYEE** entity in Figure 2.16 would be called **employee** and the table corresponding to the **EMPLOYEE QUALIFICATION** entity would be called either **employee_qualification** or **employeeQualification** to cope with the restriction that spaces are not allowed in SQL names.

Column names must be unique within a table, so it is possible to have an **effective_date** column in both the **employee_grade** table and in the **assignment** table, distinguishing between the two if necessary by using 'dot notation', for example, **employee_grade.effective_date** for the **employee_grade** table and **assignment.effective_date** for the **assignment** table. It is common practice to name foreign key columns with the same name as the column that they correspond to in the table that is referenced by the foreign key. Following this approach the **assignment** table would have two foreign key columns – **payroll_number** referencing the **employee** table and **name** referencing the **department** table. Because of the large number of 'name' columns that normally appear in a database, many designers would use **department_name** for the second case, but this means that there is not an overall consistent approach to naming. One recommended approach to the naming of foreign keys is to concatenate the relationship name, the 'distant' entity name and the 'distant' column name to give names to the foreign key columns that fully explain their role. In this case, the two foreign key columns in the **assignment** table would be called **of_employee_payroll_number** and **to_department_name**.

Each column is defined with a datatype, such as **CHAR(10)**, a fixed-length string of 10 characters; **VARCHAR(10)**, a variable-length string with a maximum length of 10 characters; **DATE**, a calendar date; and **DECIMAL(5,2)**, a number such as '234.56'. If the domain for each attribute was specified as part of the conceptual data model, it is usually fairly straightforward to determine the appropriate datatype. If domains have not been specified then it is normally necessary to review some specimen data in order to determine the appropriate datatype.

There has to be an explicit primary key declaration for each table (naming the column or columns in the table whose values uniquely identify a row in the table). If required, there must also be explicit foreign key declarations (naming the column or columns that comprise each foreign key) to implement each relationship from the table to another table.

Another important element of the first-cut database design is the specification of the physical file storage for the database. Database management systems manage the actual storage of data but most provide mechanisms for the designer to control the allocation of tables to particular physical structures. These physical structures may be called tablespaces, filegroups or some other name. It is possible to allocate more than one table to a single tablespace and in some database management systems it is possible to split a large table over a number of tablespaces. The allocation of tables to tablespaces is determined principally by the likely volumes of data for each table and how data is to be collected from different tables to answer the anticipated queries. These are not trivial questions to answer.

Optimised database design stage

The first-cut design gives a database design that closely resembles the conceptual data model. Such a design should be robust, easy to understand and meet all the data requirements of the business areas being supported. However, within the stated requirements for any information system are a number of non-functional requirements that specify performance targets for the overall system, such as the maximum time a user must wait after submitting a request for information (a query on the database) before that information is available. It may be necessary for the database designer to enhance or move away from the first-cut design to improve the performance of the database.

The two main strategies for improving performance of a database are to:

- make use of the built-in facilities of the database management system;
- compromise on the design of the logical schema.

Two facilities provided by most database management systems are the ability to cluster data and the ability to create indexes. Data clustering means arranging data on the disk in such a way that logically related data is placed as closely together as possible. This improves performance because fewer disk-access requests are required to answer queries on the database or to update data. An index provides the database management system with an alternative way to access data other than searching through all the physical records associated with a particular logical table. A database index is analogous to the index at the back of this book. It enables the database management system to know where to go to access any particular piece of data. An index may be built on a single column or on multiple columns from the same table. Using an index improves retrieval performance by reducing the number of disk accesses required to query the data. Database update is, however, slowed down if data is indexed; each database update requires updating the index (which normally requires some restructuring of the complete index) as well as updating the main data file. Changes to the clustering of data and the addition or removal of indexes are the equivalent of altering the schema at the internal level of the three level architecture. These changes can be made without affecting the schema at the logical level and without affecting the application processes.

Physical data independence is maintained and data clustering and indexing can, therefore, be altered once the database is in use.

On the other hand, a compromise to the design of the logical schema affects data independence. Such a compromise is often called denormalisation. You will recall that our aim is to design a logical schema that is in Boyce–Codd normal form; indeed, we may even seek to design a logical schema that is in a higher normal form. The rationale for this is that it provides only one place to store any item of data, reducing data redundancy and eliminating the possibility of data inconsistency (at least within that single database). This means, however, that data that may be logically related is dispersed throughout the database. Collecting this dispersed data together to answer any particular query can require a large number of disk access requests, which can in turn impact performance. Denormalisation can involve returning 'repeating groups' to their master table (or relation). It can also mean joining two tables that are often queried together. Introducing new columns to hold data that can be derived from other data already held elsewhere in the database can also be considered as denormalisation. An example of this would be the recording of the total cost of an order where the costs of the individual items ordered are already recorded. Whilst denormalisation can improve retrieval performance, it can slow down update performance (data needs to be recorded in more than one place) and introduce the possibility of inconsistency (because the users or the application programs need to manage the duplicated updates). Denormalisation should, therefore, be avoided if possible; if used, all decisions to denormalise should be carefully documented.

SUMMARY

This chapter has taken a detailed look at the development of databases. First the database concept and the three level schema architecture were introduced. Having taken a brief look at the overall database-development process, we then looked in more detail at the information requirements analysis phase. We saw examples of top-down development of a conceptual data model and the bottom-up relational data analysis process. Finally we looked at the way that a conceptual data model is translated into a physical database design.

3 What is Data Management?

This chapter starts by looking at what can happen if data is not adequately managed. It then looks at the responsibilities of a data management function and the separate roles within that function. It finishes by looking at the benefits that data management can bring to an enterprise and the relationship between data management and enterprise architecture.

THE PROBLEMS ENCOUNTERED WITHOUT DATA MANAGEMENT

At its simplest, data management is the management of data, information represented in a formalised manner suitable for communication, interpretation or processing. This far-reaching but simple statement implies that all aspects of the management of data, including the storage of data in a file or a database to support a limited set of business processes, are 'data management'. However, data management as a formal term is normally associated with the provision of an enterprise-wide service. The definition that has been in use within the BCS Data Management Specialist Group for some time is:

> Data management is a corporate service which helps with the provision of information services by controlling or co-ordinating the definitions and usage of reliable and relevant data.

From this definition it can be seen that data management is a far-reaching function. It is involved with the definition of data, to enable that data to be shared between information systems and become a corporate resource. It is also involved with the management of the data in active information systems to ensure that it is reliable (that is, of good quality) and that the relevant data is available to the users that need it.

Data management, and its 'big cousins' information management and information resource management, can be compared to other corporate business functions, for example, personnel and finance. The data management function looks after the data resource in the same way as the personnel department looks after the personnel in the organisation and the finance department looks after the organisation's money. I have used the term 'data management function' here because the data management responsibility may not reside in a single organisational department. The management structures needed for data management are discussed in Chapter 11.

It is important to recognise that the majority of data does not 'belong' to the data management function, as indeed the majority of personnel within a company do not 'belong' to the personnel department. The management of a large proportion of the data is normally the responsibility of the different functional departments in the organisation. The data management function should, however, provide the essential quality control of the enterprise's data and be recognised as an authoritative source of information about the organisation's data.

Only very few organisations have managed to implement an effective corporate data management function. The remainder are counting the costs of ineffective or non-existent data management. These costs come from the development of information systems to meet narrow departmental or business function and process needs without recognising that each information system in an organisation should be a subsystem of a larger integrated enterprise-wide federation of information systems designed so that the appropriate information is provided to the appropriate user in the appropriate place at the appropriate time. At the heart of such a federation of information systems is the requirement to share data; for this to happen, there has to be common enterprise-wide definitions of data and a co-ordinated enterprise-wide control of the actual live data. In other words, there has to be data management as defined by the Data Management Specialist Group and this data management has to be properly resourced, supported and managed in order to be effective.

Aside: Unless an organisation is prepared to replace all its information systems with a single enterprise resource planning (ERP) system, any enterprise resource planning system that is introduced is yet another system that needs to share data with other information systems. The introduction of enterprise resource planning systems does not remove the need for effective data management. Indeed, it probably exacerbates the data management problem.

Without effective enterprise-wide data management in place within the organisation:

- *The information systems within the enterprise cannot be interfaced.* Because they have not been defined and developed to work together, the information systems cannot be 'joined' other than at the most rudimentary, technical level.
- *Data is not shared between the information systems.* Even if it is possible to technically connect the information systems, it is still usually impossible to share data between those systems because of the incompatible data definitions in use in the disparate information systems.
- *Communication breaks down and information gets lost.* Without true data sharing, it becomes impossible for departments to obtain the information they need to carry out their jobs effectively within the necessary timeframe.

- *Data is unnecessarily transcribed and rekeyed.* If there is a need for information to be shared between incompatible information systems the only option that is often available is to have the information from one system rekeyed into the other system or systems. This is not only very resource-intensive but there is a danger of the data being incorrectly transcribed if the definitions are ambiguous or the concepts underlying those data definitions are incompatible.

- *The wheel keeps being reinvented.* A substantial portion of the time and cost of the development of any information system is taken up with the analysis of the information and data requirements and the subsequent development of the database to meet those requirements. Without effective data management, this effort is required for each new information system irrespective of whether the same or similar information or data requirements have been analysed before. With enterprise-wide data management in place, the new information system can reuse existing data definitions, producing savings in both time and cost of the development of the new system. Implementing data management specifically to save system-development costs is unlikely to lead to an increase in information sharing across the enterprise, whereas if data management is implemented to improve information sharing there is almost certainly going to be a reduction in system-development costs in the long term.

- *The competitive edge of the organisation is reduced.* If information is delayed or lost, for example, because the mechanisms for the sharing of data between information systems are inefficient or are not even provided, the ability of the organisation to provide an efficient service to its customers, and thus to compete with its rivals, will be impeded.

- *Frustration sets in.* Users of information systems who consistently find that they do not have the right information at the right time to carry out their job effectively soon become frustrated. The staff of the IT or IS department who are providing support for those users find that they are constantly being criticised and themselves become frustrated at their inability to provide an effective service. The IT or IS department staff involved in the development of new and replacement systems find themselves having to develop from scratch systems whose requirements overlap systems developed before either by themselves or their colleagues. They also become frustrated.

The requirement for information is changing all the time. Where data is poorly or ambiguously defined, it may be difficult to respond to requests for new information or information presented in a different manner. Real business opportunities may be lost as a result of the inability to respond quickly to changing requirements. There are many situations where information exists in systems as data but is not accessible to the users within the right time frame.

Such costs impact on the business, the users of the information, as well as on the IT or IS department, who provide the technical infrastructure to provide the information to the users.

DATA MANAGEMENT RESPONSIBILITIES

From the Data Management Specialist Group definition, it can be deduced that data management is a corporate service that:

- *strategically* supports the corporate definition, management and use of business data;
- *operationally* supports the development and maintenance of computerised information systems.

To meet its remit to provide strategic and operational support to the organisation, the data management function has a number of responsibilities. The key areas amongst these responsibilities are:

- achieving recognition of data, both structured and unstructured, as an enterprise-wide valuable business resource;
- improving the quality of the data held within the enterprise's information systems and ensuring that there are procedures in place to maintain the quality of the data;
- facilitating information sharing across the business by the provision of corporate data definitions and support to systems-development teams to ensure that these definitions are used;
- making the various levels of management within the business accountable for the development and ownership of data definitions – it is within the business, not in IT or IS, that the real meaning of data and information is known;
- achieving a single source for reference data to support all the information systems within the enterprise – this includes internal reference data, such as product codes and prices, as well as external reference data, such as UN country codes.

The degree of accountability that the data management function has depends on its reporting level in the organisation. The lower the position in the organisational hierarchy, the more limited the responsibilities are likely to be. It naturally follows that the more limited the responsibilities are, the less impact the data management function can have on the organisation's use of data and, thus, the benefits reduce accordingly.

To fulfil the above responsibilities, the data management function needs to identify the specific activities that it needs to carry out and then obtain sufficient resources to perform the activities. These activities are shown in Figure 3.1.

FIGURE 3.1   *Data management activities*

An important early activity for the success of any data management initiative is to educate all concerned about the importance of data management to the organisation and the role that they play in data management. This education, of course, involves the staff directly involved in the data management function. It must also be directed towards the business and user community at all levels, from senior management through to the end-users of the information systems who may be responsible for collecting and inputting data, and also at the technical staff in the IT or IS department who need to follow and use the products delivered through data management. If application development is 'outsourced' then those involved in the procurement procedures must also be made aware of the importance of data management so that they can ensure that adherence to the data management standards is included in the contracts with the development company.

Another important early task is to develop the organisation's data management policy and strategy. The policy document sets out what the business expects from the data management initiative and how business managers, end-users of the information systems and the IT or IS staff relate to the data management staff. This needs to be endorsed at the highest level within the organisation. Once the policy is endorsed, it is possible to develop the strategy of how to meet the data management goals and targets.

One of the principal tasks of data management is to develop the corporate data definitions for the organisation. Key to this is the development of a data model, or a set of data models, that encapsulate all of the business organisation's information needs. The data definitions can then be derived from these models. Each data definition must be 'owned' by an appropriate business authority, and data management must seek out a suitable owner. The data models and the ownership are the 'front of house' facets of data definition. Behind the scenes, there needs to be a number of standards covering the way that data models are to be developed, the format that data definitions are to take and the way that data 'objects', such as entities, attributes, tables and columns, are to be named.

Data management is a complex activity and it is doubtful if much will be achieved without some automated tool support. There is a need, therefore, to identify and procure these tools and a need to have procedures in place to ensure that the tools are used consistently and that the information stored in the tools is available when required.

If data management is to be successful, it must influence the way that data is defined and handled in any new or replacement systems. It is very important, therefore, that the data management staff interact with and support the system-development staff. It is too easy for systems developers to see any standards, including standard corporate data definitions, as constraints on their freedom of action and, maybe, a potential source of delay to the completion of their project. The interaction between data managers and system developers must be managed so that the system developers see the data managers as a positive resource that are of benefit to their project.

Once data management is up and running, the data management staff probably have a greater knowledge than the business staff of what data and information is available within the organisation, where it is available and how it is used. The data management staff can, therefore, provide a valuable information service to the business and to the IT or IS staff. They can, in effect, provide a 'one-stop shop' for information about information and data.

As with any other function, functional management has to be in place to ensure that all of these activities are co-ordinated and facilitated. There must be adequate resources to carry out the activities. The activities must be prioritised and planned so that the service provided by the data management function provides the support to the organisation that is expected and required.

Figure 3.2 shows the key deliverables to be expected from each of these activities.

The IT or IS department is often cast in the role of 'advocate' for the creation and implementation of a data management function. It is often the view of the business that the management of data is solely the responsibility of the IT or IS staff. Certain aspects of physical data management, such as database administration, do naturally fall within the overall IT or IS responsibility, but the management of data and its associated information, as an asset to enable the business to exploit its huge investment in data, is very much the responsibility of the business and, as such, the business must sponsor it and be involved in it.

Rather like a vehicle (as in Figure 3.3), the 'data management front wheel' may steer us down a particular path, but only the 'business rear wheel' can provide the power to drive us forward.

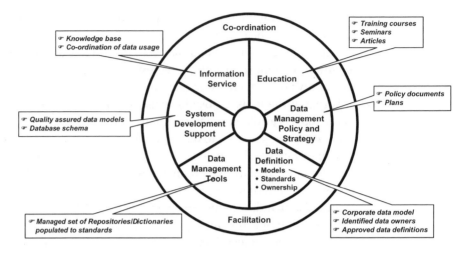

FIGURE 3.2   *Data management deliverables*

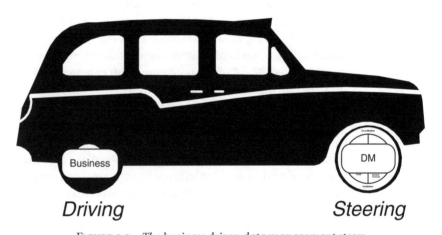

FIGURE 3.3   *The business drives; data management steers*

ROLES WITHIN DATA MANAGEMENT

The Data Management Specialist Group has identified three distinct roles within the data management function, known as data administration, database administration and repository administration. In its publication 'Data Management', the Central Computer and Telecommunications Agency (1994b) showed the relationship between data management, these three roles and the broader information-management function using the diagram in Figure 3.4.

The information management roles that are outside the scope of data management include process management, which looks at the business processes that use data; system management, which is the management of the computer systems that support the business processes; and business information support, which provides a service to the business users to enable

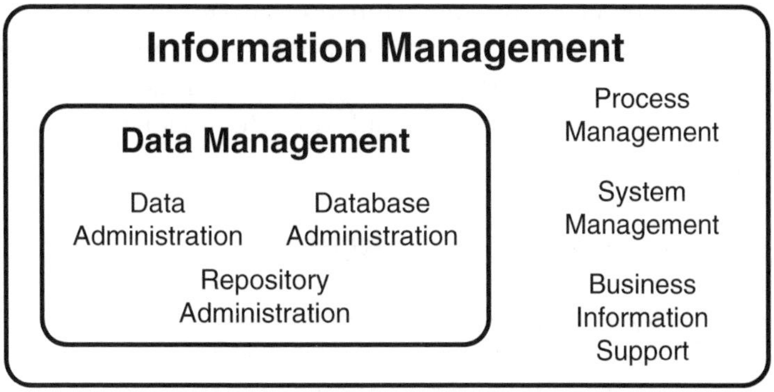

```
┌─────────────────────────────────────────────────────────┐
│              Information Management                       │
│                                          Process         │
│   ┌──────────────────────────────┐      Management       │
│   │       Data Management         │                      │
│   │                               │      System          │
│   │     Data         Database     │      Management       │
│   │ Administration  Administration│                      │
│   │                               │      Business         │
│   │       Repository              │      Information      │
│   │      Administration           │      Support         │
│   └──────────────────────────────┘                      │
└─────────────────────────────────────────────────────────┘
```

FIGURE 3.4   *The relationship between data*
management and information management

them to exploit the information available. System management is now more commonly known as IT service management.

Data administration is concerned with mechanisms for the definition, quality control and accessibility of an organisation's data. This is the role that takes a corporate view of data as it is used by the business. It is a policy-making role, in that it must set down the rules and procedures for data definition, data quality and data usage, but it may also be involved in developing, on the business's behalf, draft data definitions, carrying out data quality audits and the consequent cleansing of the data. It is often called upon to provide advice and expertise on data modelling to system-development projects. Alternatively, it may be called upon to assure the quality of data models developed by system-development project staff. Data administration is the least technical of the three data management roles. Further discussion of the areas included within the responsibilities of the data administration role is provided in Chapter 4 to Chapter 8.

Database administration is concerned with the management and control of the software used to access physical data. Database administrators carry out the day-to day administration of the various databases and their associated database management systems. Routinely this involves monitoring the performance of the database, removing or archiving data that is obsolescent and maintaining backups in case of emergencies. It may also involve reordering or restructuring the database to improve performance. Database administration may also be called upon to provide expertise on physical database design to system-development projects. Alternatively, it may be called upon to assure the quality of physical database designs to ensure that they conform to corporate standards. See Chapter 9 for further discussion of the database administration role.

Repository administration is concerned with the management and control of the software in which 'information about information' is stored, manipulated and defined. As such, it is a role whose scope is the internal support of the data management function and I normally refer to repository administration as being the 'provision of database administration specifically to support data administration'. It is the most technical of the three data management roles. See Chapter 10 for further discussion of the repository administration role.

THE BENEFITS OF DATA MANAGEMENT

Many benefits are claimed for data management. Nearly all these benefits make sound business sense and can be recognised as such. Unfortunately, not all of them can be related to direct cost savings. It therefore requires a degree of faith on the part of senior management that, when starting a data management initiative, the end result justifies the cost and the effort.

Every organisation is different. It is useful to consider the potential benefits in two areas:

- those that are business related;
- those that are related to information technology and systems.

It may be possible to identify tangible business-related benefits (a financial 'return on investment') that follow on from the implementation of data management, for example, staff savings through a reduction in rekeying of data or a reduction in the cost of marketing mailings through the eradication of duplicate customer data. However, the most significant benefits to the business are likely to be intangible. There will almost certainly be an improvement in the overall efficiency and effectiveness of the organisation as a result of both the improvement in data quality and the increased availability of information achieved by the improved sharing of data between information systems. This will, in turn, lead to an enhanced level of customer service, improving the organisation's competitive edge.

The benefits from data management related to information technology and systems will be more tangible than the business-related benefits. The reuse of information and data analysis products (data models, etc.) and data definitions will result in an increase in productivity in systems development, leading to cost savings. They will enable the sharing of data which will lead to the business benefits. Because of the use of common data definitions and a common approach to the management of data in general, there will also be savings in the cost of the maintenance of applications.

THE RELATIONSHIP BETWEEN DATA MANAGEMENT AND ENTERPRISE ARCHITECTURE

If an organisation is far-sighted enough to implement data management then there is also a good chance that the organisation has embraced the concept of enterprise architecture. In general, enterprise architecture is about understanding the different elements that make up the enterprise, including the people, the information, the processes, the communications and, very importantly, how those elements interrelate. By implementing an enterprise architecture, an organisation attempts to determine how these elements work together to meet its current and future goals.

There are a number of enterprise architecture frameworks publicly available via the internet, including:

- US Department of Defense Architecture Framework (DoDAF)
  see www.dod.mil/cio-nii/docs/DoDAF_v1_Volume_I.pdf;
- UK Ministry of Defence Architecture Framework (MODAF)
  see www.modaf.com;
- Open Group Architecture Framework (TOGAF)
  see www.opengroup.org/togaf;
- Framework for Enterprise Architecture developed by John Zachman
  (also commonly known as the Zachman Framework)
  see www.zifa.com.

DoDAF and MODAF are specifically targeted at the defence communities of the respective nations. Both of these architecture frameworks see the overall enterprise described using a number of separate views, particularly an operational view (organisations, locations, processes, information flows, etc.), a systems view (interfaces, data specifications, protocols, etc.), and a technical standards view (the supporting standards and documents). TOGAF is an enterprise architecture framework, developed by members of The Open Group Architecture Forum (www.opengroup.org/architecture), that uses models at four levels: Business, Application, Data and Technology. TOGAF can be used by any organisation that wishes to develop an enterprise architecture.

DoDAF, MODAF and TOGAF look at various aspects of an enterprise from different viewpoints. The Framework for Enterprise Architecture developed by John Zachman exemplifies this idea. His framework consists of six columns – data ('what'), process or function ('how'), network ('where'), people ('who'), time ('when') and motivation ('why') – and five rows – the scope or conceptual view (the planner's view), the business model or conceptual view (the owner's view), the system model or logical view (the designer's view), the technology model or physical view (the builder's view), and the detailed representations or out-of-context view (the subcontractor's view). To complete the enterprise architecture each intersection of row and column requires its own model.

All of these enterprise architecture frameworks involve the specification of information or data, or both, at a number of different levels. It is highly likely, therefore, that there will need to be close co-operation between the data management function and whoever is responsible for the development of the enterprise architecture.

SUMMARY

This chapter started by looking at the problems encountered when there is no data management. The formal definition of data management was presented, followed by the responsibilities of a data management function and the activities and deliverables associated with those responsibilities. The three roles within data management (data administration, database administration and repository administration) were then introduced. The business-related and systems-related benefits of data management were discussed and the chapter concluded by looking at the relationship between data management and enterprise architecture.

4 Corporate Data Modelling

This chapter looks at the subject of corporate data modelling and sees how it differs from project or business-area level data modelling. Along the way, we introduce further data modelling concepts that are particularly useful when modelling at the corporate level. Three approaches to the development of a corporate data model and six principles of corporate data modelling are introduced and discussed.

WHY DEVELOP A CORPORATE DATA MODEL?

In many respects a corporate data model is very similar to the project-level conceptual data model we described in Chapter 2. It comprises definitions of the things of significant interest to the business (the entities), definitions of what we need to know about those things (the attributes) and the associations between them (the relationships). A corporate data model is different because its scope extends beyond a single project; ideally it extends to cover the data requirements of the whole business.

There is no definitive role for a corporate data model. Whilst each 'corporation' has specific motives for the development of its corporate data model, the most common reason is to facilitate the sharing of data between applications or information systems. Irrespective of the reason for the development of the corporate data model, the 'corporate data model initiative' will only be successful if the intended role of the corporate data model is clearly understood across the whole enterprise.

There are a number of questions to be addressed when embarking on the development of a corporate data model:

- *What is the definition of 'corporate'?* It is my view that 'corporate', in the context of a corporate data model, should mean the entire enterprise. It is not unknown, however, for those who seek to avoid being involved in (or, as they see it, constrained by) data management to see 'corporate' as equating to 'the corporate headquarters', so not applicable to them in their particular business area.

- *What is 'corporate data'?* Again, it is my view that, in the context of a corporate data model, 'corporate data' covers all the data used by the enterprise. The corporate data model should, therefore, cover all of the enterprise's data requirements. There are many, both within the business and within the IT or IS staff who are supporting them, who believe that the data generated in their business area is only of use to them and it should, therefore, be outside the scope of the corporate data model. A counter-argument is that nobody can be sure that any data has only local relevance until the data requirements of the whole enterprise have been analysed and documented.

- **Is the corporate data model to be used as ...**

   ...a business model? In this role the corporate data model will not necessarily be used as the basis for information systems development. It expresses a view of data from the perspective of the business. Such a model could be used, for example, to inform business process reengineering.

   ...a database design model? In this role the corporate data model will be used to inform a common database design. This common database design, or appropriate subsets of it, can then be used in all future information systems design. This will ensure that data is commonly and unambiguously defined in all information systems, facilitating the sharing of data across those systems. Note, however, that if a common database design is to be used, then it will not be possible to optimise the database design as discussed in Chapter 2. Any optimisation to enhance the performance of one application program will almost certainly adversely affect the performance of other application programs.

   ...an interface design model? In this role the corporate data model provides a standard with which all information systems must comply at their interfaces with other information systems. The intention is not to direct the design of the databases in the individual information systems, so allowing optimisation to enhance performance, but to direct how data must be presented to other information systems when there is a requirement to share data with those other information systems. This approach means that there has to be some extra processing to translate the data from the definitions used in the design of the database to the definitions specified by the corporate data model, and vice versa. In this way, each information system appears to the other information systems as if they were using a common database design based on the corporate data model.

MORE DATA MODELLING CONCEPTS

Figure 4.1 is a copy of Figure 2.16, the final conceptual data model we developed when working through Chapter 2. This model only uses the basic data modelling concepts of entity, attribute and relationship. For many purposes these are sufficient, but there are two further concepts that will definitely be needed in the development of a corporate data model and may be useful when modelling at the project level:

- entity subtypes;
- the specification that two or more relationships are mutually exclusive.

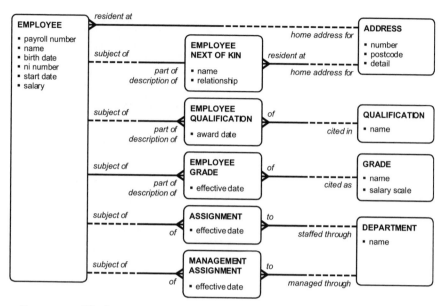

FIGURE 4.1   *The human resources conceptual data model developed in Chapter 2*

Entity subtypes

Entity subtyping is a method of expressing the idea that there may be differences as well as similarities between instances of an entity and that there may be groups of instances that share some of those differences. For example, some of the employees of a company may be employed full-time whilst the other employees are only employed part-time.

In Figure 4.2, there are two new entities, **FULL-TIME EMPLOYEE** and **PART-TIME EMPLOYEE**. They are entities in their own right, so we use the same entity notation – the 'soft-cornered' box. We identify them as subtypes of **EMPLOYEE** by placing the new entities within the **EMPLOYEE** box. **EMPLOYEE** is known as the supertype of **FULL-TIME EMPLOYEE** and **PART-TIME EMPLOYEE**. A subtype may itself be subtyped, that is it may itself act as the supertype of further subtypes. A hierarchy of supertype and subtype entities is sometimes known as a generalisation hierarchy.

The entity subtypes of an entity supertype are mutually exclusive. In our example, an employee is either employed full time or part time, but not both. Furthermore, every instance of the supertype is also an instance of one of the subtypes. There is no instance of the supertype which is not also an instance one of the subtypes. Every employee is employed either full time or part time; there is no other form of employment. Another rule of subtypes is that the mutually exclusive nature extends for all time. This means that, for our example, a part-time employee can never become a full-time employee or vice versa.

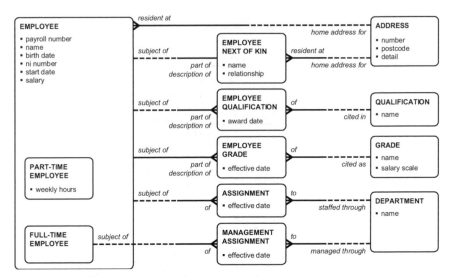

FIGURE 4.2   *Entity subtypes*

> *Aside*: In real life this may not be true. The implication of model-
> ling these as subtypes is that the transfer of a full-time employee to
> part-time employment is treated as a new employment. The full-time
> employment record is closed and a new employee record is created. You
> might consider that this is not a sensible approach – and you would
> be correct – but these subtypes of **EMPLOYEE** enable me to demonstrate
> the principles of subtyping, even if the situation is somewhat artificial.

Entity subtypes may have attributes or relationships in their own right. For
part-time employees there is a need to record the number of hours they
are contracted to work each week, but there is no requirement to record this
information for full-time employees. Thus, **PART-TIME EMPLOYEE** has a *weekly
hours* attribute. There is also a business rule that only full-time employees
may manage a department. This is represented by moving the relationship
between **EMPLOYEE** and **MANAGEMENT ASSIGNMENT** so that it is between **FULL-
TIME EMPLOYEE** and **MANAGEMENT ASSIGNMENT** such that:

Each **FULL-TIME EMPLOYEE** may be
  subject of one or more **MANAGEMENT ASSIGNMENTS**

Each **MANAGEMENT ASSIGNMENT** must be
  of one and only one **FULL-TIME EMPLOYEE**

Although the attributes or relationships that are specific to a single entity subtype are shown explicitly in the model, each subtype also implicitly inherits
all the attributes or relationships of its supertype. The attributes *payroll
number, name, birth date, NI number, start date* and *salary* apply to both of
the subtypes **FULL-TIME EMPLOYEE** and **PART-TIME EMPLOYEE**. The relationship

between **EMPLOYEE** and **ADDRESS** also applies between **FULL-TIME EMPLOYEE** and **ADDRESS** and **PART-TIME EMPLOYEE**e and **ADDRESS**, so that:

✳ Each **FULL-TIME EMPLOYEE** <u>must be</u>
    resident at <u>one and only one</u> **ADDRESS**

✳ Each **ADDRESS** <u>may be</u>
    home address for <u>one and only one</u> **FULL-TIME EMPLOYEE**

and:

✳ Each **PART-TIME EMPLOYEE** <u>must be</u>
    resident at <u>one and only one</u> **ADDRESS**

✳ Each **ADDRESS** <u>may be</u>
    home address for <u>one and only one</u> **PART-TIME EMPLOYEE**

Entity subtypes are useful in that they enable the data modeller to indicate real-world differences between groups of entity instances. They show explicitly in the conceptual data model how real-world 'things' may be classified. They are also useful in that they enable the clear specification of constraints in the model, such as the constraint that the hours to be worked each week are only to be recorded for part-time employees and the constraint that only full-time employees are allowed to manage a department. Without the use of subtypes these constraints would need to be expressed in words, which may later be misunderstood or missed altogether.

Mutually exclusive relationships

Another useful technique is the ability to indicate where only one of two or more relationships applies for any one instance of an entity. These are known as mutually exclusive relationships, and are usually marked on a conceptual data model diagram with an arc, commonly known as an 'exclusive arc'.

Figure 4.3 introduces a new entity, **PROJECT**, so that employees can be assigned to projects as well as departments. There are no restrictions constraining employees to only be assigned to projects managed by their own department; employees can be assigned to projects managed by departments other than their own. Assignments to both departments and projects are to be recorded. In our previous model, the **ASSIGNMENT** entity had only one attribute, *effective date*. This was adequate when assignments were only to departments, but for assignments to projects we need to know the start and end dates of the assignments. So the **ASSIGNMENT** entity now has two attributes, *start date* and *end date*. The **ASSIGNMENT** entity also has a relationship to the **PROJECT** entity as well as to the **DEPARTMENT** entity. These two relationships are crossed by an arc at the **ASSIGNMENT** entity end, indicating that they are mutually exclusive as far as **ASSIGNMENT** is concerned.

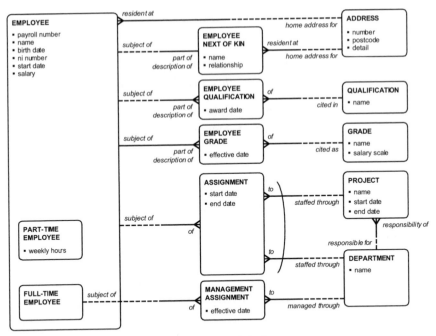

FIGURE 4.3 *An exclusive arc*

These mutually exclusive relationships are read as follows:

✱   Each ASSIGNMENT must be *to* one and only one DEPARTMENT
OR *to* one and only one PROJECT

✱   Each DEPARTMENT may be *staffed through* one or more ASSIGNMENTS

✱   Each PROJECT may be *staffed through* one or more ASSIGNMENTS

Exclusive arcs are useful in enabling the data modeller to indicate a real-world situation – the exclusive nature of relationships between entities. The arc also explicitly shows the clear specification of a constraint in the model: for any one instance of the entity only one of the mutually exclusive relationships may be recorded. In the real world, an assignment can be to either a department or a project, but not to both. This means that, within any database, an assignment record may be associated with either a department or a project record but not both.

The mutual exclusivity shown by the exclusive arc in Figure 4.3 involves two relationships and the mutually exclusive ends of these relationships are both 'mandatory' (must be) and 'many' (one or more). Mutual exclusivity is not restricted to the 'mandatory many' type of relationship ends. A set of mutually exclusive relationships may include relationship ends that are 'many' (one or more), 'one' (one and only one), or a mixture of both. However, a set of mutually exclusive relationships must include ends that are either all 'mandatory' (must be) or all 'optional' (may be); a mixture of mandatory and optional is not allowed.

Mutually exclusive relationships or subtypes?

When developing a conceptual data model, it is sometimes difficult to decide whether to use the subtyping technique or to mark relationships as being mutually exclusive. This is because the two concepts are really saying the same thing in different ways. With subtyping, we are saying that the instances of the supertype may be classified into distinct groups; with mutually exclusive relationships, we are saying that each relationship only applies to certain instances of the relevant entity – the instances of that entity are grouped according to the relevance of the relationships.

For example, instead of using the exclusive arc to indicate that assignments may be either to a department or to a project but not to both, as in Figure 4.3, we could have subtyped ASSIGNMENT into DEPARTMENT ASSIGNMENT and PROJECT ASSIGNMENT, as in Figure 4.4.

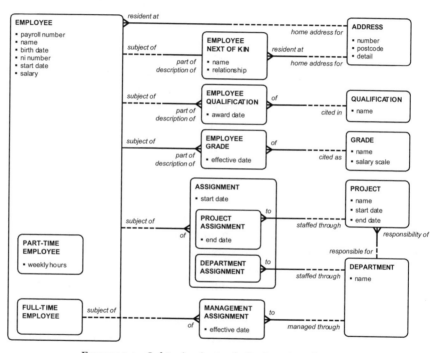

FIGURE 4.4   *Subtyping instead of using an exclusive arc*

It could be argued that this model is better than that in Figure 4.3 because the fact that we only need to know the end date of assignments to projects is explicitly shown by having ***end date*** as the only attribute of the PROJECT ASSIGNMENT subtype of ASSIGNMENT.

These relationships are now read as follows:

Each DEPARTMENT ASSIGNMENT <u>must be</u>
to <u>one and only one</u> DEPARTMENT

✳   Each **DEPARTMENT** <u>may be</u>
                staffed through <u>one or more</u> **DEPARTMENT ASSIGNMENTS**

✳   Each **PROJECT ASSIGNMENT** <u>must be</u> *to* <u>one and only one</u> **PROJECT**

✳   Each **PROJECT** <u>may be</u>
                staffed through <u>one or more</u> **PROJECT ASSIGNMENTS**

Entity subtypes can often be replaced by a set of mutually exclusive relationships. Exclusive arcs, identifying mutually exclusive relationships, can always be replaced by subtypes. You may, therefore, question why we have the exclusive arc notation. Indeed, some data modelling notations, such as IDEF1X (see Appendix A), do not have an exclusive arc notation. It is, then, necessary to use entity subtypes to show the 'mutually exclusive relationship' concept. There are two benefits of having the exclusive arc. The first is that it can be used as a shorthand notation as the model is being developed: you realise that there is some exclusivity and wish to record it; later you come back to the model and, if necessary, introduce the more-detailed entity subtypes. The second benefit comes about because using an exclusive arc instead of a set of entity subtypes provides a less cluttered and easier-to-read model. It could, therefore, make it easier to discuss a model with business people if the entity subtypes are replaced by exclusive arcs. The model with the more detailed entity subtypes is not lost; it is just not exposed to the business.

THE NATURE OF A CORPORATE DATA MODEL

In Chapter 2, we saw the development of a conceptual data model that recorded the information requirements of a specific business area to inform the development of the database that is at the heart of an information system to support that business area and only that business area. This information system, like most information systems, supports a limited set of users carrying out a limited set of business processes. We also saw how the technique of relational data analysis could be used to complement that model. However that conceptual data model is developed, it is restricted to that subset of the total information requirements of the enterprise that is required to support the current business processes or the business processes under consideration, for that restricted business area.

This approach to data modelling, therefore, provides a data model that, within the bounds of a single project, is relatively easy to understand but leads to a database design that is usually based on the current use of information and data. Any requirement to store new 'data items' or to change the 'business rules' that apply to information or data means a change to the conceptual data model, with subsequent changes to the database structure and the application programs that access the structure. The problem is often compounded because a database supporting a single system is normally optimised to improve the performance of the applications developed for that system. In the worst case, the scale of the changes to the system required when the business processes change may be so prohibitively costly, in both time and money, that the systems start to constrain rather than enhance the business.

The scope of a corporate data model must extend beyond a single information system or business area. In my view, any attempt to produce a corporate data model using an approach similar to the development of the conceptual data model of a single project is bound to fail, especially if the purpose of the initiative is to develop a corporate data model that forms the basis of the database design for all future systems. There are two interrelated reasons for this:

- Since the complexity of the corporate data model is proportional to the complexity of the enterprise, for a very complex organisation the corporate data model could be exceedingly large and exceedingly complex, requiring many years (or decades) of development. It is also very probable that because of its complexity and its size the finished product will be unintelligible to all except those who have been intimately involved in its development.

- Physical database design and application development must be postponed until the development of the corporate data model is completed. If it is not, the organisation will be continuously developing legacy systems as the development of the corporate data model overtakes the development of the systems.

A corporate data model, by definition, has to cover many different business areas. If the corporate data model is to be used as the basis for all future database design, it also has to be stable. A corporate data model, therefore, has to cope with:

- the different, sometimes conflicting, uses of information and data required by the different business areas;

- the uncertain nature of the future information and data requirements across the enterprise.

Information and data is used in many different ways by the many disparate business areas within an enterprise. Whilst a single project, supporting one business area or a single set of business processes, could produce a conceptual data model encapsulating that functional area's use of information, this becomes increasingly more difficult the broader the scope of the data model. In the development of a conceptual data model to support all of an enterprise's activity – to inform the development of a large number of inter-operating systems – I believe that it will become necessary to develop a data model that is ever more generic or abstract in nature. The implications of this are discussed later. Examples of the different uses of information that lead to this increasing 'genericity' of a corporate data model include:

- **Differences between departments over the meaning of the term 'customer'.** For the finance department, a customer is someone who has placed an order and needs to pay for the goods or services ordered, whilst for the sales and marketing department a customer could be someone that they are working with to develop a relationship so that they will place an order at some time in the future. Furthermore, for the finance department the customer is the department of the 'customer organisation' who is responsible for paying the invoice, whilst for the sales and marketing department the customer could be the person within the 'customer organisation' with the power to make purchasing decisions.

- **Overlapping roles.** For a company selling computer equipment and consumables, another company can be both a supplier, for example, supplying the paper to be sold, and a customer, for example, by buying computers to manage its own operations. For a finance company or a bank, an employee may also be a customer.

Also, in any enterprise there is some uncertainty over the future data requirements of the enterprise. If there is not to be continual reengineering of the information systems, their databases must have sufficient in-built flexibility to be able to store and distribute new information. The corporate data model must, therefore, reflect the requirement that databases derived from the corporate data model must be able to store data about 'objects', activities and concepts that have never before been identified or are based on rapidly changing 'business processes' that are updated as procedures are adapted to meet new circumstances. The database structures should be static over time, but capable of accommodating business change.

A corporate data model can either be very large, with very many entities in the model, and very detailed and specific, or else can be relatively small, with very few entities, and very abstract or generic. A corporate data model that is large and specific encapsulates all the business rules and is expressed using names and terms that are familiar to the business. It is a good model with which to discuss data requirements with the business, but any databases designed with such a model as their basis would be unlikely to cope with business change. A corporate data model that is small and generic leads to stable database designs that cope with business change, but its generic nature means that it is not a suitable vehicle for discussions with the business.

Generic data models and their implications are discussed further in Appendix C.

HOW TO DEVELOP A CORPORATE DATA MODEL

I have identified three possible approaches to the development of a corporate data model: a bottom-up approach that I call 'attribute trawling'; the joining of multiple project or area data models; and a top-down approach to the development of a single model.

Attribute-trawling approach

This approach involves studying all the existing information systems, collecting the data definitions from those systems (which are probably not documented, so will need to be extracted from the schema definitions held by the database management system) and, once all the definitions are collected, sorting them out so that good, reusable definitions are obtained. These can then be documented in a corporate data model.

There are three major problems with this approach:

- There may be some areas of the enterprise, or some business processes, that are not currently supported by information systems; there will, in consequence, be a gap in the analysis.
- It is well known that many information systems do not actually meet the users' expectations or needs; the data definitions gathered during this exercise will, therefore, be of dubious quality.
- It is unclear how the data definitions will be analysed and compared; there may just be too many to be handled without automated support and such support is not readily available.

For these three reasons, I do not recommend 'attribute trawling' as an appropriate method for the development of a corporate data model.

Joining project or area models

This approach involves the independent modelling of the information or data requirements of the separate business areas within the enterprise. These models are then amalgamated to form an enterprise-wide corporate data model. This is the approach recommended by many authors. However, this approach often fails, even when a common set of modelling standards are used.

The reason for these failures is exactly because the models are developed independently of each other. Although the models may have been developed to common standards, the reason for the failure was the absence of a common 'theme' in the models. There are often no easily identifiable common points where the models could join. What is needed is a common theme.

> *Aside*: I have personal experience of two corporate data modelling initiatives where the 'join project or area models' approach was taken but which failed as soon as an attempt was made to amalgamate the first two independently developed models, and there were a significant number of other models waiting to be amalgamated later.

Hence I also do not recommend the joining of project or area models as an appropriate method for the development of a corporate data model.

Building top-down

Building top-down implies the development of a single conceptual data model that, from its inception, is intended to cover the complete information and data requirements of the whole enterprise.

If the intention is to model separate project or business areas independently and then to join the models, and it is discovered that a common theme is needed, this implies that there has to be some modelling before the project or business area requirements are themselves modelled. In effect, this is the development of a 'framework' model, probably based on the core business of the enterprise. If, for prioritising or staffing reasons, it is necessary to model project or business area requirements separately then the 'framework' model can be used as the skeleton for the separate project or business area models, with the local requirements becoming the flesh on the skeleton. It is then easier to amalgamate the separate models.

It is my view, therefore, that the best approach is to build the corporate data model 'top-down', starting from a core or framework model that represents the major objects and concepts of the business. It can then be used as a skeleton and 'fleshed-out' with the requirements of the individual project or business areas.

Top-down starter models

The problem with starting the top-down development of a corporate data model is determining the most appropriate 'starter model'. Picking up a blank sheet of paper with the intention of modelling the information or data requirements for a large and complex organisation is a daunting prospect. It is useful to have an outline of a model to start with. There are many such models that can be used. Figure 4.5, Figure 4.6 and Figure 4.7 show just three of the possible top-down starter models.

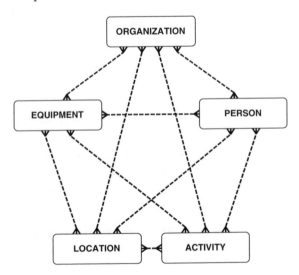

Figure 4.5   *A first top-down starter model*

The entities in this first model represent the major concepts in any business and they are all interrelated. The problem is in the detail of these optional many-to-many relationships. Resolving them will take many hours of detailed modelling. There will almost certainly be a need to identify and record subtypes of the five main entity types.

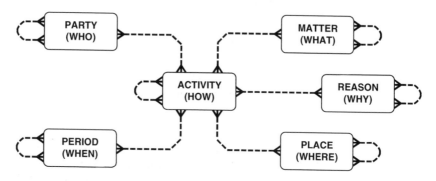

FIGURE 4.6   *A second top-down starter model*

In this model, the entities represent the 'what', 'where', 'when', 'who', 'why' and 'how' of all businesses, recognising that the common link is the 'how' – the activities of the business. As before, the development of this model probably requires subtyping of the six main entities and resolution of the many-to-many relationships.

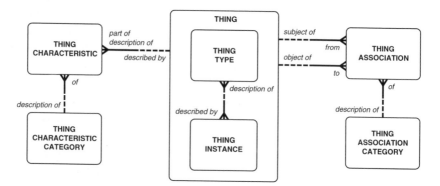

FIGURE 4.7   *A third top-down starter model*

Figure 4.7 shows what is probably the ultimate generic model. The **THING INSTANCE** and **THING TYPE** entity types need further subtyping, as may the **THING ASSOCIATION** and **THING CHARACTERISTIC** entity types. The relationships may also require refinement. Note that the relationship between **THING INSTANCE** and **THING TYPE** is a many-to-many relationship. It is possible that a real-world object may simultaneously be of more than one real-world type. This is particularly true of people.

CORPORATE DATA MODEL PRINCIPLES

As a result of leading the development of a corporate data model, I have developed six principles for the development of corporate data models. These principles are:

- develop the model 'top-down';
- give primacy to the core business;
- cover the whole enterprise;
- future-proof the model;
- develop cooperatively;
- gain consensus, not perfection.

Develop the model 'top-down'

In the previous section of this chapter, we looked at various options for developing a corporate data model. We saw that the best approach is to develop the corporate data model using a 'top-down' modelling approach. This, therefore, becomes our first principle.

Give primacy to the core business

Clearly, a corporate data model must be developed with the core business of the enterprise uppermost in the minds of the developers. If the corporate data model is to be for an enterprise whose main business is selling goods to retail customers, the core of the corporate data model should be based on sales and products and not on the data requirements of the human resources department. This ensures that the model is correctly focused. Awareness that the core business has been given primacy should also appeal to senior management, adding weight and authority to the development of the corporate data model.

It is only possible to give primacy to the core business if it is clearly defined. For some enterprises this is not so and it is difficult to identify an initial focus for the modelling effort.

The developers of the corporate data model need to be aware that by giving primacy to the 'core business' there is a danger of the model becoming too focused, thus making it extremely difficult to include other business areas within the model later on.

Cover the whole enterprise

Despite giving primacy to the core business, a corporate data model must be able to support the information needs across the full breadth of the enterprise. This ensures that the model covers all business viewpoints and that no data requirements are missed.

The resultant model could potentially cover a vast scope, particularly if the enterprise is very complex. This presents a major challenge to the modeller. Whilst developing a section of the model to support one business area, the modeller must be constantly considering all other business areas to ensure that decisions are not being made for one area that will disadvantage other areas. The modeller needs, therefore, to have an extensive knowledge of all the business areas within the corporation. This may determine which members of staff can be used to help develop the corporate data model.

Future-proof the model

For a corporate data model to be of real value, it must be stable over time; it must be 'future-proofed'. The model must, therefore, represent the true underlying nature of the information and data used in the business and not how that information or data is used at the time of the analysis. Provided there are no major changes of business purpose, the underlying nature of the information or data used in the business is unlikely to change, but the way that information and data is used and processed is often subject to change. To demonstrate this principle, I work through an example taken from my time in the Army.

Figure 4.8 shows a snippet of a model from the documentation for a proposed system that was intended to support the issue of stores to deployed units.

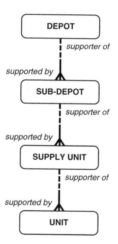

FIGURE 4.8   *The supply-chain model*

This snippet has two major flaws:

- It ignores the fact that a unit within the supply chain that supplies stores (be it a depot, a sub-depot or a supply unit) is also a unit that 'consumes' stores.
- It replicates the supply-chain hierarchy in use at the time of the analysis. It was unfortunate that by the time the system was implemented, all of the sub-depots had been closed as a cost-saving measure!

The model in Figure 4.9 provides us with a more stable solution. It uses entity subtyping to recognise that supply-chain units may also be consumer units. It also allows levels of supply-chain units to be added or removed; although the data may change, the data model, and the resulting data structure, is stable.

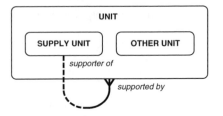

FIGURE 4.9   *The improved supply-chain model*

But this is not very helpful if we need to include a number of different business areas, as illustrated in Figure 4.10.

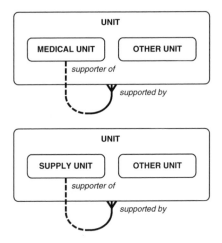

FIGURE 4.10   *More than one type of support?*

Here we see that as well as support from the supply chain units we may also have dedicated medical units to provide support. We need a way of bringing these two models together. One approach is shown in Figure 4.11.

This is technically correct, but now we have the various classifications of support units explicit in the model and, therefore, explicit in the database structure. Any change – addition or removal – of a classification requires a change to the model, which then needs to be reflected in database structures and application programs.

To ensure that changes in business practices which cannot be predicted – such as a change to the classifications of support units – can be handled without expensive changes to the corporate data model that, in turn, require expensive changes to database structures and application programs, our future-proofed design needs to be more generic, as shown in Figure 4.12.

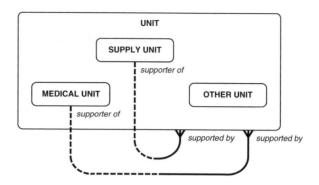

FIGURE 4.11   *The combined support model*

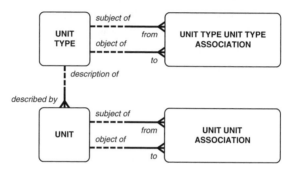

FIGURE 4.12

Because of the 'genericity' that comes with future-proofing, the advantages of model stability, database-design stability, interface-design stability and cost saving need to be balanced with the loss of explicit business information within the model, the increased run-time processing load and the need to manage data as well as data definitions. These issues are discussed in more detail when we discuss data models in Appendix C.

Develop cooperatively

It is impossible for a data management or corporate data modelling team to develop a corporate data model in isolation. Co-operation is essential. The data modellers must consult widely with subject-matter experts in the various business areas in the enterprise and with the technical people who are familiar with the existing information systems or who will be responsible for the development of future systems.

This co-operation ensures commitment both to the development of the corporate data model and to its subsequent use to inform systems development, enhancing the ability to share data. It is an unfortunate by-product of any collaborative activity that progress is slowed down by the collaboration.

Gain consensus, not perfection

There is a danger that a corporate data modelling team will seek to develop the perfect model. This is laudable, but may lead to a delay in the implementation of effective data management. The team should be prepared to publish and support a model that is deemed to be 'fit for role' by all business areas, even if it is not perfect. Although such a model may not be perfect, agreement to a model that can be used across the enterprise is gained earlier than it would have been otherwise. Iterative 'tweaking' of the model by the corporate data modelling team – attempting to develop the elusive perfect model – achieves no good purpose for the business. But strong management of the corporate data modelling team is needed to avoid it; some data modellers are never satisfied and always try to improve their models.

Of course, despite all the advantages of not necessarily seeking out the perfect model, a model that is not deemed to be 'fit for role' should not be accepted. Development and refinement must continue until a model that is deemed to be 'fit for role' is developed.

A FINAL THOUGHT

Figure 4.13 shows a familiar triangle used to illustrate the trade-offs between three competing aims – quality, speed and cheapness.

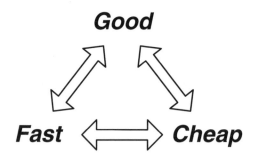

FIGURE 4.13   *The trade-off triangle*

You can only ever have two of these three. If you need a high-quality corporate data model quickly, it will be very expensive. If you need a high-quality corporate data model without paying a lot of money, it will take a long time to produce. If you need a corporate data model quickly and you cannot afford to pay much for it, the model will be of poor quality. The trick is to pick the best two for your particular situation.

But remember, 'People forget how fast you did something, but not how well you did it.'

SUMMARY

This chapter introduced the concept of a corporate data model by looking at the purpose of such a model. Two new data modelling concepts, entity subtypes and the exclusive arc, were then introduced. The way that the broad scope of a corporate data model affects its form and composition was then discussed. Three approaches to the development of a corporate data model – bottom-up attribute trawling, joining project or business area models and taking a top-down approach – were discussed. We then established six principles of corporate data modelling: develop the model 'top-down'; give primacy to the core business; cover the whole enterprise; future-proof the model; develop cooperatively; and gain consensus, not perfection.

5 Data Definition and Naming Conventions

Developing data definitions that can be used as corporate standards is seen by many as the primary role of the data administrator. Data definitions should be developed using conventions or guidelines that specify what constitutes a data definition and how the names of data 'objects' are to be formed. This chapter introduces definition and naming concepts applicable to structured data that is to be implemented using a relational database management system.

THE ELEMENTS OF A DATA DEFINITION

Guidelines are essential to ensure that each data object – entity, attribute, relationship, table, column, etc. – is documented to a particular standard. This standard must provide the minimum acceptable level of descriptive information about data that is to be made available to all the potential users of that data. These potential users are probably first and foremost the developers of future systems, but they may also be people from the business who are interested in knowing what data is available and where.

Although it is possible to suggest what descriptive information about data should be available, these guidelines probably need to be specific to the organisation. This enables the guidelines to cover those aspects of data definition that are important to the management of data within that particular organisation. It is difficult to be prescriptive as to what should be included in a data definition.

Most data definition frameworks or guidelines are based on what is loosely called a 'data item' – roughly equating to a field in a file record, to an attribute in a conceptual data model and to a column in an SQL schema. The elements of such a data definition framework should include as a minimum:

- a name or label;
- a significance statement;
- formats;
- valid value lists or validation criteria;
- valid operations;
- ownership details;
- usage details;
- source;
- comments;
- configuration information.

Fundamental to this standard is that each data item should have a name that uniquely identifies the data item. Naming conventions are discussed later in this chapter. Where there is the possibility of more than one name being applicable, one name must be considered as the primary name and all the other names should be recorded as aliases or synonyms. Each data item should also have a comprehensive and accurate description of the item. It is preferable if the description is held in the form of a significance statement – a statement of why the data item is deemed to be significant to the business. If the data item has no significance to the business there is no reason for it to be defined; couching descriptions in terms of the significance of the data to the business helps develop a description that is meaningful to the business, which in turn helps system developers ensure that the data is unambiguously understood when used by application programs.

Details of the format of the data should be included in the definition. This may simply be a statement that the data is currency, a number, a date or a string of characters; but it may also include details of any restrictions that need to be applied, for example, the maximum length of a string of characters.

It is also essential to include lists of valid values or a statement of any validation criteria that may be applied to the data. For some data items, there may be a predetermined list of valid values. For 'Gender', the valid values may be restricted to 'Male' and 'Female', or may be 'Male', 'Female' and 'Unknown'; for 'Staff Category', the values might be 'Full-time Employee', 'Part-time Employee' and 'Contractor'. For other data items, validation criteria may be needed. For 'Salary', the validation criterion might be 'greater than £0 and less than or equal to £100,000'; for 'Surname', the validation criterion might be 'only include the characters A–Z, a–z, space, hyphen and apostrophe'.

The operations that it is valid to carry out on the data should also be recorded. It is, for example, valid to multiply a length by a number to give a greater (or smaller) length. It is also valid to multiply a length by another length, to give an area. It is valid to multiply a currency amount by a number to give another currency amount, maybe as part of a currency-exchange transaction. It makes no sense, however, to multiply a currency amount by another currency amount, and so such an operation would not be valid. For data that comprises strings of characters it is important to record where it is valid to concatenate that data with other string data.

Ownership details should be recorded. Ownership exists at two levels – ownership of the data definition and ownership of the data values. The owner of the data definition is the person in the organisation who has the authority to say that this data should be held and that this definition is the appropriate definition for the data. It should be the responsibility of the owner of the data definition, not the data administrator, to obtain agreement for the data definition across the organisation. The owner of the data definition may also be the owner of the data values once they are recorded, but it may be more appropriate to assign this ownership role to another person (or group of people). Data ownership should not be confused with data stewardship, which is a task normally carried out by the data administrators. Data steward-ship involves the maintenance of the data definition on behalf of the owner of the data definition.

Where the data that is defined by this definition is used should also be recorded. This will generally be in the form of a list of the information systems that use data that is the subject of the data definition.

The source of the data definition should be included in the definition. The source may be the owner of the data definition, or it may be that the data administrator has developed the data definition using knowledge gained during the analysis of the data requirements. Alternatively, it could be that the definition originated in a procedural manual or some other documentation.

It may be necessary to record some extra comments to expand or clarify some other element of the definition. Only in exceptional cases should it be necessary to add extra comments; it should really be possible to include all the detail necessary under the other headings.

Finally, the data definition should include information to enable versions of the definition to be controlled. This may include details of the original author and the date of the authorship plus details of any subsequent modi-fications.

It is important to understand the form of the 'data item' to which a defini-tion built to these standards applies. Is it the definition of a field, an attribute or a column? Is it a definition of the format, structure and values that may be applied to more than one attribute? If it is the latter, then it is not a field, attribute or column definition, but is a definition of the equivalent of a domain in the relational model of data – a definition of 'a pool of values that an attribute may take'.

Examples of two 'data item' definitions are shown in Figures 5.1 and 5.2. The definition in Figure 5.1 has validation criteria and a set of valid operations, whilst that in Figure 5.2 has a set of valid values.

The data definition elements listed above are those suggested for the defin-ition of a 'data item' or domain. The concepts behind these data definition elements can be adopted to provide the conventions for the definition of other data objects, such as entities, relationships and tables. For example, the definition of an entity could include its primary name, any aliases for the primary name, the relationships the entity has with other entities (preferably expressed as sentences reading from the entity being defined), the attributes of the entity and the descriptions of any unique identifiers. An example of an entity definition constructed using these elements is in Figure 5.3.

Name or Label	Salary
Significance Statement	has significance as the annual salary, expressed in whole pounds Sterling, paid to an employee of the company before the addition of any extra payments for overtime and/or performance bonuses and before the application of any statutory deductions
Format	Currency
Value List	Not applicable
Validation Criteria	> 0
Valid Operations	multiply by number; answer is currency divide by number; answer is currency add currency; answer is currency subtract currency; answer is currency divide by currency; answer is ratio
Ownership	HR Director
Users	HR Management System, Payroll System
Source	Interview Deputy HR Manager, 15 Sep 06
Comments	None
Date created	15 Sep 06
Author	K F Gordon
Date last updated	3 Feb 07

FIGURE 5.1   *A data definition with validation criteria and valid operations*

Name or Label	Relationship
Significance Statement	has significance as the description of the personal relationship that exists between an employee and another person
Format	Character
Value List	Spouse Partner Child Parent Distant relative Friend
Validation Criteria	None
Valid Operations	None
Ownership	HR Director
Users	HR Management System
Source	HR Manual Edition 3 Section 3-44
Comments	Spouse now includes Civil Partner
Date created	27 Jun 02
Author	J Smith
Date last updated	20 Jan 06

FIGURE 5.2   *A data definition with valid values*

Each **EMPLOYEE NEXT OF KIN**

    has significance as the person nominated by an employee as the person to be notified in the event of any emergency involving that employee

Each **EMPLOYEE NEXT OF KIN**

    may also be known as an **EMPLOYEE EMERGENCY CONTACT**

Each **EMPLOYEE NEXT OF KIN**

    must be part of description of one and only one **EMPLOYEE**
    must be resident at one and only one **ADDRESS**

Each **EMPLOYEE NEXT OF KIN** has attributes:

    name
    relationship

No two **EMPLOYEE NEXT OF KIN** can have the same combination of:

    part of description of one and only one **EMPLOYEE**
    name

FIGURE 5.3   *An entity definition*

DATA NAMING CONVENTIONS

The purpose of a data naming convention

A data naming convention should be developed to provide consistent, unique and meaningful names for all existing and new items within the enterprise's common data resource. A consistent approach to data naming should be applied across the enterprise to help achieve unambiguous understanding of data. Data names need to be both unique and meaningful to the business; unique so that the data objects to which they refer can be unambiguously identified and meaningful so that the terms used in the names are terms familiar to the business. Technical terms and abbreviations should be avoided wherever possible.

The data names should, however, also aid communication between all those involved in the use and development of information systems; they must be meaningful to those involved in systems analysis and design as well as to the business.

Consistent, unique and meaningful names can only be achieved if the conventions are well known and easily understood and followed. The conventions must be enforceable.

A typical data naming convention

All data naming conventions rely on using terms, which may be either single words or a number of words, in a precise and predefined manner. Key to this in all naming conventions is what is known as the class word or term. This is also sometimes known as a representation term. Typical class words might be, for example, 'identifier', 'number' and 'text', providing an indication of the form or the representation of the data.

The typical data naming convention that I describe provides names for 'data items' constructed of three terms:

- a mandatory prime term that provides the context of the data, which normally means the entity or table holding the 'data item';
- one or more optional modifier terms that are used to make the meaning of the data explicit;
- a mandatory class term that indicates the 'class' of the data.

Examples of some names constructed using this convention are:

Employee Height

Employee Hair Colour

Employee Eye Colour

Employee Birth Date

Employee Employment Start Date

Employee Qualification Effective Date

Employee Qualification Issuing Authority Name.

In these names, 'Employee' and 'Employee Qualification' are prime terms; 'Hair', 'Eye', 'Birth', 'Employment Start', 'Effective' and 'Issuing Authority' are modifier terms; and 'Date', 'Height', 'Colour' and 'Name' are class terms.

With very few exceptions, abbreviations should not be used in the names of objects that are part of a conceptual data model. The only exceptions should be where an abbreviation has achieved common usage and the full term is seldom, if ever, used, for example, UN instead of United Nations. Because of constraints in the database management system software, it may be necessary to abbreviate 'physical' names of tables and columns in an SQL schema. The naming convention should include, therefore, a standard approach to abbreviating names when the SQL schema is being derived from the conceptual data model. Appendix D provides an example of a full data naming convention.

Problems associated with data naming conventions

There are basically two problems with data naming conventions: they can be over-prescriptive and they may not deliver what is expected. Some organisations have decided to adopt the prime-modifier-class term approach to data naming but have then produced a very restricted list of acceptable class terms. The worst case I have seen had only 11 class terms – 'amount', 'quantity', 'code', 'identifier', 'name', 'text', 'rate', 'dimension', 'volume', 'weight', 'date' and 'time'. Within this convention, the name 'Employee Height' would need to be replaced with 'Employee Height Dimension' (i.e. 'Height' has now become a modifier term) and 'Employee Hair Colour' would become 'Employee Hair Colour Name' ('Hair Colour' now being the modifier term). Whilst data names developed using such a restricted set of class terms are very precise they do produce names that appear to those who are not managers to be very idiosyncratic. Exposure of data names such as 'Employee Hair Colour Name' to the business community can bring the whole data management initiative into disrepute. Whilst I believe that there should be a standard list of acceptable class terms, I do believe that this list should not be too restrictive.

There is a view that the correct use of a data naming convention enables the identification, through common names, of common 'data items' in different data models. I call this the 'utopian view of data modelling'. Data modelling is largely a subjective activity. Whilst the use of a naming convention to ensure a consistency of approach to the naming of data objects is good practice, it is unlikely that the use of a naming convention alone will lead to the development of identical names by modellers operating independently of each other who are modelling similar business concepts. One modeller might use the name 'Prospect' for an entity that another modeller might quite legitimately call 'Potential Customer'.

The chance of the development of identical or similar names is improved if the naming convention is supported by a thesaurus or controlled vocabulary. A data naming thesaurus contains a list of approved terms, their meanings and their allowed uses as prime, modifier or class terms. It may also include details of terms that are 'broader than' or 'narrower than' an individual term, making it easier to select the appropriate term to use in any particular circumstance. It also contains a list of disallowed terms and the appropriate approved terms to use in their place. For example:

- 'Customer' may be used as a prime term, and is a narrower term than 'External Party' and a broader term than 'Potential Customer' and 'Actual Customer'.
- 'Prospect' is disallowed as a prime term; use 'Potential Customer'.

SUMMARY

This chapter has introduced the concepts of data definition and data naming, and why guidelines or conventions for these need to be in place. Suggestions were given for the detail needed for a data definition and examples were provided. The prime-modifier-class term data naming convention was described and some problems associated with naming conventions were discussed.

6 Metadata

WHAT IS METADATA?

This chapter introduces the concept of metadata and describes its role in data management and elsewhere.

Put very simply, metadata is 'data about data' or 'data that describes other data'. This is a very broad definition of metadata and, in consequence, the term 'metadata' is used in a number of different contexts, principally as:

- metadata for data management;
- metadata for content management;
- metadata for describing data values.

METADATA FOR DATA MANAGEMENT

The classical data management view is that metadata in some way describes the types of data stored in a database. Table and column definitions for a database schema managed by an SQL database management system are metadata. Constraint definitions are also metadata. Rules for accessing data in the database and for maintaining the quality of the data are metadata. Conceptual data models and the data definitions derived from them are also metadata. The relationships in a conceptual data model are metadata. Details of the ownership and source of data definitions are metadata. Any other information that helps business users and system developers with understanding what data is recorded in the enterprise's databases and where it is recorded is metadata.

Metadata may be held on paper (so is not really 'data' according to our definition from Chapter 1) or held electronically. Paper-based metadata may be made available to staff in manuals containing, for example, glossaries of business terms that support the use of the data, descriptions of the information systems owned by the enterprise and the data held by each system, and conceptual data models of the databases for the systems. Electronically held metadata may be stored in the enterprise's information systems. This metadata is used to support the management of the data held in the individual systems, for example, the system tables used by a database management system to hold details of the logical schema of the database and the metadata held by a data warehouse describing the schemas of the operational systems that feed the data warehouse. Metadata may also be held electronically in separate stand-alone systems to support data administration. These separate systems are often called data dictionaries or repositories. They are discussed in more detail in Chapter 10.

METADATA FOR CONTENT MANAGEMENT

Increasingly, the term metadata is also being used to describe data that describes the content of documents held in libraries and other archives and the content of web pages. A typical example of this use of the term metadata is the Dublin Core Metadata Element Set, often informally known as the Dublin Core ('Dublin' is Dublin, Ohio, USA, the home of the Online Computer Library Center, and not Dublin, Ireland).

The Dublin Core is a standard for describing information resources – video, sound, image, text and web pages – that may be used in many different contexts. The first version of the Dublin Core was designed for simple resource discovery. It has 15 metadata elements, each of which is optional and may be repeated:

- **title** – a name by which the resource is known;
- **creator** – a person, an organisation or a service;
- **subject**;
- **description** – which may include an abstract table of contents, reference to a graphical representation of the content or a free-text account of the content;
- **publisher**;
- **contributor**;
- **date**;
- **type** – whether the resource is a moving image, a still image, sound, text, etc.;
- **format**;
- **identifier** – for example, a Uniform Resource Identifier (URI) or an International Standard Book Number (ISBN);
- **source**;
- **language**;
- **relation** – any related resources;
- **coverage** – spatial, temporal or jurisdiction;
- **rights** – for example, Intellectual Property Rights (IPR), copyright and various property rights.

Another version of the Dublin Core, the Qualified Dublin Core, has been developed. There are three additional elements (**audience, provenance** and **rightsHolder**). Some of the simple Dublin Core elements may also be qualified; for example, the **date** element may be qualified to be **available, created, dateAccepted, dateCopyrighted, dateSubmitted, issued, modified** or **valid**.

The Dublin Core is not the only standard for content management. Amongst the many others available are the Standard for Learning Object Metadata published by the Institute of Electrical and Electronics Engineers (IEEE), the Resource Description Framework (RDF) specifications from the World Wide Web Consortium (W3C), and the Agricultural Metadata Element Set (AgMES) from the Food and Agriculture Organisation (FAO) of the United Nations.

METADATA FOR DESCRIBING DATA VALUES

As the ability to store multimedia data – moving images, sounds, still images, text, etc. – in a database becomes increasingly available, there is a need to store extra data that describes the content of the multimedia data or how the multimedia data is to be processed by an application when it is retrieved from the database. This extra data is also known as metadata.

Some of this metadata may be held as part of the multimedia itself. Still images (line drawings, photographs, etc.) may be stored and exchanged in a number of different formats, including JPEG (Joint Photographic Experts Group File Interchange Format), GIF (Graphics Interchange Format), BMP (Windows bitmap format) and TIFF (Tagged Image File Format). All of these standard formats embed metadata within the file itself; the BMP and TIFF formats provide contrasting approaches to the embedding of metadata within a file.

A bitmap file in BMP format contains four blocks of data. The first block is the **Bitmap Header** which identifies the file as a bitmap file; the second block is the **Bitmap Information** which stores more detailed information about the bitmap image such as its height and width; the third block is the **Color Palette** which stores the definition of the colours being used; and the fourth block is the **Bitmap Data** which describes the image, pixel by pixel, starting from the bottom left corner. The first three of these four blocks of data is embedded metadata.

In a TIFF file, the embedded metadata is held in the file header in the form of tags. These tags indicate, for example, the size of the image, how the image data is arranged and whether image compression has been used.

The purpose of the embedded metadata in these still image file formats is to describe how the images contained in the files should be processed and displayed. The same is true with embedded metadata in other multimedia file types, for example, video clips, audio files or documents in proprietary word-processing formats.

It is generally impossible to query a multimedia data file to find out about its content. You cannot, for example, browse a number of JPEG files to find those that include photographs of dark-haired men without displaying the images held in the files. If there is a requirement to sort through a number of images to find those of people with, for instance, a particular hair colour or another identifying feature then this information must be held as data in the database alongside the multimedia file. There may, therefore, be additional columns in the database to hold hair colour, eye colour, body shape, etc. The data held in these additional columns is also known as metadata.

SUMMARY

This chapter has introduced the concept of metadata. It has also described its importance in data management (where the metadata describes the types of data stored in a database and includes data definitions and information about them), in content management (where the metadata describes the content of documents held either on paper or electronically) and as additional information about multimedia data values (where the metadata may describe the content of the multimedia value, how the multimedia value is to be processed, or both).

7 Data Quality

In Chapter 1, we showed the importance of high-quality information to a business and, hence, that it is important that the underlying data is of good quality. In this chapter we investigate further the issues surrounding data quality. We look at the completeness and correctness dimensions of data quality and how to bring about an improvement in data quality.

WHAT IS DATA QUALITY?

The word quality means different things in different contexts. When talking about the quality of a dish served as part of a meal in a restaurant I could be talking about the very essence of that dish – the ingredients that the chef uses to create it. On the other hand I could be talking about its character once it has been prepared – its texture, its aroma, how spicy it is, etc. But in discussing the quality of a particular dish on a plate about to be served the chef is expressing an opinion as to how well that dish comes up to expectations – the extent to which it is fit for eating, the purpose for which it was created, or if it meets the restaurant's standards.

It is in this last sense – its 'fitness for use' or its 'goodness' or otherwise – that we use the term quality when talking about data quality. Olson defined data quality by saying that 'data has quality if it satisfies the requirements of its intended use' (Olson, 2003). He then went on to say:

> It lacks quality to the extent that it does not satisfy the requirement. In other words, data quality depends as much on the intended use as it does on the data itself. To satisfy the intended use, the data must be accurate, timely, relevant, complete, understood, and trusted.

ISSUES ASSOCIATED WITH POOR-QUALITY DATA

In their report entitled 'Data Quality and Integrity', the Butler Group (2004), an independent provider of IT research, analysis and advice, said that 'businesses have failed and will continue to do so, because they neglect to take seriously the management of data quality and integrity issues.'

For their Global Data Management Survey, PricewaterhouseCoopers (2004) surveyed 452 large and medium-sized companies in the UK, US and Australia. They found that only 34% of the companies surveyed claimed to be 'very confident' in the quality of their data.

Olson (2003) identified some areas in which costs are created and opportunities lost through poor data quality. These are:

- transaction rework costs, for example, needing a department to handle mishandled orders and shipments;
- costs incurred in implementing new systems, for example, errors in data increase the cost of implementing an enterprise data warehouse;
- delays in delivering data to decision makers, for example, having to manually massage information before it can be released to managers;
- lost customers through poor service, for example, customers not returning because of receiving incorrect shipments;
- lost production through supply-chain problems, for example, the wrong quantity of parts is ordered from a supplier.

Poor data quality is common across all business areas and has a major impact on customer service, revenue and profits. As shown in Chapter 1, poor-quality data leads to poor-quality information. Poor-quality data has a direct impact on an organisation's decision-making ability.

THE CAUSES OF POOR-QUALITY DATA

Poor-quality data can arise for a number of reasons, some technical and some human (although even the technical reasons can probably be traced back to some human error):

- databases having inappropriate schemas;
- errors being made on data entry;
- data decaying over time;
- data being corrupted when moved between systems;
- lack of understanding of the data when it is used.

As discussed in Chapter 2, databases should be designed so that there is no unnecessary duplication of data. They should also be designed so that they can cope with changes in requirements without major cost implications. Update anomalies, which can lead to data inconsistency, are avoided when there is no unnecessary duplication of data. Data inconsistency can lead to inaccurate information being presented to users. When databases are not designed to cope flexibly with future data requirements and the redesign of the database is too costly for the enterprise, there is a potential for reducing the overall data quality because 'work-arounds' are developed that overload columns in the database. Columns are then used to hold data which they were not designed to hold. Often these 'work-arounds' are not properly documented; knowledge about the meaning of data is held within the heads of a small number of users. Databases must be designed with flexibility and data quality in mind, even if this is at the expense of performance.

There can be a number of reasons why errors are made on data entry. Some of these reasons are accidental and some are deliberate. Accidental data-entry errors, for example, mistyping a date or a name, is the most common source of poor-quality data. The number of these accidental data-entry errors is sometimes increased because insufficient thought has been given to the way that data is entered. Spelling errors, for example, can be reduced by providing the user with a set of valid values from which to select an option. Another source of data-entry errors is where the system is designed so that values are needed for some data but those values are not actually available. Users then either enter fictional data so that they can complete the process or abandon the data entry until the data values are available.

The value of some data decays over time. This is particularly true of databases supporting human resources operations. The qualifications held by employees are normally recorded when they are first employed but it is very seldom that a human resources department has procedures in place to ensure that this data is regularly checked and updated. An employee can, therefore, work hard to gain new qualifications and yet these are not recorded in the company's information systems. A search to find employees with appropriate qualifications for a task may well miss the most appropriately qualified employee. In another environment, the stock figures in a retail store's database are normally amended to take account of the arrival of new stock and of sales, but the stock figures can be inaccurate if they are not regularly adjusted to take account of pilfering and shoplifting.

Perfectly good data can be corrupted when it is moved between systems, for example, when extracted from operational systems to feed a data warehouse. This corruption is generally because the documentation of the feeder systems has not been kept up to date as they have been modified and, consequently, inappropriate transformations and cleaning procedures have been applied to the data.

Finally, there is a danger that data may not be understood when it is presented to users. This is normally caused by the documentation being out of date or metadata being missing or ambiguous.

THE DIMENSIONS OF DATA QUALITY

There are two main dimensions of data quality – completeness and correctness. Completeness assesses the extent to which the data reflects the real-world situation. Correctness, on the other hand, assesses whether the data complies with the appropriate constraints and validation rules and whether it accurately reflects the real-world situation. These two dimensions of data quality apply to both metadata and occurrence data, as shown in Figure 7.1.

When considering the quality of metadata, all the data models, all the names for the data 'objects' and all of the physical implementations (specified using data definition languages (DDL) such as the data definition capabilities included in SQL) must be assessed in terms of completeness and correctness.

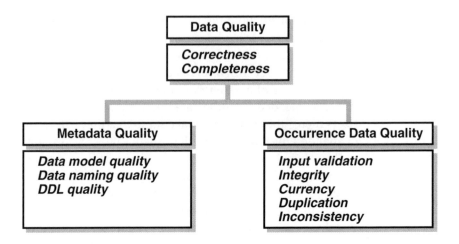

FIGURE 7.1   *The dimensions of data quality*

When considering the quality of occurrence data, the data used by the business, there are a number of key factors to be considered:

- **Input validation** – ensuring, wherever possible, that data is validated on input; it should be impossible to input an invalid date such as 35 October 2006 or to input a birth date for an employee that would imply that they were only two years of age when they started their employment with the company.
- **Integrity** – ensuring that data meets all the data integrity rules; no payroll numbers are duplicated, for example.
- **Currency** – ensuring that data is up to date; that changes in employee circumstances have been recorded.
- **Duplication** – ensuring that there is no logical duplication of data and that any physical duplication is properly managed.
- **Inconsistency** – ensuring that data remains consistent; this is generally achieved by managing duplication correctly.

DATA MODEL QUALITY

An initial starting point for ensuring that data is of good quality is to have a conceptual data model that is both complete and correct. There are a number of approaches that may be taken to the assessment of the quality of a conceptual data model; some of these approaches are purely qualitative, whilst others are quantitative, applying statistical techniques to the numbers of entities, attributes and relationships in the model. Many of these approaches have been reviewed in (Genero and Piattini, 2002).

An easily applied qualitative model for the assessment of the quality of a data model amongst those reviewed by Genero and Piattini is that proposed by (Reingruber and Gregory, 1994), which is shown in Figure 7.2.

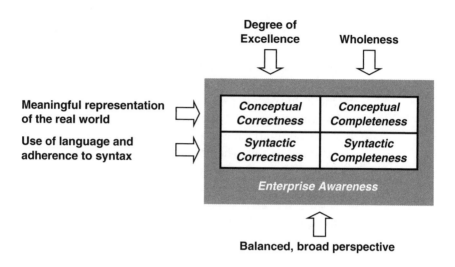

FIGURE 7.2   *The five dimensions of data model quality*

In this model, Reingruber and Gregory have augmented the correctness and completeness dimensions with two further orthogonal dimensions – the syntactic dimension and the semantic dimension. The syntactic dimension addresses how the modelling language and its syntax have been used whilst the semantic dimension addresses the relationship between the model and the data requirements of the business area that the model represents. Applying these orthogonal dimensions together, we get the four dimensions of syntactic correctness, syntactic completeness, conceptual correctness and conceptual completeness. Reingruber and Gregory have added a fifth, overarching, dimension that they call enterprise awareness. This recognises that any data model for a specific business area or set of business processes should be seen as a subset of the enterprise or corporate data model. It is the enterprise awareness dimension that is most often overlooked by data modellers working as part of project teams involved in the development of information systems.

IMPROVING DATA QUALITY

In their 'Data Quality and Integrity' report, the Butler Group (2004) reported that:

> Too many businesses are caught up in a cycle of managing the downstream impact of data quality with disproportionate resources when compared to implementing a proactive, ongoing data quality strategy. In short, data quality has to start before the physical data actually exists: prevention is better than cure.

This implies that to achieve effective, enduring data quality an enterprise needs to implement a set of procedures and a culture within the organisation that promotes and sustains good-quality data. Data quality must be the responsibility of a senior business manager. There is no point in having a project to cleanse the data without putting in place the environment to maintain the data in a clean state.

English (2002) has proposed a methodology (or, in his words, a 'value system') called Total Quality Data Management (TQdM) that has been developed to achieve just this. The name of this methodology has now been changed to Total Information Quality Management (TIQM), although the principles remain the same. An overview of the methodology is shown in Figure 7.3.

The first process, P1, looks at the quality of the design of the databases (that is, the quality of the data definitions) and of the overall information architecture, both from a technical perspective and from a customer-satisfaction perspective. The second process, P2, looks at the data itself. Again there is a technical perspective – does the data comply with the rules – and a customer-satisfaction perspective. The third process, P3, measures the costs of the poor-quality information in terms of reduced profit and revenue. The fourth process, P4, cleans the existing data, giving corrected and good-quality data. The fifth process, P5, improves the enduring information processes to ensure that the data is maintained at good quality. The sixth process, P6, is about effecting a cultural transformation so that there can be long-term information- and data-quality improvement.

The technical perspective of process P2 involves a set of techniques known as data profiling. This involves searching through the data looking for potential errors and anomalies, such as similar data with different spellings, data outside boundaries and missing values. For small volumes of data, profiling can be carried out by copying the data into a spreadsheet program and manipulating it using the spreadsheet facilities. Reordering a date column exposes invalid dates. Duplicate names can be identified if a name column is sorted alphabetically. Using filters can make it easy to see incorrect values outside a given range. For larger volumes of data, profiling can be carried out by writing appropriate SQL queries or by using visualisation tools that display graphs or charts based on the data. For very large data volumes, these techniques are time-consuming and are unlikely to find any but the most obvious errors or anomalies. There are, however, a number of data-profiling tools on the market that can speed up the process. These tools will not clean the data and they may not even identify the individual dirty data values. But they will provide details of the categories of dirty data that are present so that cleansing may then be applied.

Although much of the work to improve data quality is undertaken by technical data management staff, data quality is primarily a business issue. Unfortunately, it is often difficult to get the business to recognise that there is a problem. Although there may be information-architecture reasons that cause or allow poor-quality data, much of the poor-quality data arises through poor

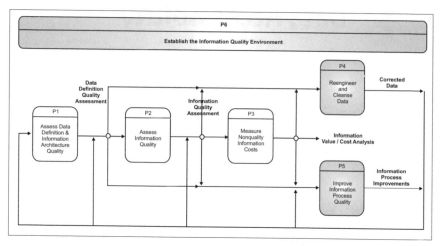

FIGURE 7.3   *Total Quality data Management methodology*

processes associated with the handling of information in the business. As the Butler Group (2004) identified:

> A typical response to data quality problems is to blame the IT department. Not only is this not helpful, it is not actually correct. Data quality needs to be seen as a business problem, not an IT problem.

Once poor-quality data has been cleaned, good data quality can only be maintained through a concerted effort by all in the business who create and use data. This will not only require the development of appropriate procedures, but it will also require an enterprise-wide education programme and a change in the overall culture of the organisation so that the importance of good-quality information and data is recognised.

SUMMARY

This chapter has defined data quality. It has looked at possible causes of poor data quality and looks at how data quality can be improved. It has identified the dimensions of data quality and has looked at data quality from the perspectives of both metadata, including conceptual data models, and occurrence data.

8 Data Accessibility

This chapter brings together three related topics, data security, data integrity and data recovery. Although the mechanisms to control security, integrity and recovery of data are normally controlled and managed by database administrators, the overall policies for the security, integrity and recovery of data fall within the remit of the data administration function.

DATA SECURITY

Data security is about protecting the database against unauthorised users. This is to maintain privacy, to ensure that data is not seen by those who are not entitled to see it, and also to ensure that data is not wilfully corrupted.

There should be an enterprise-wide data security policy in place. This policy should specify the degree of security protection to be applied to the different categories of data in the enterprise and who should have access to what data. The policy should be clear and concise so that all involved in the management of data can easily understand their role in the maintenance of the security of that data.

The policy is then enforced through the use of the security mechanisms provided both by the operating systems and the database management systems in use in the enterprise's information systems. The data security mechanisms available include access controls and encryption. Additionally, audit trails may be put in place to track who did what in the event of a breach of security.

Access controls

Most users only need access to a subset of the available data to carry out their duties. They should, therefore, have authorised access to that data and be prevented from accessing the rest of the data. This is where access controls come in.

Access controls rely on authentication procedures such as logins and associated passwords. Groups of data access rights are then granted to individuals, or to groups of individuals with the same or similar roles, based on their logins.

The aim of access control is to ensure that database users can only create, read, update or delete data relevant to their role. One of the functions of the database management system is to provide the facilities to enable this to be achieved. For example, SQL has a subset of the language that is the data control language (DCL) in addition to the data definition language (DDL), the part of SQL that allows for the creation of tables and the various constraints, and the data manipulation language (DML), which allows data to read, inserted, updated or deleted. Access to data or any database object (table, procedure, etc.) is restricted to the creator of the object, usually the database administrator. The creator of an object becomes its owner. No other users can access an object, say to read or update the data, unless privileges associated with that object have been given to that user. The data control statements in SQL allow for the granting and of revoking these privileges, which fall into three groups:

- table privileges;
- function and procedure privileges;
- database object privileges.

Table privileges allow the user to access specific base tables and views (the SQL name for virtual tables) and, maybe, specific columns within those tables. The privileges may be to **SELECT** (i.e. read) data, to **INSERT** (i.e. create) data, to **UPDATE** data or to **DELETE** data. There is an additional 'privilege', **ALL PRIVILEGES**, that allows the user to create, read, update and delete data. The **SELECT, INSERT** and **UPDATE** privileges can apply either to whole tables or to specific columns; the **DELETE** privilege can only apply to whole tables, that is only whole rows can be deleted. Typical table privilege statements are shown in Figure 8.1.

```
GRANT ALL PRIVILEGES ON employee
      TO human_resources;

GRANT SELECT ON employee
            (payroll_number, surname, salary)
      TO department_head;

GRANT UPDATE, INSERT ON qualification
      TO user27;
```

FIGURE 8.1   *Table privilege statements*

Function and procedure privileges allow users to execute stored SQL-invoked routines. These are routines that may be written in SQL (using the syntax for functions and procedures) and with the program code stored as part of the logical schema. Alternatively they may be written in some other pro-gramming language, such as C, with their definition stored as part of the logical schema. The privilege statement in Figure 8.2 allows the human resources department to execute a function that calculates the current age of an employee.

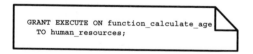

```
GRANT EXECUTE ON function_calculate_age
      TO human_resources;
```

FIGURE 8.2   *A function privilege statement*

Database object privileges control which users can create or alter database structures. These privileges are not part of the SQL standard but are provided by some vendors of database management systems. These privileges are normally reserved for database administrators. In fact, if these privileges are not restricted to database administrators it will be almost impossible to have enterprise-wide management of data. The privilege statement in Figure 8.3 allows the human resources department to create tables within their database.

```
GRANT CREATE table
    TO human_resources;
```

FIGURE 8.3   *A database object privilege statement*

All of these privileges may also be granted to all users by using the pseudo authorisation identifier **PUBLIC**.

Another way that access to data can be controlled is through the use of virtual tables or views. This becomes extremely powerful when combined with access controls. For example, instead of providing department heads with **SELECT** access to the **payroll_number**, **surname** and **salary** columns of the **employee** table it is possible to create an appropriate view for that data and grant access to that view, as shown in Figure 8.4.

```
CREATE VIEW employee_salary
    AS
    SELECT payroll_number, surname, salary
    FROM employee;

GRANT SELECT ON employee_salary
    TO department_head;
```

FIGURE 8.4   *A view statement and an associated table privilege statement*

Another example of the use of views is to restrict access to data for a particular user, for example, so that an employee can see their own employee record but no others. This can be achieved as shown in Figure 8.5 (assuming that a user's authorisation identifier is their payroll number).

```
CREATE VIEW single_employee
    AS
    SELECT *
    FROM employee
    WHERE payroll_number = USER;

GRANT SELECT ON single_employee
    TO PUBLIC;
```

FIGURE 8.5   *A user-specific view statement
and an associated table privilege statement*

Discretionary and mandatory access controls

There are two levels of access control:

- Discretionary Access Control (DAC) is where the users who are granted access rights are allowed to propagate those rights to other users.
- Mandatory Access Control (MAC) is where access rights cannot be changed by the users.

The access control mechanisms described above, including their use with views, provide Discretionary Access Control. The privileges may be granted and revoked, and once given privileges and the authority to grant them onwards, there is no limit to their propagation amongst users. Under Discretionary Access Control, a user could accidentally or maliciously provide access to create, read, update or delete data to unauthorised users. Consequently, Discretionary Access Control provides a very low-level of data security, yet the use of views and the granting and revoking of privileges are the most common data security mechanisms in use.

Mandatory Access Control needs to be applied where an environment with trusted security is needed. In Discretionary Access Control, the user (which may be the database administrator) who created an object can grant access rights to other users. In Mandatory Access Control, the access rights are set by the security administrator and are not under the control of the users.

A popular model used in Mandatory Access Control is the Bell–LaPadula Model, developed by David Bell and Len LaPadula for the US Department of Defense. Consider a situation where the organisation holds data at three security levels, secret, confidential and public, so that secret is the most sensitive and public is the least sensitive; that is, secret is more sensitive than confidential and confidential is more sensitive than public. Objects in the database are given a security label – one of the specified security levels, secret, confidential, public. That is the level at which the object is classified. Each user or role (known as a subject in the Bell–LaPadula Model) is given a security clearance – again, one of the specified security levels, secret, confidential, public. This is the highest level of classification that the subject can access. The model then imposes two restrictions on access to data, as follows:

- A subject with a clearance at a given level of classification may not read a database object or data labelled at a higher classification level; that is, there is 'no read up'.
- A subject with a clearance at a given level of classification must not write to any database object labelled at a lower classification level; that is, there is 'no write-down'.

With this model, therefore, users can only view data at or below their own security level; confidential users can view confidential or public data, but may not view secret data. On the other hand, users can only create data at or above their own security level; confidential users can create confidential or secret data but may not create public data. This second restriction prevents a user from accidentally or maliciously writing highly classified data, say secret data, to a table that is of a lower, say public, classification, which would then be available to subjects with a lower clearance.

Multilevel security

Using a model such as the Bell–LaPadula Model, Mandatory Access Control could be applied to a complete database. For example, all data within the database can be considered as being secret (even though some, probably most, of it should realistically be of a lower classification) and the control is then applied via the operating system. Only subjects with appropriate clearance are allowed access to the database. Applying multilevel security to the whole database in this way is often known as ' system high'. A far greater degree of security can be achieved through the use of multilevel security within the database. This is achieved by applying security labels to database objects, tables, columns, etc, and to the data itself. In the case of the data, a security label is applied to each row, so all data in that row is at the same classification level.

One of the implications of the application of multilevel security to database objects and data is that two users (or one user with two different roles, each having a different clearance) may get different answers to the same query applied to the same set of data. Consider a table with 1000 rows of data, where 50 rows are labelled as having a secret classification, 100 rows are labelled as having a confidential classification and the remaining rows are labelled as having a public classification. A general query on that table returns 850 rows of data for a subject with a public clearance, 950 rows of data for a subject with a confidential clearance and all 1000 rows for a subject with a secret clearance. The subject with only public clearance is not told that they are denied access to 150 rows; the database management system responds as if there are only 850 rows in the table. Problems can arise when only some of the data in a secret or confidential row should be labelled at that higher level, and most of the data in the row should really be labelled as public. The user with public clearance is then denied access to data that only warrants a public label and should, therefore, be available to them. In the worst case, if they believe that some data about 'x' should be available to them but they do not see that data they may infer that there is some other data about 'x' that is of a higher classification and this may, of itself, be a breach of security. For this reason, the design of a database where multilevel security is to be implemented requires considerably more care than for a 'system high' or unclassified database. At one time, a major database management system vendor was publicly saying that the design of a multilevel secure database would cost 14 times the cost of a standard database. I am not aware that these figures were ever verified through surveys or controlled studies, but they do provide an indication of the extra care that needs to be taken when designing a database with internal multilevel security.

Encryption

The access controls discussed above are applied by the database management system, but it is possible to use the operating and file-management systems to directly access the data files, thus bypassing the database management system and its security controls. Generally, the average user cannot make sense of these files – the information held within them is of a proprietary format designed by the database management system vendor. However, there are two ways that the data in these files could be compromised. A copy could be taken of the files and then used with another instance of the database management system software to access the files. Under these circumstances, the only danger is that the data is read by someone unauthorised to do so. Alternatively, a determined 'hacker' with the right knowledge could access these files in situ without going through the database management system. In this case, the 'hacker' could corrupt the data as well as reading it.

To prevent either of these situations, the database could be encrypted. Either the whole database could be encrypted or the encryption could be applied to just some of the data. The encryption of the whole database is the simplest option, but it affects the overall database performance; the database needs to be unencrypted every time some data needs to be read and re-encrypted every time some data is updated. The alternative is to only encrypt data in columns that need encrypting, such as columns holding credit card details. Some database management systems come with a built-in ability to encrypt some or all of the data; others provide encryption as an extra module. There are also stand-alone database encryption software products available from third-party vendors.

Audit trails

Most database management systems include facilities to maintain audit trails of database operations, recording what database objects were accessed by whom and when. Some even allow the audit trail to record what data was changed. Audit trails do not prevent unauthorised access, but they do provide information that allows security breaches to be detected. As such they help to promote data security.

DATA INTEGRITY

Whereas data security is about protecting the database against unauthorised users, data integrity is about protecting the database against authorised users. As stated in Chapter 2, one of the roles of a database management system is to allow constraints on data to be defined and to enforce those constraints. It is these constraints that ensure that the data remains consistent and complies with the business rules.

Integrity constraints fall into two categories: those that are inherent in the underlying model of the database management system and those that are encoded into the logical schema.

The inherent constraint rules for all relational databases are, for example:

- All candidate keys are unique; that is, no duplication is allowed.
- No component of the primary key is allowed to be null; this is known as 'entity integrity'.
- Foreign key values must not be unmatched; this is known as 'referential integrity'.

If you purchase a product that claims to be a relational database system, you can expect that if one or more columns is declared as a candidate key and an attempt is made to insert a duplicate set of values into those columns then the insert will be rejected and an appropriate message given to the user. Similarly, if there is an attempt to insert a set of values into the primary key columns of a table where one or more value is missing the insert should be rejected, as should an attempt to insert an unmatched foreign key.

Declaring `payroll_number` as the primary key of the `employee` table in the logical schema therefore ensures that payroll numbers are unique and are always present. Declaring the combination of `number` and `post_code` in the `employee` table as a foreign key referencing the `address` table ensures that only combinations of `number` and `post_code` values that already exist in the `address` table can be inserted into the `employee` table.

Primary key and foreign key constraints are not the only constraints that can be encoded in the logical schema. It is possible to write more general constraints, some of which can be extremely complex, such as:

- The only allowed values for the `relationship` column in the `employee_next_of_kin` table are 'Spouse', 'Partner', 'Parent', 'Child', 'Distant Relative' and 'Friend' – this is an example of a constraint that applies to a single column of a table.
- The difference between the `start_date` value and the `birth_date` value in the `employee` table must be between 16 and 60 years – all employees must be between 16 and 60 years of age when they are first employed – this is an example of a constraint that applies to more than one column of a single table.
- The `effective_date` value in the `employee_grade` table must be later than or equal to the `start_date` of the related employee – this is an example of a constraint that applies to columns in more than one table.

Once constraints have been defined, any attempts to insert data or to update existing data in a way that does not comply with a constraint are rejected. Thus the data within the database retains its integrity, allowing the users a level of confidence in the quality of the data. Data integrity controls are necessary to ensure that data is of high quality, but data integrity controls are not, of themselves, sufficient to maintain the quality of the data.

DATA RECOVERY

Data recovery is about restoring the database to a state that is known to be correct after a failure. Policies must be in place whereby the risks to the data is assessed and then adequate provision is made to ensure that it will be possible to restore the data if necessary. The implementation of these policies must be monitored; when there are no failures from which to recover, it is very easy to overlook the need to prepare for the worst.

Causes of failure

The types of failure that need to be considered can be classified as:
- transaction failures;
- system crashes;
- media failures.

A transaction is a logical unit of work; all or none of the operations within the transaction must be completed to ensure that the database remains in a consistent state. Partial completion leaves the database in an inconsistent state. Thus, there are four properties of transactions, known as the ACID properties, that all database management systems are required to maintain. These are:
- *Atomicity* – either all operations of the transaction are reflected properly in the database, or none are.
- *Consistency* – execution of a transaction in isolation preserves the consistency of the database.
- *Isolation* – each transaction is unaware of other transactions executing concurrently in the system.
- *Durability* – after a transaction completes successfully, the changes it has made to the database persist even if there is a system failure.

For example, in a transaction to transfer funds from an account, X, to another account, Y, within a bank there are two operations: a debit from account X and a credit to account Y for the same amount. Executing either one of those operations on its own is unacceptable; the database will show an incorrect total for the sum of the funds held by the bank. So both these operations must be committed to the database, and hence be held in persistent storage (i.e. on the disk). Alternatively, in the event of failure to complete the whole transaction, those operations that have been completed must be rolled back so that the database is returned to the state that it was in before the transaction started.

Transaction failures can be further classified into those that are the result of logical errors and those that are the result of system errors. Logical errors occur where there is an error in the data input or the transaction will violate some constraint, for example, if there are insufficient funds in account X to be transferred to account Y. System errors are where the system has entered a state where it cannot complete the transaction, for example, if account X has been debited but for some reason writing to account Y is prevented. In the case of logical errors it is necessary for the user to resubmit the transaction with data that is acceptable. In the case of system errors, however, the system itself should attempt to re-execute the complete transaction on behalf of the user.

System crashes occur when there is some fault with the hardware or there is a bug, either in the database management system software or in the operating system software. The result is that any data held in volatile memory, perhaps as part of a transaction, is corrupted. Data that is already in persistent storage should not be corrupted. System crashes could also be caused by external factors, such as a power cut.

Media failures typically occur when a block on a disk loses its data as a result of some malfunction during a read from disk operation or a write to disk operation.

Recovery mechanisms

Being prepared to recover data after a failure requires that there is some degree of redundancy of data. This redundancy is purely physical; it is not logical redundancy, which could lead to update anomalies. There are a number of forms that this physical redundancy may take.

The commonest form of physical redundancy that allows for recovery after transaction failures is the database log. The log records all the changes to the data held in the database, usually recording both the old and new values of the data. The log record of a change to the data is created before the database itself is modified. When it is necessary to return the database to the last known consistent state that existed before the failure the log is consulted to discover those operations that must be undone and those operations that must be redone.

The main technique used to recover after system or media failures is to restore a backup of the database. A backup is where the contents of the database and its log are copied onto another storage medium such as a magnetic tape, usually using a utility provided as part of the database management system software. Such backups may be full backups or incremental backups. Incremental backups only record the changes since the last backup. A backup plan could be, therefore, that a full backup is taken at a set time once a week and on the following days only incremental backups are taken. For example, if a full backup is taken at 3 am each Monday morning, the incremental backup at the same time on Tuesday morning records just the changes since 3 am Monday, the Wednesday incremental backup records just the changes since 3 am Tuesday, and so on.

There are a number of alternative approaches to using backups. These alternatives could be used instead of backups altogether or could be used to augment a backup strategy. One alternative is to have a standby database, a 'near-identical' copy of an operational database, on a remote server. It is described as 'near identical' because there will always be a slight delay in the posting of changes to the standby database. A standby database will, of course, contain all the errors that exist in the data in the main operational database. Another alternative technique is to employ disk mirroring. This is where another copy of the data is held on another storage device. Both the primary and secondary storage devices are managed by the same instance of the database management system software and modifications are made to both devices simultaneously. Disk mirroring is only really useful to recover from a media failure. A system failure that affects the primary device will almost certainly also affect the secondary device. Disk mirroring should only be used to augment a backup strategy and should not be used instead of backups. Yet another alternative is to employ data replication, where data is held in more than one operational database. This is discussed in more detail in Chapter 12 in the context of distributed databases.

SUMMARY

Mechanisms for the application of data security, data integrity and data recovery have been discussed. Whilst database administrators maintain these mechanisms, data administration is responsible for the development of the relevant security, integrity and recovery policies.

9 Database Administration

This chapter provides an overview of the roles and responsibilities of database administrators. It also provides a more in-depth view of one of the jobs carried out by database administrators, the monitoring and tuning of the performance of a database.

DATABASE ADMINISTRATION RESPONSIBILITIES

Database administration is concerned with the management and control of the software used to access physical data. The database administrators, often called DBAs, look after the database management systems in use to record the organisation's data.

Database administrators are responsible for:

- development and maintenance of technical standards covering the database administration function;
- physical database design;
- the management of the database management system software;
- database administration education and training.

Technical standards

Just like any other business function, the database administration function requires its own technical standards to govern its processes and procedures. These standards need to be developed with data sharing and interoperability across the whole enterprise in mind and also need to consider the handling and storage of unstructured or multimedia data as well as the more normal structured data. As well as covering all the activities undertaken by the database administrators themselves, these standards also need to include how application development teams can test the databases they are developing or test their application programs with existing databases. The standards must also specify how end users are to access data.

Database physical design

The general principles of physical database design were covered in Chapter 2. It is the responsibility of the database administration function to provide the expertise to the enterprise on all matters that impact on database design. In an ideal situation, database administrators who are part of the enterprise-wide data management function design all the enterprise's databases, basing these designs on the corporate data standards. If, however, database design is decentralised to application development teams the central database administration team should have the responsibility for reviewing and approving the database designs. This ensures that the designs do not contravene the enterprise's data standards, irrespective of whether they have been developed by in-house application development teams or by external service or software providers. As part of this review process, the database administrators need to be in a position to resolve conflicts between application teams where databases are to be shared. They also need to ensure that the database designs can cope with future data requirements. This implies that there has to be a high level of agreement and collaboration between the data administration and database administration functions.

It is unfortunate that in many cases good database design is sacrificed in the pursuit of enhanced performance. To achieve fast response to queries, the database design may become too tightly coupled to the application design. This not only reduces the scope for data sharing in the short term, it can also lead to data inconsistency and other forms of poor-quality data and could also lead to an inability to cope with future business change.

The database administrators need to be thoroughly familiar with the principles, both theoretical and practical, underlying the various database management systems in use within the enterprise. For example, if relational database management systems are in use (and they almost certainly are), the database administrators need a deep understanding of relational theory and specific detailed knowledge of the particular database management system products in use.

The management of the DBMS software

The duties of a database administrator include:

- management of the security of the database through the correct establishment of new users, the granting of appropriate access rights to users (see Chapter 8) and the investigation of security breaches;
- monitoring of the performance of the database and tuning to improve performance where necessary;
- guarding against catastrophic database failures by taking regular database backups (see Chapter 8) and rehearsing the associated recovery procedures;
- management of upgrades or changes to the database management system software, for example, to take account of new features provided by the software.

Education and training

Database administrators must maintain their own expertise and constantly need to update their training and education. They need theoretical education on database issues. In some cases, this is to understand the underlying theory of the particular database management systems in use; in other cases, it is to understand the advances being made in the field of databases, such as the introduction of structured types and collection types into SQL (see Chapter 12) and the impact that has on database design. They also need detailed training on the database management system products they are managing. Such training may cover the day-to-day activities of administering users and their access rights and backup and recovery techniques to more advanced topics such as database configuration and tuning and how database instances may be incorporated into a federated distributed data system.

The database administrators may also be called upon to provide advice on the training required by different categories of database user.

PERFORMANCE MONITORING AND TUNING

Database administrators should not wait for users to complain about poor performance; they should be constantly monitoring performance and taking appropriate remedial action to ensure that the users receive a good level of service. Nevertheless, however proactive the database administrators are in identifying potential performance problems and taking action to prevent them, they still need to be ready to respond to unexpected poor performance; no matter how hard you try to prevent it, unplanned poor performance problems are always likely to occur.

Not all performance issues that appear at first sight to be due to poor database performance are in fact caused by the database; there may be more general system performance issues or there may be something in the application program code that is having an affect on the overall performance. If the poor performance is down to some general system issue, the database administrator needs to collaborate with the system manager to overcome the problem. If the poor performance is down to something in the application code, the database administrator may need to offer advice as to how the code may be rewritten to overcome the problem. This is particularly so if the problem is with embedded database queries hosted within the application code; the query may well be expressed in a way that is inherently inefficient. Database administrators need to be able to guide application developers as to how to write efficient database queries. The database administrator has to be aware, however, that there may be factors other than embedded database queries that cause poor performance. For example, the use of poorly designed loops within the application code itself can impact on the performance of the system, giving the impression that there is a database performance problem.

If, after investigation, it is found that the database is the cause of the poor performance there are a number of steps that the database administrator can take to rectify the situation. Most, if not all, database management system vendors provide tools for the database administrator to analyse the performance of the database and to then tune the database. These vendor-provided tools tend to be for the database management systems sold by that vendor only, but a number of third-party vendors also provide tools, some of which can be used across a heterogeneous environment of mixed database management systems.

The following actions within the control of the database administrator may be used to alter performance:

- the allocation of memory as buffer, or data cache, to store data that is often queried to reduce the number of disk reads required;
- the allocation of tables, or parts of tables, to files and the allocation of those files to disk space;
- the extent to which database transactions are logged; writing to a log consumes resources, but logs are essential in the event that the database needs to be recovered;
- the application of locks in multiuser situations, so that when a user is accessing some data, that data is locked to prevent another user reading incomplete data or attempting to apply a conflicting update; minimising the possibility of deadlocks (two or more applications holding locks on data that others need to be able to proceed) or reducing the timeout interval (the time an application process can be suspended);
- the use of indexes and the clustering of data, as discussed in Chapter 2.

All of these parameters may be set during the initial setting up of the database, but they can also be altered when the database is in use.

Another option is to denormalise the database, moving away from the logical design to improve query performance. This was also discussed in Chapter 2. This affects data independence, slows down update performance whilst improving retrieval performance, and increases the possibility of inconsistent data. Denormalisation should be avoided if at all possible.

SUMMARY

In this chapter, we have looked at the roles and responsibilities of database administrators, including the development of database administration standards, the physical design of databases, the management of the database management software once it is in use and education and training. We also took a deeper look at the monitoring of the performance of the database and the actions that can be taken to improve performance.

10 Repository Administration

As we saw in Chapter 3, repository administration is concerned with the management and control of the software in which 'information about information' is stored, manipulated and defined. A repository administrator is, therefore, providing a database administration service to the data management function. The repository administrator needs to follow all of the database administration procedures and techniques discussed in Chapter 9. This chapter expands on the roles of repositories or other software associated with the handling of metadata.

REPOSITORIES, DATA DICTIONARIES, ENCYCLOPAEDIAS, CATALOGS AND DIRECTORIES

There are a range of systems, or subsystems, available that have the common primary purpose of storing, manipulating or defining metadata – 'information about information' – but they appear under a number of different names, such as repositories, data dictionaries, encyclopaedias, catalogs and directories.

The last of these two, catalogs and directories, are usually provided as part of a database management system; each directory or catalog is, therefore, associated with a single database instance. Data dictionaries and encyclopaedias are normally associated with tools that are used to support software engineering; an instance of a data dictionary or an encyclopaedia is often associated with a single software development project. Repositories have a broader role and are normally associated with corporate data management initiatives.

As an integral part of a database management system, directories and catalogs are usually associated with physical data as shown in Figure 10.1. Directories and catalogs document the data definitions and the schemas that are used to store the data.

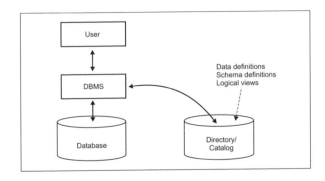

FIGURE 10.1   *The role of directories or catalogs*

They also provide the mappings between the logical and internal schemas, and between the logical and external schemas if the external schema concept is supported. Although their primary role is to implement and manage the physical data-storage environment, they may also be used to manage the database access controls. Despite their close association with a database management system and the physical data environment, directories and catalogs can also be used to record more conceptual information, such as the conceptual data models, about the database.

Increasingly, system development is supported by computer aided software engineering (CASE) tools. These tools usually have a sophisticated user interface that allows the analyst or developer to produce a range of software-engineering diagrams, such as conceptual data models, data flow diagrams and process models. These tools are normally associated with one particular software engineering methodology and produce their diagrams using one notation. Some allow the SQL data definition language statements for the logical schema to be automatically generated from the metadata for the conceptual data model. Most CASE tools maintain the integrity between the different models so that, for example, something cannot be depicted on a data flow diagram that is not supported by the conceptual data model.

An encyclopaedia or data dictionary that supports the CASE tool environment is designed specifically for that purpose. Like any other database, it has a schema that is based on a conceptual data model. In this case, the conceptual data model is a metadata model that reflects the object types, properties and associations required by the methodology that the CASE environment supports. It is not usually possible to modify this model and it may not even be known to you. The data structure of the encyclopaedia or data dictionary is fixed; any attempt to alter the structure of the encyclopaedia or data dictionary is likely to interfere with the coupling between the user interface, the CASE application code and the underlying database.

As can be seen from Figure 10.2, the encyclopaedia or data dictionary is only accessed via the user interface and the CASE tool environment, but there may be a built-in import/export facility to interface with other tools or dictionaries.

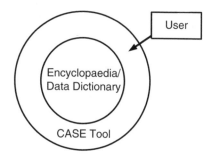

FIGURE 10.2   *The relationship between a CASE*
tool and its encyclopaedia or data dictionary

Unlike the encyclopaedia or data dictionary supplied as part of a CASE tool, a fully functional repository is based on a flexible information or metadata model. The metadata model and the schema definition of the repository should be available so that the underlying data structure can be modified. This allows an enterprise to add new concepts to the repository to adapt the concepts already supported by it so that the repository structure can match the methodology in use within the enterprise, even if that methodology has been developed in-house. Many of the products available today that are now called repositories were once known as data dictionaries.

A repository should be capable of storing many different types of model (see Figure 10.3) and have a significant level of functionality such that it can fully support the data management activities and co-ordinate the complete 'set' of data management tools. First and foremost, a repository is a software tool to assist data managers to carry out their activities. In theory, it is possible to implement a paper-based repository using some type of manual storage, but in practice the complexity of information we need to control and store using the repository soon makes the non-automated approach impossible to manage.

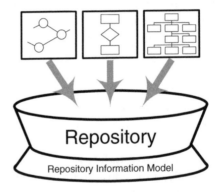

FIGURE 10.3 *The architecture of a repository*

The data management repository provides a centralised source of information about the data of the enterprise. The information held in this repository is of use throughout the enterprise. To optimise its use, it must have interfaces with the other tools that use or manage data, but this can be very difficult to achieve in practice because of the differing environments in which the tools reside and the various personnel who are responsible for them. Nevertheless, a well-structured and well-maintained repository becomes a reference point for information which should be readily accessible to all, whether by direct interrogation or the use of reports generated from the repository.

REPOSITORY FEATURES

The repository acts as an encyclopaedia of knowledge about the organisation and its goals, structure, functions and processes. Conceptual data models and process models should be stored in the repository, as well as information about design details and the different types of data and data structures in use across the enterprise.

The scope of a repository is shown in Figure 10.4. The repository should be capable of dealing with the definition of multiple object types with differing properties and complex relationships. It should provide facilities to handle multiple names for objects in a controlled manner. It should support such things as database design and code generation. It should be possible to partition the repository to represent different views of information, corresponding to different stages in the software development life cycle. It should be possible to maintain effective version control.

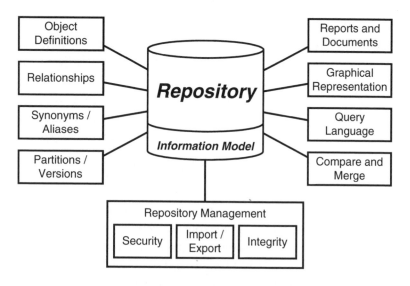

FIGURE 10.4　*The scope of a repository*

The repository should have an easy-to-use query language, should have compare and merge facilities, should be able to represent information in graphical format and should be able to generate formal documents. It should be able to import and export information to and from other products, such as CASE tools.

A repository should be perceived as a database of information. The procurement of a repository should follow the procedure for the procurement of any software, as outlined in Figure 10.5. Good design is essential if the user requirements are to be satisfied. Ideally, therefore, we should discipline ourselves to produce a suitable conceptual model based on an analysis of the requirements. This will provide a blueprint for the repository that we can use to evaluate the available products.

When evaluating repositories it is important to look at the functionality and flexibility of the products available. The following questions are a small sample of those that should be asked:

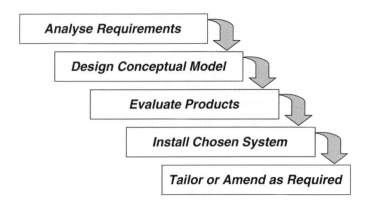

FIGURE 10.5 *The repository procurement process*

- What properties can be defined for each object type?
- How does the repository deal with multiple names?
- Is it possible to support multiple views or versions?
- Is it possible to tailor the information model?
- Are there any performance implications in doing so?
- Does the repository support different types of database management systems?
- What types of relationship are supported?
- What types of query can the repository answer?
- Is the query language easy to use?
- How does the repository import or export information?
- What standard reports are offered?
- Can report layouts and terminology be tailored?
- How easy is the product to install and maintain?
- How easy is the product to use?
- Is it menu-driven? Does it have online help facilities?
- What features for maintaining integrity and security are there?

The data management staff should not only have authority to select and manage a repository but should also be part of the evaluation process for other systems development software tools in order to ensure correct links can be provided with the repository and that the principles of data management can be upheld.

THE REPOSITORY AS A CENTRALISED SOURCE OF INFORMATION

By setting up a repository, data management is setting up a centralised source of information – a knowledge base – that is of potential use to everyone in the organisation. This is shown in Figure 10.6. As well as information about the data of the enterprise, many repositories also contain other information that is useful to information systems developers, such as process definitions, business rules and interface definitions.

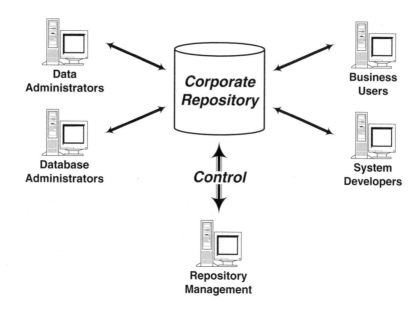

FIGURE 10.6   *A repository as a centralised source of information*

Careful consideration must be given to the methods by which use of this knowledge base can be optimised. The repository has great potential as a vehicle for dissemination of information both in the form of reports and as an online knowledge base of information.

The type of access we give to users can play a critical part in the success of the repository. Decisions on who is allowed to update the repository and under what circumstances are highly dependent on the planned use of the repository. For example, update of the repository with data analysis informa-tion could be limited to the data administration function, but if the repository is to be highly integrated in the system development process that approach may prove unacceptable to the system development teams.

As with any other database, the data held in the repository must be of high quality if it is to be useful. The data management team has a fundamental duty to ensure that the information in the repository is accurate and correct and that it is subject to quality assurance.

Of equal importance to the design of the actual repository, is the design of the repository infrastructure – the technical environment in which the repository is used. If the infrastructure is set up correctly, the repository should be integrated into the working practices of the IT or IS department and those other departments that are going to make use of it. Each repository user should be provided with an appropriate level of support. This may take the form of menu-driven-processing, online help, skeleton screens, tailored reports, customised queries, etc. Training must be geared to meet the needs of the different types of user. It may be useful to develop modular in-house training courses to satisfy these requirements. If the repository is easy to use it is more likely to be readily accepted by its potential users.

METADATA MODELS

Any system that holds metadata, irrespective of whether it is called a repository, a data dictionary or some other name, needs a database designed to hold that metadata. The conceptual data model for such a database is known as a metadata model. Metadata models are described in more detail in Appendix E.

SUMMARY

This chapter concentrated on the systems that a repository administrator is responsible for. The differences between directories and catalogs, encyclopaedias and data dictionaries, and repositories were discussed. The features of a repository and the way that a repository can be used as an enterprise-wide knowledge base were explored in more detail.

11 The Management of Data Management

This chapter looks at the skills and techniques required by data administrators, database administrators and repository administrators. It also explores some options for the placing of the elements of the data management function within the enterprise's organisational structure.

TECHNIQUES AND SKILLS FOR DATA ADMINISTRATION

Data administration is often situated in a highly technical environment. Data administrators need to be able to communicate with skilled IT or IS technicians but they also need to be able to communicate with business-oriented managers and end-users. The ideal data administrator should have knowledge, experience and expertise in a variety of areas relating both to the organisation and to the IT or IS environment. The skills that are required by a data administrator are shown in Figure 11.1.

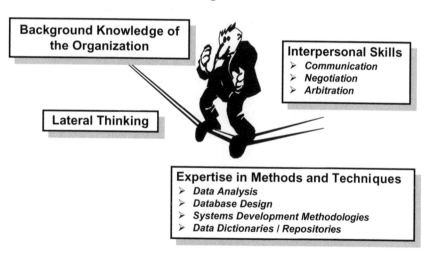

FIGURE 11.1   *The data administration skill set*

An understanding of the organisation is essential. The data administrator needs an in-depth knowledge of:

- the structure of the organisation;
- the products or services developed or sold by the organisation;
- the major competitors of the organisation;
- the business strategy of the organisation;
- the internal politics within the organisation;

- the management practices and procedures;
- the relationship between different departments within the organisation;
- the relationship between different companies in a group.

An understanding of data analysis, data modelling, database design and administration and, of course, data dictionaries or repositories is extremely useful, but the level of expertise required is dependent on the tools and techniques in use. If the data management staff are responsible for the development of methodologies or for the use of software tools this also impacts upon the level of technical expertise required.

Communication is a fundamental skill, as a data administrator needs to talk to personnel throughout the organisation at all levels. The data administrator needs to be able to promote data management, interview staff at all levels in order to understand the need for data, make formal presentations, write clear and concise reports and be comfortable in all communication activities. Good negotiating skills are also essential as there are many issues concerning the use of data to be resolved.

To be able to understand complex and often ill-defined problems, and to resolve them, is an essential skill of a data administrator. So it is useful for the data administrator to be a lateral thinker, able to take a number of differing views, put them together and produce an innovative practical solution.

Unfortunately, not many organisations are able to recruit skilled data engineers with good communication and negotiating skills who are brilliant lateral thinkers and have a detailed knowledge of the organisation. If I was asked to rate these four areas in order of importance when seeking a recruit for data administration, the order would be:

(i) business knowledge;

(ii) interpersonal skills;

(iii) lateral thinking;

(iv) data engineering knowledge.

The deep understanding of the business required by a data administrator can only be acquired through experience over a long time; which implies that data administrators should be appointed from within the organisation. Good interpersonal skills and lateral thinking are inherent; some people have them, others do not. Knowledge of data analysis, data modelling, database design and administration and data dictionaries or repositories can be taught quite easily once someone is in post. It should not, therefore, be an essential prerequisite for appointment as a data administrator. The post-appointment teaching required may be delivered in-house or through formal courses.

TECHNIQUES AND SKILLS FOR DATABASE ADMINISTRATION

The skills required by a database administrator are very different from those required by a data administrator. The good database administrator is an information technology professional who has:

- a detailed product knowledge of the database management systems in use within the enterprise;
- the ability to pay attention to detail;
- diplomacy.

Database administrators are normally trained to work with one or more specific database management systems. Indeed, most of the major database management system vendors, such as Oracle, Microsoft (with SQL Server) and IBM (with DB2) now offer certification for database administrators. Whilst certification is helpful because it indicates that the database administrator has gone through a formal training programme so that they know the facilities provided by the product and the product-specific procedures for the database administration tasks, certification is not necessarily an indication of ability. The deep product knowledge that enables the database administrator to cope with the unexpected situation can only come from experience.

The personal skills required of a database administrator are the ability to pay attention to detail and diplomacy. The first of these comes because there is a lot of detail involved in the administration of a database. Carrying out tasks in the right order at the right time is vital, as is the maintenance of meticulous records. Diplomacy is required because the database administrator needs to deal with questions and requests from business management and end-users, and these requests may sometimes be difficult, if not impossible, to fulfil.

In the case of the database administrator, the technical skills and knowledge should take precedence over the personal skills. The fundamental duties involve getting the best out of the database management systems in use in the organisation.

TECHNIQUES AND SKILLS FOR REPOSITORY ADMINISTRATION

Since there is similarity between the two roles, the techniques and skills required by the repository administrator are very similar to those required by the database administrator. The repository administrator is an IT professional, trained to work with the specific repository software that is in use. Again, attention to detail is required. The main difference is that, where the database administrator needs to interact with business management and end-users, the repository administrator is principally interacting with data administrators.

THE POSITIONING OF DATA MANAGEMENT WITHIN THE ENTERPRISE

There is no perfect solution to where the data management function, or its sub-functions, should be situated within an organisation. It may well be within IT/IS; it may be outside it. It might report to the board within one organisation and in another it might be part of the IT/IS technical support. Data management often evolves in an organisation long before it is officially recognised as such.

There may be situations where an organisation has two levels of data management – one strategic and one operational. This could be implemented by two distinct but related units or by a centralised data management unit and some type of local project or business-area data manager responsibility. The former could have a co-ordinating role or could be much more actively in control – perhaps by seconding trained staff onto different project teams as local experts.

Company politics can also play a significant part in the decisions over the placing of a data management function. It may receive substantial backing from the management, enabling it to be established at the optimum level for the particular organisation. Alternatively, lack of management commitment may mean data management comes in via the back door and has to fight hard for recognition and appropriate positioning.

The position and structure of the data management function may change as the needs of the organisation change. Something that starts off as being seen to operate purely at the operational level may become more strategic at a later stage or vice versa. Whatever the position and structure, it has an effect on the potential goals and objectives of the data management team. It may also influence the areas of responsibility quite considerably.

There are a number of aspects to consider when positioning a data management function. In a 'green field' situation where the data management function is newly introduced, it may be possible to choose the optimum position. For most organisations, it is a case of trying to balance long-term planning, short-term needs and available resources to try and provide the most effective data management function with a growth potential.

Figures 11.2 to 11.6 show some possible organisation structures. They are only representative of a much larger number of possible structures. The figures are not necessarily complete and are used only to demonstrate various options and their advantages and disadvantages.

In the option shown in Figure 11.2, the data management function reports to the board via a business planning/strategy unit. This makes it a strategic rather than an operational function, providing it with strong business links. It probably has an independent budget and is likely to be managed by someone with a business background. The remit of the data management function would potentially include additional responsibilities relating to the management of information – in particular, the way that information is distributed within the organisation.

The function is on a similar level to the IT/IS department and is well-placed to co-ordinate data management requirements. However, it may not necessarily be well placed to deal with some of the more technical issues which affect the operation of the IT/IS department and may experience difficulty implementing data management within projects effectively. As such there

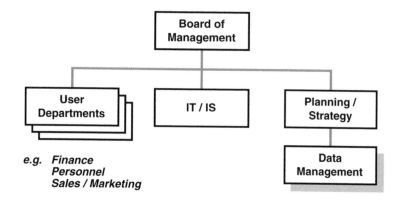

FIGURE 11.2 *Business-based data management*

is a requirement to implement some additional data management function within the IT/IS department.

Figure 11.3 shows the data management function positioned within IT/IS but independent of the systems development function. In this position, it is probably in one of the optimum positions to carry out both a strategic and an operational role. It has direct contact with the business independently of systems development. It is likely to have some form of independent budget, it is most probably managed by someone with an understanding of IT/IS and it should interface well with the other departments within IT/IS.

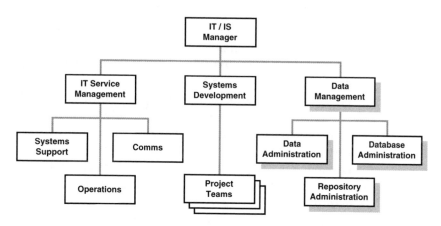

FIGURE 11.3 *Independent data management in the IT/IS department*

However, data management is often perceived by other IT/IS departments as a hindrance to their activities, causing them additional work and potentially delaying projects, forcing them to overrun deadlines. This can be overcome by the centralised data management function operating very much as a service function to the other IT/IS areas, particularly the business analysts involved in systems development projects and those involved in managing the current systems. By providing a service it does not put an extra workload on the development staff and provides them with positive help in the systems development phases.

In Figure 11.4, the data management function is situated within the systems development area, where it is in a reasonable position to carry out its operational activities. It can easily support the project teams as both areas are under the systems development manager.

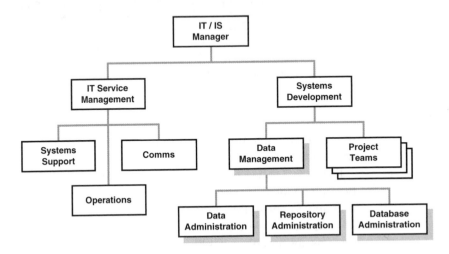

FIGURE 11.4   *Data management within systems development*

As in the structure in Figure 11.3, the function could provide a centralised service to all the project teams, or could consider having a trained 'local' data manager in each project team. If this approach is adopted, it is recommended that this person still reports to the manager of the centralised data management function, otherwise he or she may well get caught up in other project-oriented development activities when deadlines become pressing.

The major disadvantage of the structure in Figure 11.4 is the difficulty that the data management function may experience in obtaining independent access to the business. It is perceived by the business as an IT/IS development-support function rather than as a corporate data management asset with expert knowledge of the data and information available to the enterprise.

Figure 11.5 shows a data management function dispersed across the elements of the IT/IS department. The physical and organisational separation of the data administration function from the database administrators makes it more difficult to manage and control the mapping between conceptual design and physical implementation. However, the database administrators may feel that being placed organisationally alongside the technical-support function has significant advantages to compensate for this. There is always a need for database administration and systems programming to liaise closely regarding the implementation and operation of databases.

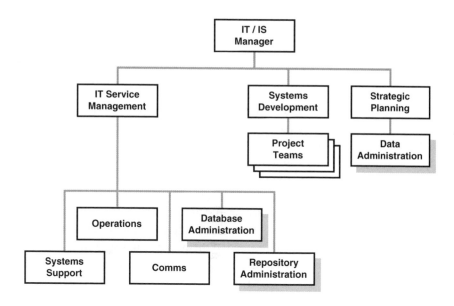

FIGURE 11.5 *Dispersed IT/IS based data management*

On the other hand, the placement of data administration directly within a strategic planning or similar function means that it is very well placed to perform its role. It can still support the systems development process whilst maintaining independent links with the business and sustaining a corporate profile.

If the IT/IS operation is distributed within an organisation, it is necessary to consider a network of data management units. Each unit should be autonomous and report to the 'local' management team. This is the situation shown in Figure 11.6.

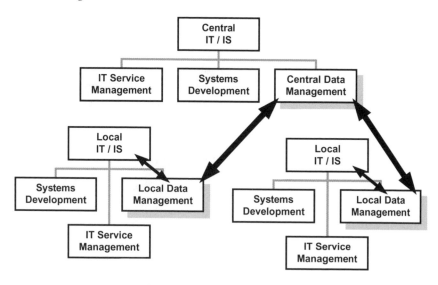

FIGURE 11.6 *Distributed data management*

However, there is a need to ensure that the separate units work collectively towards a set of corporate goals. It is necessary to ensure that a consistent set of standards and working practices are adopted in line with a common policy and strategy. It is also important to identify how corporate, common and local data are identified, documented and maintained. It is critical that there be good communication between the various data management units and that individual data managers are made accountable for complying with corporate policy.

This presents the local data managers with a problem. In effect they have two masters, which is never good management practice. They have their immediate masters, the local IT/IS managers, whose requirements they need to meet and who are probably responsible for writing their annual perform-ance assessment. This relationship is shown in Figure 11.6 by the narrower of the two double-headed arrows. At the same time they have a functional responsibility to the central data manager, as shown by the thicker of the two double-headed arrows.

SUMMARY

This chapter has looked at the business knowledge, personal skills and data engineering expertise needed by data administrators and the deeper technical knowledge and personal skills needed by database and repository administrators. Some possible options for the positioning of the data man-agement function and its data administration, database administration and repository administration elements within the organisational hierarchy were also investigated.

12 Industry Trends and their Effects on Data Management

This chapter looks at a number of fads, developments and initiatives that are affecting the way that data is managed. The topics discussed are the use of application packages, the distribution of data and databases, data warehousing and data mining, object orientation, multimedia or unstructured data and, finally, web technology.

THE USE OF PACKAGES

For most business processes, there are now application packages that can be bought 'off the shelf'. A bought-in financial package can handle sales order processing, purchase order processing, general ledger and much more. A human resources package includes recruitment management, payroll, training management, and so on. Many organisations have a strategy of using these 'off-the-shelf' application packages wherever possible, as this is normally seen as a relatively cheap option for delivering speedy business benefit.

Most application packages provide the functionality that the package designer thinks is appropriate for a broad range of businesses. The database underlying these packages is designed to support the functionality provided by the package. It is highly unlikely that the requirement to share data was taken into account when the package was being designed. In an environment where off-the-shelf application packages are used, it is, therefore, difficult to share data between systems. This is especially true if the organisation is to be supported by a mixture of bespoke systems and packaged systems or by packaged systems from different vendors. It is not unknown, however, for data not be shareable between packages or systems from the same vendor. If off-the-shelf application packages are to be used and there is to be data sharing, a 'bespoke interface' or a set of bespoke interfaces must be developed.

Where application packages are to be procured to support business requirements, there are a number of issues that need to be addressed from a data management perspective:

- Is a reliable conceptual data model or logical schema available for the package? If not, it will be impossible for the data management team to assess the difficulty of sharing data between this package and the rest of the enterprise's systems before it is procured and implemented.
- Does the package match the functional and data requirements of the business? Business users easily identify if the package does or does

not meet their functional and local data requirements but they are unlikely to consider any wider requirement to share data.

- How will the corporation handle the effects of the introduction by the vendor of new versions or releases of the package? New versions may introduce a requirement to reengineer interfaces.

The questions above are based on the assumption that the selected off-the-shelf package meets the business users' requirements. Increasingly, however, packages are being bought that do not quite match the functional requirements – the designer of the package envisaged a slightly different set of processes and procedures for the business area to those in use within the organisation. This is a result of the application of the Pareto Law, also known as the 80:20 principle, to package requirements. This principle says that 20 per cent of the work that we do produces 80 per cent of our income. In the context of the procurement of software, this is taken to mean that 80 per cent of the functionality we need only requires 20 per cent of the total cost. Getting the extra 20 per cent of functionality, to give us everything we need, costs that extra 80 per cent. The assumption is, therefore, that to save money we accept a package that provides 80 per cent of the functionality we require and adapt our procedures and processes to match the product we have bought. This seldom works out in practice, but even if it did nobody seems to take into account the cost of changing the well-established business procedures and practices. The normal situation is that once the package has been bought we discover that the business is not prepared to change the way it works and the off-the-shelf package has to be 'tailored' to meet the full business functionality. There are substantial financial costs in implementing this tailoring. However, a package that has been tailored is no longer an off-the-shelf package; it is now a 'bespoke' product.

To use an off-the-shelf package within a federated system always requires the development of an interface so that the package's data can be shared with other packages and systems and, probably, requires that the package's functionality also has to be tailored to meet the existing business processes and procedures.

When the true costs of developing, maintaining and managing interfaces as well as the tailoring required by the business area are included in the cost–benefit analysis, off-the-shelf application packages often turn out to be a more expensive option than bespoke development. All of this is also true for enterprise resource planning packages, which were briefly discussed in Chapter 1.

Aside: I was once told that a study had been undertaken looking at the average whole-life cost overruns for systems development based on bespoke software, on the one hand, and for systems development based on the use of off-the-shelf application packages, on the other hand. The study found that the average whole-life costs for bespoke development ran three times over budget but that the average whole-life costs for a development with an off-the-shelf application package ran 14 times over budget. Unfortunately I have not been able to track down any details of this study.

DISTRIBUTED DATA AND DATABASES

Our discussion of database architecture in Chapter 2, and particularly the three level schema architecture, was based on the assumption that all the data would be held in a single database at a single site. Such an arrangement is the logical solution for a small organisation that is based at a single site. A large enterprise that is geographically dispersed could still use a single centralised database and the users could access that database from the terminals or personal computers on their desks over a communications network. On the other hand, the enterprise could opt to have its data and databases distributed throughout its sites.

There are two principal reasons why the enterprise may choose to distribute its data. The first of these is a conscious decision to distribute data as a result of a business requirement to have data held closer to where it is used, probably to ensure that work is not disrupted by communications failures. The second reason, the most likely reason, is that there are many existing systems dispersed throughout the enterprise, each of which has its own database. In this case, there is probably a desire to see this data managed as a cohesive whole; we need the ability to share data between legacy systems.

In both these situations, the distributed system should provide greater reliability and availability of data with a reduced response time for any particular query. Reliability is improved because the probability that any one site is working at any particular time is improved since any single equipment failure should not bring the system down. In the event of a failure of any one component of the system, the remainder can continue to operate. Availability is improved for similar reasons. If data is replicated, which we discuss below, availability is improved even more.

If we wish to distribute data (top-down distribution), we need to consider an approach to deciding what data is to be stored where and how that data is managed so that it appears as a cohesive whole. Similarly, if we wish to integrate data from existing distributed independent systems (bottom-up integration) so that it appears as a cohesive whole, we need to know how that integration is approached and how it is managed after integration. Using the terminology from the three level schema architecture, in the top-down distribution scenario we start with a single logical schema (the global logical schema) and break it down so that we have a number of local logical schemas. In the bottom-up integration scenario, we start with a number of local logical schemas and derive a global logical schema. In both cases, it is the responsibility of the 'distributed database management system' to know how the various local logical schemas map to the global logical schema and to manage the distribution of the actual data.

The perfect distributed database system?

Chris Date, a well known author and lecturer on relational database issues, has stated (Date, 2003) a fundamental principle and 12 rules (or objectives) for distributed databases. His fundamental principle is:

> To the user, a distributed system should look exactly like a nondistributed system.

The user in this fundamental principle, and in the 12 objectives below, is not necessarily the 'end-user', the human sitting at the terminal. Anyone or anything that accesses the database is considered to be a user, including application programs. By extension, therefore, the application programmer should see the distributed database as a single non-distributed database. The programmer should not need to say 'get data X from site Y'. The instruction to 'get data X' should be sufficient; the 'distributed database management system' should then know that it needs to go to site Y to get the data.

Date's 12 objectives are:

- *Local autonomy* – local data is owned and managed locally, with local accountability and security; no site depends on another for successful functioning.
- *No reliance on a central site* – all sites are equal, and none relies on a master site for processing or communications.
- *Continuous operation* – installations at one site do not affect operations at another; there should never be a need for a planned shutdown; adding or deleting installations should not affect programs or activities; likewise, portions of databases should be able to be created and destroyed without stopping any component.
- *Location independence* (also known as *location transparency*) – users do not have to know where data is physically stored; they act as if all data is stored locally.
- *Fragmentation independence* (*transparency*) – relations or tables can be fragmented for physical storage, but users are able to act as if data was not fragmented.
- *Replication independence* – relations or tables and fragments of relations or tables can be represented at the physical level by multiple, distinct, stored copies or replicas at distinct sites; replicas are transparent to the user.

- *Distributed query processing* – local computer and input-output activity occurs at multiple sites, with data communications between the sites; both local and global optimisation of query processing are supported (that is, the system finds the cheapest way to answer a query that involves accessing several databases).
- *Distributed transaction management* – single transactions are able to execute code at multiple sites, causing updates at multiple sites.
- *Hardware independence* – distributed database systems are able to run on different kinds of hardware with all machines participating as equal partners where appropriate.
- *Operating system independence* – distributed database systems are able to run under different operating systems.
- *Network independence* – distributed database systems are able to work with different communications networks.
- *Database independence* – distributed database systems are able to be built of different kinds of databases, provided they have the same interfaces.

If you consider those 12 objectives, you may think that they are difficult to achieve. It could well be that, for many years to come, most distributed data systems will consist of a number of individual databases federated in such a way that, to the end user only, they appear as a single system.

Top-down fragmentation and partitioning

The development of a set of local logical schemas from a global logical schema involves using the techniques of fragmentation and partitioning. Fragmentation is the splitting of a table (or relation) into fragments, each of which represents a distinct subset of the data required at one or more specific sites. Partitioning then involves combining fragments so that all the fragments required at a particular site are grouped into a partition.

Fragmentation can be vertical, horizontal or hybrid. Vertical fragmentation involves assigning each column of the table to one (and only one) fragment. There is one exception to this: the primary key column(s) must appear in each fragment so that the original table can be reconstituted from the fragments. Horizontal fragmentation involves the assignment of the rows of the table to one (and only one) fragment. Hybrid fragmentation is a combination of the vertical and horizontal fragmentation where a vertical fragment is further fragmented horizontally or a horizontal fragment is further fragmented vertically.

Figure 12.1 shows an example of vertical fragmentation. At the top is a table of personnel data. Beneath are two vertical fragments. The fragment on the left has the `birth_date` and `salary` columns whilst the fragment on the right has the remaining columns.

payroll_ number	surname	first_name	birth_date	salary	department	grade
AY334	Watson	Barbara	1952-12-06	20340	Finance	4
AY478	Wilson	John	1953-07-03	13436	Production	5
BZ987	Smith	Joe	1964-02-24	35625	HQ	1
CA446	Jones	Phil	1974-05-05	27750	Production	2
CX137	Rogers	Jenny	1970-01-10	27750	Finance	2
DJ777	Phillips	Henry	1974-05-05	22570	Finance	3
EX115	Thompson	Brian	1979-06-11	21785	Production	3
FJ678	Harrison	Roger	1988-04-27	14300	Finance	4
FL233	Smith	Jane	1989-08-25	12725	Production	5

payroll_ number	birth_date	salary
AY334	1952-12-06	20340
AY478	1953-07-03	13436
BZ987	1964-02-24	35625
CA446	1974-05-05	27750
CX137	1970-01-10	27750
DJ777	1974-05-05	22570
EX115	1979-06-11	21785
FJ678	1988-04-27	14300
FL233	1989-08-25	12725

payroll_ number	surname	first_name	department	grade
AY334	Watson	Barbara	Finance	4
AY478	Wilson	John	Production	5
BZ987	Smith	Joe	HQ	1
CA446	Jones	Phil	Production	2
CX137	Rogers	Jenny	Finance	2
DJ777	Phillips	Henry	Finance	3
EX115	Thompson	Brian	Production	3
FJ678	Harrison	Roger	Finance	4
FL233	Smith	Jane	Production	5

FIGURE 12.1   *Vertical fragmentation*

In Figure 12.2, the larger vertical fragment is further fragmented horizontally so that there is a fragment for each department. The end result is, therefore, a hybrid fragmentation.

payroll_ number	surname	first_name	birth_date	salary	department	grade
AY334	Watson	Barbara	1952-12-06	20340	Finance	4
AY478	Wilson	John	1953-07-03	13436	Production	5
BZ987	Smith	Joe	1964-02-24	35625	HQ	1
CA446	Jones	Phil	1974-05-05	27750	Production	2
CX137	Rogers	Jenny	1970-01-10	27750	Finance	2
DJ777	Phillips	Henry	1974-05-05	22570	Finance	3
EX115	Thompson	Brian	1979-06-11	21785	Production	3
FJ678	Harrison	Roger	1988-04-27	14300	Finance	4
FL233	Smith	Jane	1989-08-25	12725	Production	5

payroll_ number	birth_date	salary
AY334	1952-12-06	20340
AY478	1953-07-03	13436
BZ987	1964-02-24	35625
CA446	1974-05-05	27750
CX137	1970-01-10	27750
DJ777	1974-05-05	22570
EX115	1979-06-11	21785
FJ678	1988-04-27	14300
FL233	1989-08-25	12725

payroll_ number	surname	first_name	department	grade
BZ987	Smith	Joe	HQ	1

payroll_ number	surname	first_name	department	grade
AY334	Watson	Barbara	Finance	4
CX137	Rogers	Jenny	Finance	2
DJ777	Phillips	Henry	Finance	3
FJ678	Harrison	Roger	Finance	4

payroll_ number	surname	first_name	department	grade
AY478	Wilson	John	Production	5
CA446	Jones	Phil	Production	2
EX115	Thompson	Brian	Production	3
FL233	Smith	Jane	Production	5

FIGURE 12.2   *Hybrid fragmentation*

Any fragmentation must be lossless and disjoint. Lossless means that no data must be lost. Recombining the fragments provides all the data. Disjoint means that each data value (other than the primary key values in the case of vertical fragmentation) appears in only one fragment. The fragments shown in Figure 12.2 meet these criteria.

All of these fragments can be grouped into a single partition to be allocated to the database that is local to the human resources department. This partition happens to be equivalent to the original table, but that is coincidence.

Each of the departmental horizontal fragments can form partitions that are allocated to the departmental databases. This implies that some of the data is replicated. The replication is of complete fragments, not individual data values.

The aim of fragmentation and partitioning, and any associated decisions about replication, is to organise data so that it is placed closest to where it needs to be used.

Bottom-up integration

The techniques of fragmentation and partitioning for the top-down decomposition of a global logical schema to create a number of local logical schemas are well documented. They are included in most texts that cover distributed data and distributed databases. Unfortunately, there is no commonly agreed process for integrating a number of local logical schemas into a single global logical schema. The task is the equivalent of developing a corporate data model by joining project or area models that was discussed in Chapter 4. You will recall that this approach to the development of a corporate data model was rejected because of its high failure rate.

The development of a global logical schema through the direct combination of a number of local logical schemas is equally likely to fail. The formats used for common data items may well be different in the disparate local schemas; for example a date may be held as text using the **CHARACTER VARYING** datatype in one system and using a **DATE** datatype in another system. Columns with the same name in two local schemas can represent entirely different concepts; for example, a column named **description** in the **product** table in one system may hold the names by which the products are known, whereas the **product** table in another system may have two columns, **designation** and **description**, where **designation** holds the formal names of the products and the **description** column holds additional information that amplifies the designation where necessary. Columns with entirely different names can represent identical concepts; for example, columns named **sex** and **gender** in different systems may both have the same valid values – 'Male', 'Female' or 'Unknown'. Identification of these common concepts could be made more difficult through differences in coding. For example, the concepts 'Male', 'Female' and 'Unknown' may be coded as M, F and U in one system, as 0, 1 and 99 in another system and as 1, 2 and 0 in yet a third system. To make matters worse, these codings might not even be documented. The identification of all these issues is normally only achieved by getting together subject matter experts from the business and database experts for each of the databases in question so that they can talk through the issues in great detail. Even then some problems can be overlooked.

The situation can be eased if there is a common understanding of the global data requirements that the global logical schema is to represent. Then it is a case of identifying how each of the individual data requirements is handled in each of the local logical schemas and arranging a mapping to a common representation of the requirement in the global logical schema. It looks as if an integration project of this kind is more likely to succeed if there is an existing data management initiative and a corporate data model within the organisation.

The management of replication

When looking at the concepts of fragmentation and partitioning, we saw that some or all of the data may be replicated in a distributed data system. Replication is duplication of data and one of the fundamental principles of database design is that duplication of data should be avoided. This is what the normalisation process we saw in Chapter 2 is about – the removal of duplication to avoid update anomalies. Replication, however, is acceptable because it is managed duplication; replication implies that we have management procedures in place to ensure that the collective distributed database remains consistent.

Replication may be:

- full or partial; and
- synchronous or asynchronous; and
- subject to master–slave or update-anywhere updating.

Full replication is where the entire data, including all updates, is copied to every database instance within the distributed system. In partial replication, only data that it is deemed necessary to hold at a site is copied to the database supporting that site.

Synchronous replication is where all the copies of the data are held in a strictly consistent state. Any update at any one site is copied to all the other sites that require it and all sites, including the originating site, commit that update to their databases simultaneously. If any one site cannot commit the data to its database then no site, including the originating site, is allowed to do so. In asynchronous replication, the individual databases are allowed to become inconsistent for a time with the intention that all sites become consistent eventually. The time that databases are inconsistent may be very short, fractions of a second, say, but in an environment where data is being constantly updated the databases may never actually be totally consistent. The time delays and the degree of consistency are largely dependent on the capacity, quality and reliability of the network that connects the sites.

Master–slave updating is where one site, the master, has control of all updating. Any site that wishes to update data informs the master, which then propagates the update to every site, including the site that originated the update. All sites then commit the update to their database. Update-anywhere is a form of updating which does away with the reliance on a central site, the master. Each site is now aware of the location of all the replicas and passes updates to sites with replicas as necessary. Both master–slave and update-anywhere updating can be used with either synchronous or asynchronous replication.

DATA WAREHOUSING AND DATA MINING

A data warehouse is not just a large collection of data. At its simplest, it is a copy of transactional data – that is, the data created in the operational systems used by the enterprise. This copied data is specifically structured to make it easy for the data to be queried and analysed. Senior management can use this copied data to monitor the progress of the business and, hence, to make strategic decisions that affect the future of the business.

Although, at its heart, a data warehouse holds copies of transactional data, to make it easier to analyse and query that data a data warehouse also holds some aggregated or summarised data – copied data that has been processed in some way. Most data warehouses also hold a considerable amount of human-readable metadata to help management and other users understand the data in the warehouse.

A data-warehouse architecture

Figure 12.3 shows a typical data-warehouse architecture. On the left are the operational systems used by a supermarket chain: for example, the electronic point-of-sale (EPOS) systems visible at the checkouts, the stock-ordering systems and the human resources systems. The data is copied to the data warehouse using extraction, translation and loading (ETL) processes, where the data is copied from the operational systems (extraction), converted from the structure and formats of the operational systems to the structure and formats of the data warehouse (translation) and then written to the data warehouse (loading). The translation process might include cleaning of the data if there is any doubt as to its quality. This cleaning might, for example, include the substitution of statistically determined values for missing data.

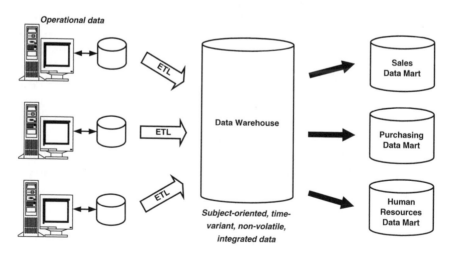

FIGURE 12.3   *A typical data warehouse architecture*

The data warehouse contains data that is:

- subject-oriented – the data warehouse contains copies of data that are organised so that all the data relating to the same event or other subject of interest is associated with each other;
- time-variant – the data is arranged so changes over time can be identified;
- non-volatile – once data is in the data warehouse it is never updated or deleted;
- integrated – the data in the data warehouse is from most or all of the enterprise's operational systems and is structured so that it is seen as a single collection of data.

For a supermarket, the data warehouse could record that a customer – who may or may not have a loyalty card and may or may not, therefore, be identifiable – bought two 200g tins of Brand X Baked Beans, one 415g tin of Brand Y Cream of Tomato Soup, and one own-brand uncut white loaf, and so on, as they passed through a particular checkout in a particular store at a particular time on a particular day.

This data can then be used to, amongst other things:

- compare sales between stores;
- compare sales of own-brand products against branded products;
- identify purchasing patterns for particular days of the week or times of day;
- identify relationships between product purchases – for example, it has been reported that a supermarket chain discovered that beer is more often bought by those who buy disposable nappies than by those who do not buy disposable nappies.

On the right of Figure 12.3 are a number of smaller collections of data known as data marts, each of which has a copied subset of the data in the enterprise data warehouse that is subject or business-area specific. The main difference between a data mart and the enterprise data warehouse from which the data mart has drawn its data is the reduced scope of the data held by the data mart, although each data mart may hold more or less aggregated or summarised data than is held in the enterprise data warehouse.

Since the data in a data warehouse or a data mart is a historical copy of transactional data and is not going to be updated, there is no need to worry about update anomalies. There is, therefore, no requirement for the data to be normalised. This allows the data to be structured in a way that makes it easy to query.

The multidimensional model of data

Conceptually, users of data warehouses find it easy to visualise the data as a 'cube' of three, four, or even five or more, dimensions (cubes with more than three dimensions are sometimes known as 'hypercubes'). If a company sells products at stores and the company's performance is measured over time, then the associated data can be visualised as in Figure 12.4; that is, as a cube with three dimensions (a *Product* dimension, a *Store* dimension and a *Time* dimension).

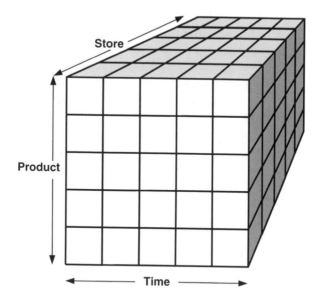

FIGURE 12.4 *A multidimensional data model*

The conceptual visualisation of data in this way is referred to as the multi-dimensional model of data. The points (cells) within the cube are where the measurements for the particular combinations of product, store and time are stored. This way, the value of the sales of a particular product (200g tin of Brand X Baked Beans) at a particular store (Store 315) over a particular time (2–3pm on Friday 20 January 2007) can be directly seen. Summing along the store dimension gives the value of all of the sales of 200g tins of Brand X Baked Beans at all of the company's stores during that hour. Summing along the product dimension gives the value of the sales of all the products sold at that store during that hour. Summing along the time dimension gives the value of the sales of 200g tins of Brand X Baked Beans at that store over the extended time period (month, year, etc.).

Once structured in this way the data can be:

- used with standard reporting tools;
- queried using OLAP (online analytical processing) techniques;
- subject to data mining.

Standard reporting

Reporting tools, for example, can provide the simple sales information over the store, period or time dimensions as described above. These tools easily support questions of the 'who ...?' and 'what ...?' variety, such as, 'which store had the greatest value of sales in December 2006?' and 'what was our best-selling product in December 2006?'

OLAP

The term 'online analytical processing' (OLAP) has been applied to a range of techniques that can be used by senior managers and knowledge workers to query historical, summarised, multidimensional data. The term is used in contrast to ' online transactional processing' (OLTP), where front-line staff are interacting with databases in the course of day-to-day operations. The data associated with OTLP is current, up to date and, probably, relational.

OLAP techniques provide the ability to answer more sophisticated questions than those provided by the standard reporting tools, such as 'what if ...?' and 'why ...?' A typical question would be 'What will happen to our sales figures if we withdraw 200g tins of Brand X Baked Beans from our product range?' The OLAP techniques are based around four basic operations that can be applied to a multidimensional cube of data: slice, dice, roll-up and drill-down.

The slice operation provides a sub-cube of data by selecting a subset of one of the dimensions. Slicing along the store dimension provides a sub-cube that contains data for a single store or a group of stores (for example, Store 315 or all the stores in the northern region, but showing the values for each product in the product range at each time period in the time range). Slicing along the product dimension provides a sub-cube that contains data for a single product or a category of products (for example, 200g tins of Brand X Baked Beans or all canned goods, but showing the values for each store at each time period in the time range). Slicing along the time dimension provides a sub-cube that contains data for a single time period (for example, 2–3pm on Friday 20 January 2007 or the whole of the first quarter 2007, but showing the values for each product in the product range sold at each store). Slicing purely selects a subset of the data that was available in the original cube without changing any of the values.

The dice operation provides a sub-cube of data by selecting a subset of two or more of the dimensions. The resultant sub-cube may, for example, contain data for a single store for a limited product range over a limited time period (for example, the value of sales of each product within the tinned goods category at Store 315 during January 2007). As with the slice operation, dicing purely selects a subset of the data that was available in the original cube without changing any of the values.

The roll-up (or aggregation) operation provides a new cube of data with the values along one or more dimensions aggregated; for example, rolling up along the product dimension gives a cube showing the total values for the sales for all products in each store in each time period. Unlike the slicing and dicing operations, the roll-up operation calculates new values.

The drill-down (or de-aggregation) operation provides a new cube of data with a more detailed view of the data along one or more dimensions. When drilling down the new cube is not formed from the existing cube of data (as it is for slice, dice and roll-up operations) but is formed from more detailed data; the assumption is that the original cube was showing aggregated data and more detailed data is held in the data warehouse. For example, if we have a cell showing, as a single value, the value of all the sales for tinned goods in all the stores in the northern region on Friday 20 January 2007, we can drill down to look at the sales by individual store, for each individual product or for each hour of the day, or for any combination of these three.

Data mining

Data mining is the application of advanced statistical and other techniques against the large volumes of data held in a data warehouse to discover previously unknown patterns in the data that may be of interest to the business. The patterns are discovered by identifying the underlying rules and features in the data. Data mining is sometimes known as knowledge discovery in databases (KDD). The techniques used in data mining include, amongst others, statistical techniques, cluster analysis and neural networks.

Statistical techniques can be used in a number of different ways. They can be applied to remove any erroneous or irrelevant data before any further analysis is carried out. Sampling techniques could be used to reduce the amount of data that has to be analysed. Other statistical techniques may be used to identify classes within data, for example, to find common shopping times and common purchases, or to find associations within sets of data, for example, discovering where products are commonly bought together. An example of using the a-priori algorithm, a statistical technique to discover associations, is given in Appendix F.

Cluster analysis is the process of finding clusters or subsets of data so that the data in the cluster (or subset) share some common property. For example, cluster analysis could be used to generate a profile of people who responded to a previous mailing campaign. This profile can then be used to predict future responses, enabling future mailings to be directed to gain the best response.

Neural networks are the computer equivalent of a biological nervous system. Each neural network is a network of processing elements called neurons. Neural networks are useful in data mining because they 'learn' as they analyse data. Once a neural network has been trained, it can be seen as an 'expert' in the category of data that it has been trained to analyse. A neural network is seen as a black box which takes a number of inputs and provides an output. The neurons in a network are arranged in layers; there are at least an input layer and an output layer, but there may well also be a number of intermediate layers that are hidden. Examples of the use of neural networks include the prediction of stock prices and the prediction of the risk of cancer.

Relational data warehouse schema

Whilst there are database management systems on the market that are based on the multidimensional model of data, it is possible to emulate the multi-dimensional view of data using a relational database management system. Our three-dimensional cube (*product, store* and *time*) could be represented using the star schema shown at Figure 12.5.

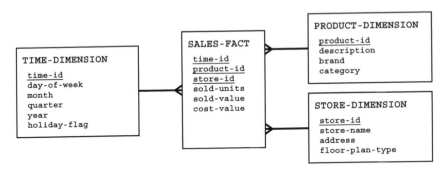

FIGURE 12.5   *A typical relational schema for a data warehouse*

At the centre of the star is a single fact table – in this case the **SALES-FACT** table. This fact table has a many-to-one relationship with each of the dimension tables, **STORE-DIMENSION, PRODUCT-DIMENSION** and **TIME-DIMENSION**.

In this schema, the fact table contains the daily sales totals, that is, the units sold, the cost value and the sale value, for each product in each store. This is as a result of a decision that was made following an analysis of the likely queries that may be made of the data. If it is likely that a user may at some time in the future wish to analyse the distribution of sales throughout a day the time dimension table needs an additional column (say 'hour'). Decisions about the granularity of the dimensions of the data warehouse are, therefore, very important. Users can only drill down to the lowest level of granularity at which data is stored. Once data has been stored in the data warehouse with the granularity of the time dimension being set as a day, it is impossible to determine the pattern of sales at different times during the day.

There are a number of things to note about this schema. The primary key of the fact table is the combination of the foreign keys that reference the dimension tables. The only non-key columns of the fact table are all numer-ical. This is important because they are to be subject to statistical analysis. The dimension tables are not normalised – there is a lot of repetition of data. Additionally, the **TIME-DIMENSION** table has a column called **holiday-flag**. This enables users to query the data to see what effect holidays have on the sales. The other columns in the time-dimension table allow for analyses that compare sales on Mondays against sales on, say, Tuesdays, January sales against March sales, first quarter sales against third quarter sales, and sales on May Day Bank Holiday 2006 against May Day Bank Holiday 2007. The

STORE-DIMENSION table has a floor-plan-type column. This allows analyses that look at the extent to which different store layouts may influence sales. Why are the fruit and vegetables by the entrance and the in-store bakeries diagonally opposite the entrance in most supermarkets?

There are possible variations on the star schema. A snowflake schema introduces a degree of normalisation into the dimensions. A galaxy schema has two or more fact tables that share one or more of the dimensions. The latest versions of SQL have introduced support for OLAP operations with a relational schema, such as a GROUP BY ROLLUP facility.

OBJECT ORIENTATION AND DATABASES

What is object orientation?

Object orientation is a programming paradigm where the world is seen as a collection of objects that exhibit both state and behaviour. The state of an object at any one time is the aggregation of the values of the object's attributes. The behaviour is the set of messages to which the object can respond. Objects respond to messages by executing methods, short pieces of program code.

Objects are grouped into classes. So, for example, within an object oriented program to manage human resources there could be an **Employee** class with attributes of *payrollNumber, title, surname, otherNames, birthDate, salary*, etc. One of the instances of this class, an object, for our human resources department has the state 'CX137, Mrs, Rogers, Jennifer Alyson, 10 January 1970, 27750'. This object also has an object identifier that is used by the system to uniquely identify the object. The object identifier is totally independent of the values of its attributes, is system generated, and is hidden from the user. This means that object orientation has no equivalent of the primary key concept of the relational model of data.

Examples of the sort of messages that instances of the **Employee** class may respond to are:

- 'What is your surname?', where the answer is generated by a method that reads the value of the *surname* attribute;
- 'What is your full name?', where the answer is generated by a method that concatenates the values of the *title, otherNames* and *surname* attributes;
- 'What is your age?', where the answer is generated by a method that calculates the difference between the current date and the value of the *birthDate* attribute;
- 'Change surname to (new surname)';
- 'Change salary to (new salary)'.

The fundamental concepts of object orientation

There are four fundamental concepts underlying the object orientation programming paradigm. These are:

- encapsulation (or data hiding);
- inheritance;
- polymorphism;
- aggregation.

Encapsulation is the hiding of the implementation of an object's data structure and methods from the user. The only way that an object can interact with other objects is through the passing of messages. It is not possible to directly query the attributes of an object to find their value. We cannot, for instance, query the *salary* attribute of the 'Jenny Rogers' object of the **Employee** class and get the result '27750', but we can send the message 'What is your salary?' to that object. On receipt of that message the appropriate method is executed and a message is returned which says 'My salary is 27750'. The principle of encapsulation goes further in that we should not even need to know that objects of the **Employee** class have a *salary* attribute. The encapsulation principle can best be explained by considering an object of the **Cube** class within a system to handle geometric shapes. This object may respond to the message 'What is the length of one of your edges?' with the answer '3m' and to the message 'What is your volume?' with the answer '27m^3', but we do not know whether objects of the **Cube** class have an *edgeLength* attribute and respond to the 'What is your volume?' message by calculating the cube of the value of that *edgeLength* attribute or if they have a *volume* attribute and respond to the 'What is the length of one of your edges?' messages by calculating the cube root of the value of the *volume* attribute. Furthermore, we should not care. Provided we know the messages that an object responds to, we know all that we need to know to be able to use that object in a program.

Inheritance is the ability of one object class to reuse the data structures and methods of another class without reimplementing them. For example, the **Cube** class can inherit the properties of the **RectangularSolid** class which, in turn, can inherit the properties of the **RegularSolid** class. Objects of the **Sphere** class can also inherit the properties of the **RegularSolid** class. All objects of the **RegularSolid** class can respond to the 'What is your volume?' message. This means that all objects of the **RectangularSolid** class (which includes all objects of the **Cube** class) and of the **Sphere** class can also respond to that same message.

Polymorphism is where different objects in different classes respond to the same message by executing different methods. For example, objects of the **Cube** class can respond to the 'What is your volume?' message by cubing the value of the *edgeLength* attribute, objects of the **RectangularSolid** class can respond to the 'What is your volume?' message by multiplying the values of the *length*, *breadth* and *height* attributes, whilst objects of the **Sphere** class can respond to the 'What is your volume?' message by cubing the value of the ***radius*** attribute, then multiplying the result by the constant $4\pi/3$.

Aggregation, which is sometimes also known as containment, is the ability to group objects to make more complex or composite objects. For example, an object of the **Department** class may hold a reference (the object identifier) to an object of the **Set** class, where each element of that set is itself a reference to an object of the **Employee** class; a department contains all of its employees.

Object oriented databases

It is important that persistent storage of objects is available in any information system that hosts object oriented application programs. Some object oriented programming environments do provide persistent storage, but it is then closely coupled to the application programs themselves. There are, however, some object oriented database management systems available on the market, but they tend to be used in fairly specialised environments, such as computer-aided design and manufacturing (CAD/CAM) and geographic information systems (GIS). Those products that are available, although following generally accepted object oriented principles, have been developed using different approaches, such as the extension of an existing object oriented programming language or the development of class libraries using an object oriented programming language, and use different syntaxes for the data definition and data manipulation languages. There are no commonly accepted standards (yet) for object oriented databases.

The Object Data Management Group (ODMG) has, however, developed a formal specification for object oriented databases. This specification includes a data definition language called Object Definition Language (ODL) and a query language called Object Query Language (OQL). There is not a single manipulation language; the manipulation of the objects needs to be programmed in an object oriented programming language such as C++ or Java. Figure 12.6 shows a simple conceptual data model and Figure 12.7 shows the ODL schema definitions to implement it.

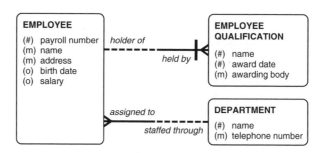

FIGURE 12.6   *A simple conceptual data model*

```
class Employee
( extent employees
  keys payroll_number, (name, address) )
{
  attribute string payroll_number,
  attribute string name,
  attribute Address address,
  attribute date birth_date,
  attribute Payment salary,
  relationship set<Employee_Qualification> holder_ of inverse Employee_Qualification::held_by,
  relationship Department assigned_to inverse Department::staffed_through,
  Payment calculate_monthly_payme nt()
};

class Employee_Qualificat ion
( extent employees_qualificati ons
  keys (held_by, name, award_date) )
{
  attribute string name,
  attribute date award_date,
  attribute Organization awarding_body,
  relationship Employee held_by inverse Employee::holder_of
};

class Department
( extent departments
  keys name )
{
  attribute string name,
  attribute string telephone_number,
  relationship set<Employee> staffed_throu gh inverse Employee::assigned_to
};
```

FIGURE 12.7   *The ODL schema definitions for the simple conceptual data model*

The **extent** is a name that is given to all the instances of this class within the particular database. This name is used by the OQL in its queries. The **keys** are not keys in the relational sense but are in fact uniqueness constraints. Remember that the equivalent in the object oriented paradigm of the relational model's primary key is the system-generated object identifier, which is hidden from the user. Note that the ODL key declarations can include relationships as well as attributes – *held_by* is part of the key of *Employee_Qualification*.

Each attribute is declared with a name and a literal type. The *payroll_number* attribute of the *Employee* class uses one of the built-in literal types, **string**, whereas the *address* attribute of the *Employee* class uses a user-defined structured literal type, *Address*.

Each relationship is declared with both a forward and an inverse traversal path in each class involved in the relationship. For example, the relationship that each EMPLOYEE may be *holder of* one or more EMPLOYEE QUALIFICATIONS and each EMPLOYEE QUALIFICATION must be *held by* one and only one EMPLOYEE is represented by the following declaration in the *Employee* class:

> **relationship** *set<Employee_Qualification> holder_of*
> **inverse** *Employee_Qualification::held_by*

and also by the following declaration in the Employee_Qualificat ion class:

> **relationship** *Employee held_by*
> **inverse** *Employee::holder_of*

The first of these declarations says that there is a relationship between *Employee* and *Employee_Qualification* called *holder_of* such that each instance of the *Employee* class may reference a *set* literal type whose elements are references to the instances of the *Employee_Qualification* class that represent the qualifications held by that employee (the forward traversal path) and to see that relationship from the other way you need to look at the specification of the *held_by* relationship in the *Employee_Qualification* class (the inverse traversal path). There can be zero, one or many elements in a set, so there may be zero, one or many qualifications recorded for each employee.

The second of these declarations says that there is a relationship between *Employee_Qualification* and *Employee* called *held_by* such that each instance of the *Employee_Qualification* class may reference an instance of the *Employee* class that represents the holder of this qualification (the forward traversal path) and to see that relationship from the other way you need to look at the specification of the *holder_of* relationship in the *Employee* class (the inverse traversal path). There can be only one employee holding each employee qualification.

Although *set* is used in these declarations for the 'many' relationships, it is not the only collection literal type that can be used. A *set* has no duplicates. If duplicates are possible, a *bag* collection type can be used. The elements of *sets* and *bags* are unordered. If there is an implied order in the 'many', a *list* collection type may be used.

Methods, such as the method to calculate the monthly payment from the annual salary, can also be specified. Only the method signature is included in the ODL specification; the methods themselves have to be implemented in another object oriented programming language. In the case of the *calculate_monthly_payment()* method, the result that is returned is of the *Payment* user-defined structured literal type.

Note that there is no explicit specification for optionality (mandatory or optional) for relationships. If it is required, optionality has to be handled through the use of methods.

Object relational databases

In the latest versions of SQL, published in 1999 and 2003, the scope has been extended to include some object-like facilities. Databases using these extended facilities are often called object relational databases. These object relational facilities include user-defined structured types and collection types, such as **MULTISETS** ('multiset' is another name for a 'bag' – a set where duplicates are allowed) and **ARRAYS**.

Figure 12.8 shows two structured types, **st_address** and **st_qualification**. (The **st_** is not necessary; it is just used as a device to distinguish a structured type from other database items with similar names.) The **st_address** structured type has five attributes (**name_or_number**, **street**, **area**, **town**, **post_code**); the **st_qualification** structured type has three attributes (**name**, **award_date**, **awarding_body**).

```
CREATE TYPE st_address
( name_or_number    VARCHAR(30),
  street            VARCHAR(30),
  area              VARCHAR(30),
  town              VARCHAR(30),
  post_code         VARCHAR(8)
);

CREATE TYPE st_qualification
( name              VARCHAR(30),
  award_date        DATE       ,
  awarding_body     VARCHAR(30)
);
```

FIGURE 12.8   *Structured type declarations*

Figure 12.9 shows the **CREATE TABLE** statements that are needed to implement the conceptual data model shown in Figure 12.6 using these structured
types. The structured types are used in the declarations of two columns in the
employee table. The **address** column is declared with the **st_address** structured type as its datatype – complete addresses are held as values in a single
column. The **qualifications** column is declared with a **MULTISET** as its
datatype, with each element of the **MULTISET** being of the **st_qualification**
structured type – the complete details of the employee's qualifications (zero,
one or many) are held as a single value and there is no longer any requirement
for a separate **employee_qualification** table.

Structured types are objects and so may have methods and may exist in
inheritance hierarchies. In Figure 12.9, we see structured types being used as
the datatype for a column. Structured types may, however, also be used as the
specification for a table and, where inheritance is involved, this ability can be
used to directly implement entity subtypes, something not previously possible. Figure 12.10 shows a revised conceptual data model that now includes
two subtypes of **EMPLOYEE**, **PART-TIME EMPLOYEE** and **FULL-TIME EMPLOYEE**.

```
CREATE TABLE department
( name                    VARCHAR(25)                  NOT NULL,
  telephone_number        VARCHAR(15)                  NOT NULL,
  PRIMARY KEY name
);

CREATE TABLE employee
( payroll_number          CHAR(5)                      NOT NULL,
  name                    VARCHAR(50)                  NOT NULL,
  address                 st_address                   NOT NULL,
  birth_date              DATE                         ,
  salary                  INTEGER                      ,
  qualifications          st_qualification MULTISET    ,
  assigned_to_department_name  VARCHAR(25)             NOT NULL,
  PRIMARY KEY payroll_number,
  FOREIGN KEY assigned_to_department_name REFERENCES department
);
```

FIGURE 12.9   *Table declarations using structured types and collections*

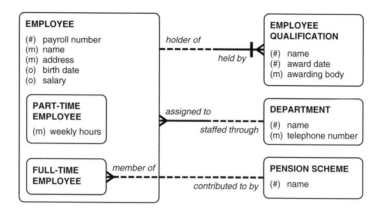

FIGURE 12.10 *Revised simple conceptual data model with entity subtypes*

Figure 12.11 shows the **CREATE TYPE** statements needed to implement this revised conceptual data model using tables based on the structured types. The **st_address** and **st_qualification** structured types are unchanged. The **st_employee** type is very similar to the previous **employee** table with two very important differences. First, there are no constraints (**NOT NULL**, **PRIMARY KEY**, etc.); constraints are applied to tables, not to types. Secondly, the attribute that will become the column that provides the foreign key to the **department** table has a different name and is of a **REF** datatype. This is explained when we see how the tables are created. The fact that **st_part_time_employee** and **st_full_time_employee** are both subtypes of **st_employee** is shown by the declaration that they are both **UNDER** **st_employee**.

Figure 12.12 shows the **CREATE TABLE** statements that use these structured types. The **employee** table has eight columns, seven from the structured type (**payroll_number, name, address, birth_date, salary, qualifications** and **assigned_to_department_ref**) and an additional column called **row_id**. This additional column holds a system-generated value of the **REF** type – the object identifier. It is also declared as the primary key. The **CREATE TABLE** statement for the **employee** table also includes the **NOT NULL** and **FOREIGN KEY** constraints.

The **part_time_employee** and **full_time_employee** tables are declared as being **UNDER employee**, i.e. as subtables of the **employee** table. The **part_time_employee** table now has nine columns, the eight columns inherited from the **employee** table and the additional **weekly_hours** column. All details of employees are automatically stored in the appropriate table, in the **part_time_employee** table for part-time employees and in the **full_time_employee** table for full-time employees. A query seeking the name and address of all the full-time employees reads the **full_time_employee** table. A query seeking the name and address of all employees reads the **full_time_employee** table for the names and addresses of all the full-time employees, the **part_time_employee** table for the

151

```
CREATE TYPE st_address
( name_or_number                 VARCHAR(30),
  street                         VARCHAR(30),
  area                           VARCHAR(30),
  town                           VARCHAR(30),
  post_code                      VARCHAR(8)
);

CREATE TYPE st_qualification
( name                           VARCHAR(30),
  award_date                     DATE        ,
  awarding_body                  VARCHAR(30)
);

CREATE TYPE st_employee
( payroll_number                 CHAR(5),
  name                           VARCHAR(50),
  address                        st_address,
  birth_date                     DATE,
  salary                         INTEGER,
  qualifications                 st_qualification MULTISET,
  assigned_to_department_ref     REF(st_department) SCOPE department
);

CREATE TYPE st_part_time_employee
   UNDER st_employee AS
( weekly_hours                   DECIMAL(5,2)
);

CREATE TYPE st_full_time_employee
   UNDER st_employee AS
( member_of_pension_scheme_ref   REF(st_pension_scheme) SCOPE pension_scheme
);

CREATE TYPE st_pension_scheme
( name                           VARCHAR(40)
);

CREATE TYPE st_department
( name                           VARCHAR(25),
  telephone_number               VARCHAR(15)
);
```

FIGURE 12.11   *Creating structured types*

names and addresses of all the part-time employees, and the `employee` table for those employees who are neither full-time employees nor part-time employees (there should not be any of these). Thus, inheritance is managed 'under the covers' by the database management system.

MULTIMEDIA AND DATABASES

When we have discussed data so far we have generally been referring to data that comprises short character strings (names, etc.), numbers and dates. This is often called structured data. Not all data is structured, however. There is another category of data that is sometimes called multimedia data and sometimes called unstructured data. This data includes line figures such as charts, graphs, and illustrations; photographs and other pixellated images that are seen as pictures by the human eye; and digitised audio and video.

```
CREATE TABLE department
    OF st_department
( REF IS row_id SYSTEM GENERATED,
  PRIMARY KEY (row_id),
  name WITH OPTIONS NOT NULL,
  telephone_number WITH OPTIONS NOT NULL
);

CREATE TABLE pension_scheme
    OF st_pension_scheme
( REF IS row_id SYSTEM GENERATED,
  PRIMARY KEY (row_id),
  name WITH OPTIONS NOT NULL
);

CREATE TABLE employee
    OF st_employee
( REF IS row_id SYSTEM GENERATED,
  PRIMARY KEY (row_id),
  payroll_number WITH OPTIONS NOT NULL,
  name WITH OPTIONS NOT NULL,
  address WITH OPTIONS NOT NULL,
  assigned_to_department_ref WITH OPTIONS NOT NULL,
  FOREIGN KEY assigned_to_department_ref REFERENCES department
);

CREATE TABLE part_time_employee
    OF st_part_time_employee
    UNDER employee
( weekly_hours WITH OPTIONS NOT NULL
);

CREATE TABLE full_time_employee
    OF st_full_time_employee
    UNDER employee
( FOREIGN KEY   member_of_pension_scheme_ref REFERENCES pension_scheme
);
```

FIGURE 12.12   *Creating tables based on the structured types*

Storing and retrieving multimedia data presents a number of challenges because of the nature of multimedia data.

- Multimedia data is usually complex.
- Multimedia data is usually large.
- Multimedia data may have many possible representations, for example, a photograph may be in JPG, PNG, GIF or BMP format.

There is often a requirement to store multimedia data with structured data. For example, the human resources department might want to store a photograph of each employee as part of their employee record; word-processed summaries of meetings may be held with data recording the dates, locations, subjects and attendees of those meetings.

The multimedia data may be stored external to the structured database, with only a reference to the multimedia stored within the database. In this way, it is possible to call up the record for an individual employee and for the application program to automatically retrieve and display the employee's photograph or, similarly, to automatically retrieve the summary of a meeting by querying the database using the subject and the date. When the multimedia data is stored externally like this, it is only partially under the control of the database management system. Users could access the multimedia data without using the database management system at all.

Alternatively, the multimedia data can be stored within the database, which means that access to the data is fully under the control of the database management system. With recent releases of the SQL standard there are two new datatypes that enable the internal storage of multimedia data: the **BINARY LARGE OBJECT** (also known as **BLOB**) and the **CHARACTER LARGE OBJECT** (also known as **CLOB**). With the **BLOB** datatype, the multimedia data is stored as a meaningless stream of bits and it is impossible to query the multimedia data itself. To retrieve the photographs of all the fair-haired employees, it would necessary to have the colour of each employee's hair recorded as structured data; there is no pattern in the bit-stream that can be used to determine whether the subjects of the photographs have fair, or any other colour, hair. With the **CLOB** datatype the multimedia data is stored as a stream of text characters. There can, therefore, be limited querying of the multimedia data. Note that most word-processing software stores documents in a proprietary format and these word-processed documents need to be stored using the **BLOB** datatype and not the **CLOB** datatype. The text of the document can be stored using a **CLOB**, but the formatting of the document is lost. One way to store a document as text (so that it can be stored using the **CLOB** datatype) is to format the document using the HyperText Markup Language (HTML), which is discussed when we look at web technology.

When storing multimedia data externally to the database, a reference to the location of the multimedia data needs to be stored in the database. Until recently, the only way to do this was to store the reference as a path reference, for example, the photograph of Jenny Rogers may be referenced as 'c:\hr_docs\photos\cx137jrogers.gif'. The photograph is still accessible to any user who knows its location and could be replaced with a more up-to-date photograph without needing to access the database, provided the new photograph is given the same name as the old photograph and is stored in the same location. If the photograph is deleted or moved the, now inaccurate, reference could remain in the database. A well-intentioned attempt to 'tidy up' the directory structure on a hard disk could cause havoc with direct references of this sort.

The latest versions of the SQL standard have yet another new datatype that helps to overcome the problems when multimedia data is stored externally. This is the **DATALINK** datatype. A column declared as being of the type **DATALINK** has values that are expressed as a URL, for example, 'file:///localhost/c:/hr_docs/photos/cx137jrogers.gif'. One advantage of this is that the multimedia data may be held remotely from the database server, maybe close to where the data is used to reduce the overall network traffic. A **DATALINK** column may be declared with special properties that, in association with some additional datalinker software, allow there to be some control of the external multimedia data. One property ensures that the multimedia file cannot be renamed or deleted; another property denies access to the multimedia file other than as a result of querying the database; and a third property ensures that if the **DATALINK** reference is deleted from the database an appropriate action is carried out, either the multimedia file is deleted or control is passed back to the normal file management system.

Another way of handling multimedia data is to use a specially designed 'package'. The ISO/IEC 13249 series of standards have created a number of standard packages that make use of the SQL structured type feature to support the handling of multimedia data, particularly for full-text documents, still images and spatial data.

The Full-Text package (ISO/IEC 13249-2, 2003) provides methods for recording and querying large streams of text. The querying can test whether the text contains a pattern (where the pattern can be a word or a phrase, can contain wildcard characters, can include Boolean (AND or OR) conditions, can test for the proximity of words or phrases, can test for a synonym of a given word, can test for words based on a given stem) or a combination of patterns.

The Still Image package (ISO/IEC 13249-5, 2003) provides methods for the recording and manipulation of images such as photographs, with the images either being stored internally, as a **BLOB**, or externally, referenced by a **DATALINK** value. The manipulation methods allow the image to be resized, scaled, rotated and displayed as a thumbnail.

The Spatial package (ISO/IEC 13249-3, 2003) provides methods for the recording and management of spatial data (points, lines and areas) within given spatial frames of reference (latitude and longitude, national grids, etc.). The principal use of this package is for geospatial and mapping applications, but its use is not restricted to this area.

DATA AND WEB TECHNOLOGY

The internet is a global federation of interconnected networks that can be used for the passing of email messages between users and for conferencing services. The internet also hosts the web, a global network of information resources. Web users 'browse' information using application programs called web browsers, such as Microsoft Internet Explorer, Netscape Navigator and Mozilla Firefox. The information resources are stored as documents written using the HyperText Markup Language (HTML).

HTML is a general-purpose display language derived from the Standard Generalised Markup Language (SGML). SGML provides a grammar for specifying formats based on standard markup notations ('markup' is the name given to the concept of combining text with extra information about the text). The markup information is provided as plain-text 'tags', so that documents formatted using SGML, or any of its derivatives, can be read by both machines and by humans.

HTML documents are held on computers known as web servers. To enable the HTML documents to be found, there is a uniform naming scheme used within the web, with each document given its own unique name, known as a Uniform Resource Indicator (URI). The documents are delivered to the browsers from the servers using a standard protocol such as HyperText Transfer Protocol (HTTP).

Because it is relatively simple to design HTML documents and web technology is easy to use, many organisations are employing the same technology to manage their business. If this technology is used exclusively within a business (i.e. it is not open to outside users) it is known as an intranet; if the technology is used to deal with a company's external customers or associates, it is sometimes known as an extranet.

HTML is purely concerned with the way that an information resource such as a document is presented by a web browser. It is not concerned with the meaning of the information contained in the document. Another markup language based on SGML is used for that purpose. That language is known as eXtensible Markup Language (XML). XML is only concerned with the definition and structure of the information in the document, having no tags to specify presentation. Further description of both HTML and XML, including some discussion of problems associated with the use of XML, are provided in Appendix G.

XML and relational databases

XML is principally a mechanism for transferring data; on receipt, an XML document can be parsed to retrieve and present the data to a user at the receiving site. However, it may be that we need to store the data from the XML document in a database at the receiver site. That data may then be used to compose another XML document for transfer to yet a different site. It is important, therefore, to recognise the requirement for the transfer of data from XML documents to databases and also the requirement to create XML documents from data in databases.

There are a number of databases on the market that store data in XML format. These are known as native XML databases (or NXDs). In a native XML database, the standard unit of storage is the XML document. As a technology, native XML databases are in their infancy and, apart from XQuery, there are no standards commonly accepted by all the vendors.

A native XML database is not the only option, however, for the storage of data contained in an XML document. XML documents, or elements of XML documents, could, for instance, be stored in relational database columns that have been declared as either **CHARACTER VARYING** or **CLOB** datatypes. The whole XML document may be stored in a single column or decomposed so that the elements are stored as individual data values. Additional support for the handling of XML documents is now available because the latest SQL standard includes a part known as SQL/XML. This new part introduces an **XML** datatype, which can be used in the same way as any other datatype, i.e. as a datatype for a column, as a variable or as a parameter for a function. SQL/XML also introduces facilities that provide for the composition of XML using data extracted from a relational database and, conversely, for the storage of data extracted from an XML document in a relational database. These facilities are described in more detail in Appendix H.

XML documents may be composed from existing data selected from a database, they may be received as a result of a business-to-business (B2B) transaction, or they may contain original data created using an XML editor. Although XML was initially developed with the limited but important job of transferring data within a web environment so that the meaning of the content was known, XML is now often regarded as the way to solve all IT problems. It is almost impossible to avoid new suggestions for the use of XML. In many cases these new uses are over sold.

Other ways to link databases and web technology

The web-user interface is a browser that uses a network (the internet, an intranet or an extranet) to access a web server. The role of the web server is to provide the information requested by the web browser. Web browsers are designed to read HTML documents, which are, by their very nature, static. Using HTML alone, it is very difficult to keep the information in the documents up to date, especially if that information is changing rapidly. What is required for web technology to be used to access databases is for the web pages to be created dynamically using data from the database. We also need the ability to do the opposite, for the user to be able to insert information into a web browser and for that information to be stored as data in a database.

We have seen that XML documents can be created by querying a relational database and, conversely, that information can be extracted from an XML document and inserted into a relational database. Furthermore, it is possible to extract the information from an XML document and insert it in an HTML page ready for display. However, XML is not the only option available when we need to interact with a database from a web browser.

It is possible, for example, to embed programs in HTML documents using a scripting language such as JavaScript or PHP. Scripting languages allow the user to input information and provide facilities for database connectivity. The popular Google search engine (www.google.co.uk), for example, has JavaScript functions embedded in its web pages.

There are also a number of interface specifications that can be used to transfer information between web browsers or web servers and databases. Some of these are proprietary whilst others are openly available specifications. An example of an openly available specification is the Common Gateway Interface (CGI). Using CGI, a web server can pass requests for data generated at a web browser to a database and then pass the database output back to the web browser. The Java Database Connectivity (JDBC) specification is another openly available specification that allows Java, a programming language commonly used to develop web-based applications, to access and manipulate data stored in relational databases.

SUMMARY

This chapter has looked a number of different areas, all of which impact on data management or are areas that data management needs to be aware of and have policies in place to deal with.

The first area considered was the use of off-the-shelf application packages. We saw that these packages are often difficult to integrate into a federation of systems where data is to be shared and that the overall cost of using an application package may be more expensive than expected due to the cost of providing interfaces and tailoring.

We then considered distributed data and databases. We looked at the reasons that data may be distributed and we looked at Chris Date's objectives for a distributed database management system. We then looked at techniques for developing both top-down distribution and bottom-up integration and completed our look at distributed data by considering how replication can be managed.

The next area of interest was data warehousing and the associated concept of data mining. We looked at the data warehouse concept within an overall systems architecture and discussed the nature of the data within a data warehouse: subject-oriented, time-variant, non-volatile and integrated. We looked at the multidimensional model of data and the OLAP operations of slice, dice, roll-up and drill-down. We briefly looked at data mining before looking at the relational data warehouse schema.

Next came object orientation and databases. We looked at the basic concepts of object orientation and then looked at object oriented databases and object relational databases. In the case of object relational databases, we looked specifically at the advances in SQL and the way that the structured type exhibits object oriented properties, enabling structured types to be used both as datatypes for columns and as the basis for the creation of tables themselves. In the latter case, we saw how structured types can provide automatic support for hierarchies.

We then looked at multimedia databases. We saw the **BLOB**, **CLOB** and **DATALINK** datatypes and briefly looked at the special multimedia packages that are being provided.

We finished by looking at data and web technology. The use of HTML and XML documents was discussed. We concluded by looking very briefly at some other approaches to link databases and web technology.

Comparison of Data Modelling Notations

This appendix compares five notations that are in common use for data modelling, with the same business scenario drawn in each notation. The notations are:

- The Ellis–Barker notation – see Figure A.1 and Figure A.2;

- The Chen entity–relationship notation – see Figure A.3;

- The Information Engineering notation – see Figure A.4;

- The IDEF1X notation – see Figure A.5;

- The UML notation for object class diagrams – see Figure A.6.

The Ellis–Barker notation

Figure A.1 shows a data model drawn using my preferred notation. This notation does not have a formal name, but I am calling it the Ellis–Barker notation because it was developed in the early 1980s by Harry Ellis and Richard Barker when they were working for CACI, an IT services company. Richard Barker then took the notation and its related methodology into the development of Oracle's CASE tool. It is this notation that he describes in his book *CASE*METHOD: Entity Relationship Modelling* (Barker, 1989). It is also used by David Hay in his book *Data Model Patterns: Conventions of Thought* (Hay, 1996).

The beauty of this notation is that it is easy to read. Harry Ellis and Richard Barker set out to develop a notation that unambiguously and accurately portrayed the data requirements yet at the same time reduced the number of interactions that the analyst would require with the users. I have used this notation with many who have never seen a data model before; they find the concepts easy to grasp and are soon able to describe the data requirements that led to the model being discussed.

The model in Figure A.1 represents the data requirements associated with the handling of orders. Some of the orders are 'call-off' orders, i.e. there are 'framework orders' in place and the customer submits orders for the products or services, the call-off orders, as required. There may also be normal orders, i.e. orders that are not called off from a framework arrangement. Hence, to allow for the recording of the call-off orders being associated with a framework order, each ORDER may be *part of* one and only one ORDER.

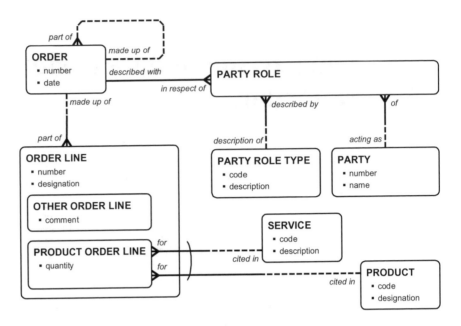

FIGURE A.1 *A data model in Ellis–Barker notation*

Parties, persons or organisations, can play different roles associated with an order. They may be the customer who placed the order, the consignee of the goods or services as they are delivered, the department to which the invoice is to be sent or the staff member who is responsible for ensuring that the order is completed. Hence, each ORDER must be *described with* one or more PARTY ROLES, where each PARTY ROLE must be *of* one and only one PARTY and each PARTY ROLE must be *described by* one and only PARTY ROLE TYPE.

The details of the order, the products or services being ordered or other comments, are included as 'order lines'. Hence, each ORDER may be *made up of* one or more ORDER LINES. Each of these ORDER LINES must be either a PRODUCT ORDER LINE, a specification of a product or service being ordered, or an OTHER ORDER LINE, to enable a comment to be added to an order. Furthermore, each PRODUCT ORDER LINE must be *for* one and only one PRODUCT OR must be *for* one and only one SERVICE.

There are a number of variations that can be used with this notation. The attributes can be omitted from the model diagram to aid readability. Attributes can be annotated with (#), to indicate it is part of the unique identifier, (m), if it is mandatory for a value to exist or (o), if values are optional. For a complete indication of unique identification, those relationships that are part of a unique identifier, sometimes called identifying relationships, are annotated with a bar across the relationship line. These additional annotations are shown in Figure A.2.

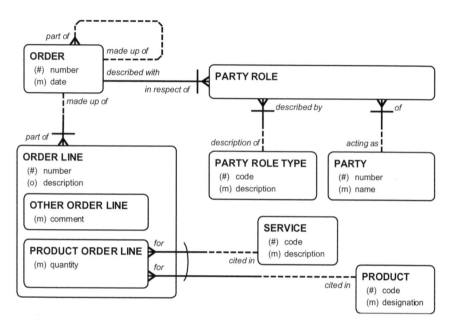

FIGURE A.2   *Ellis–Barker data model with attribute annotation and unique identifiers*

The unique identifiers for the entities shown in Figure A.2 are:

- for **ORDER** – the *number* attribute;

- for **ORDER LINE** – the *number* attribute and the <u>must be</u> *part of* <u>one and only one</u> **ORDER** relationship;

- for **PRODUCT** – the *code* attribute;

- for **SERVICE** – the *code* attribute;

- for **PARTY** – the *number* attribute;

- for **PARTY ROLE TYPE** – the *code* attribute;

- for **PARTY ROLE** – the <u>must be</u> *in respect of* <u>one and only one</u> **ORDER** relationship, the <u>must be</u> *of* <u>one and only one</u> **PARTY** relationship, and the <u>must be</u> *described by* <u>one and only one</u> **PARTY ROLE TYPE** relationship.

The Chen notation

The Chen notation in Figure A.3 was the original entity–relationship modelling notation proposed by Peter Chen in his paper *The Entity-Relationship Model – Toward a Unified View of Data* (Chen, 1976) and the notation, with some refinements, is still in use today in a number of environments.

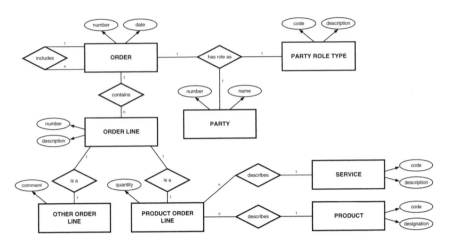

FIGURE A.3 *A data model in Chen notation*

Entities are represented by boxes, relationships by diamonds and attributes by ellipses attached to the entity boxes. Relationships can be 'n-ary', in that more than two entities may be related by a single relationship. Hence the **PARTY ROLE TYPE** entity of Figure A.1 is represented by the 'has role as' relationship in this notation.

There are no equivalents of the exclusive arc or entity subtyping. The supertype–subtype hierarchy is simulated by the two 'is a' relationships, but these do not fully cover the concept because they do not document the fact that the subtypes are mutually exclusive.

The information engineering notation

Figure A.4 shows the same business area drawn using the Information Engineering data modelling notation. Information Engineering was developed by James Martin and Clive Finkelstein in the late 1970s. It was very popular in the UK, Europe and USA in the 1980s and 1990s, where it had extensive CASE tool support. The methodology had a number of techniques which looked at data (its structure and how it changed over time) and processes and provided some cross-checking to ensure that there is a correlation between data and process.

The relationship notation is as precise as that used in the Ellis–Barker notation, but more symbols are used to impart the same message. A crow's foot with a bar across its base means 'one or more', whilst a crow's foot with a circle at its base means 'zero, one or more'. The absence of a crow's foot with two bars means 'one and only one' and the absence of a crow's foot with a circle means 'zero or one'. So, from Figure A.4, the relationship between **PARTY** and **PARTY ROLE** is read as 'each **PARTY** *is quoted in* <u>zero, one or more</u> **PARTY ROLES**' and 'each **PARTY ROLE** *references* <u>one and only one</u> **PARTY**' and the recursive relationship on **ORDER** reads as 'each **ORDER** *includes* <u>zero, one or more</u> **ORDERS**' and 'each **ORDER** *is included in* <u>zero or one</u> **ORDER**'.

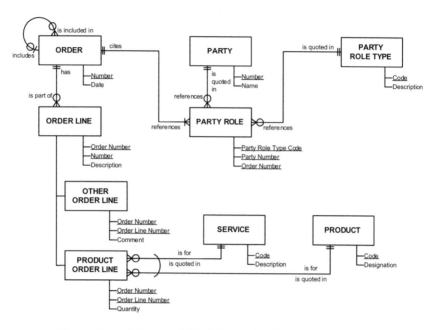

FIGURE A.4 *A data model in Information Engineering notation*

Attributes can be included on the diagram. They are listed outside the entity box, as shown, with the unique identifiers (primary keys) being underlined.

Exclusive arcs and entity subtypes are supported. The subtypes are shown separately from the supertype but connected to it by a line. There is no special notation for this line and it is possible for the subtypes to become visually separated from their supertype. Because the subtypes are external to the supertype, it is possible to include more than one set of subtypes on the same diagram. For example, a PERSON entity could be subtyped into MALE PERSON and FEMALE PERSON and at the same time could also be subtyped into EMPLOYEE and CUSTOMER. This ability to support multiple subtyping hierarchies is not possible in the Ellis–Barker notation where the subtypes are located within the supertype 'box'.

The IDEF1X notation

IDEF1X, shown in Figure A.5, is one of the family of ICAM Definition Languages (IDEF). ICAM is short for Integrated Computer-Aided Manufacturing, an initiative managed by the US Air Force. IDEF1X is a data modelling language – there was an IDEF1, an information modelling language, but this was extended and renamed as IDEF1X. Amongst the other IDEF languages are IDEF0, a functional modelling language; IDEF2, a dynamics modelling language; and IDEF3, a process or workflow modelling language. IDEF1X is now a US Federal standard and the language has become very widely used both within the US and internationally. IDEF1X is a very rich notation, encompassing many different facets of the basic entity, attribute and relationship concepts.

For example, within the language there are two different types of entity: independent and dependent. An independent entity is one that does not depend on any other for its identification and is shown on an IDEF1X diagram using a box with square corners. A dependent entity, therefore, is one that depends on one or more other entities for its identification and is shown on an IDEF1X diagram using a box with rounded corners. The entities ORDER, PRODUCT, SERVICE, PARTY and PARTY-ROLE-TYPE are independent entities; the entities ORDER-LINE (and its subtypes) and PARTY-ROLE are dependent entities.

In a full IDEF1X diagram, both types of entity have their attributes listed in two groups. The attributes above the separation line in the entity box are the 'key attributes' (or the 'primary key attributes' – the attributes that form the primary key columns in the equivalent table in an SQL implementation); whilst the attributes below the line are the non-key attributes. All attributes, key and non-key, that are part of a foreign key are marked with '(FK)'. Note the rule that all attribute names (except for those that are part of a foreign key) must be unique within the model, which means that the entity name often has to be added to the attribute name to ensure this uniqueness. Foreign key attributes can retain their original names or can be renamed when in their foreign key role.

The relationship notation is very complex. A solid line represents an identifying relationship (a relationship where all the primary key attributes of the parent entity become part of the primary key of the child entity) and a dotted line represents a non-identifying relationship. A 'blob' on the end of the relationship line is almost the equivalent of a crow's foot in the Ellis–Barker and Information Engineering notations – it represents the end of the relationship that is at the child end of the relationship (the 'foreign key end'). Unannotated, the 'blob' represents 'zero or more'; annotated with a 'P' (for positive) it represents 'one or more'; annotated with a 'Z' (for zero), it represents 'zero or one'; annotated with a number, for example '2', it represents 'exactly 2'. An open diamond at the parent end (the 'primary key end') of a non-identifying relationship indicates that the parent entity type is optional, for example, not every ORDER is included in another ORDER.

As with Information Engineering, subtypes are shown external to their supertype, but there is a specific notation to indicate the subtypes. A subtype is known as a 'category entity' in IDEF1X and the combination of a supertype and its subtypes is known as a category or generalisation hierarchy. There is, however, a specific notation for a category hierarchy. This is a circle over two bars for a complete hierarchy (where each instance of the supertype has an equivalent instance of one of the subtypes) and a circle over a single bar for an incomplete hierarchy. (An incomplete hierarchy does not meet our rule for subtypes given in Chapter 4 that every instance of the supertype

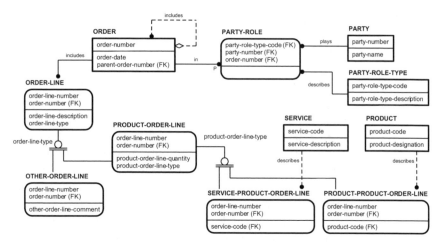

FIGURE A.5   *A data model in IDEF1X notation*

must also be an instance of one of the subtypes as well as the subtypes being mutually exclusive.) The name of the attribute in the supertype that is to act as the 'category discriminator' is alongside the category-hierarchy notation. Because the subtypes are shown external to the supertype, multiple subtyping hierarchies can be used.

There is no equivalent of the exclusive arc in IDEF1X which means that mutually exclusive relationships must be shown using subtyping. Hence we have the subtypes **PRODUCT-PRODUCT-ORDER-LINE** and **SERVICE-PRODUCT-ORDER-LINE** of **PRODUCT-ORDER-LINE** which play no role other than to relate **PRODUCT-ORDER-LINE** with **PRODUCT** and **SERVICE** respectively.

> *Aside*: Once he had seen the notation I use, an American friend of mine employed as a data modeller on a multinational project resorted to annotating one of his IDEF1X models with 'These two relationships are mutually exclusive' to get over the proliferation of unnecessary subtypes throughout the model.

Because the IDEF1X notation is very rich it is not very easy for those not involved in data modelling to understand the model. This becomes even more so, the greater the number of entities on the model. An IDEF1X model is more an expression of a logical schema than a conceptual data model that documents a business area's information requirements. The information requirements are documented, but they are swamped by a mass of detail that is really there so that the design of the database can be automated. It is sometimes difficult 'to see the wood for the trees'.

The UML class notation

The Unified Modeling Language (UML) is a set of modelling notations for object oriented analysis and design. It is not a method because each of the model types stands alone – there is no overall process in UML to tie the separate models together. There are some processes, such as the Rational Unified Process, that use UML notations but they are not part of UML. Central to all object oriented analysis and design methods is the modelling of object classes. This is very similar to data modelling and UML class models are increasingly replacing data models in software development.

Each object class is represented by a box that is split into three separate sections. The top section contains the name of the class. The middle section lists the attributes of the class. Each attribute may be annotated with its type (string, integer, date, etc.) and with a default value (but no default values are shown in Figure A.6). The bottom section contains the operations of the class – the processes that a class knows how to carry out. As we are only interested in data (that is, attributes), no operations are shown in Figure A.6.

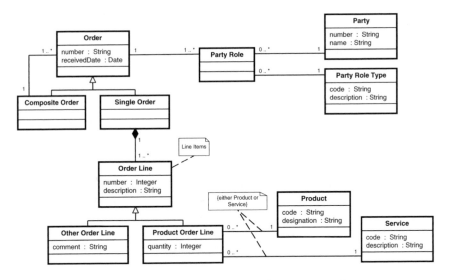

FIGURE A.6   *An object class model in UML notation*

The 'multiplicity' of each relationship (called associations in UML) is shown using textual annotations as opposed to the crow's foot, or similar, notation. The black diamond represents composition. An **ORDER** (a **SINGLE ORDER** on our class diagram) is composed of a number of **ORDER LINES**, representing the items being ordered. An **ORDER LINE** has no relevance without its parent **ORDER** and cannot be transferred between **ORDERS**.

There is a standard notation, the white arrow head, for the subclass concept. **PRODUCT ORDER LINE** and **OTHER ORDER LINE** are subclasses of **ORDER LINE**. Note that UML has no equivalent of the recursive relationship so the *part of*

– *made up of* relationship on ORDER is achieved by subclassing ORDER into COMPOSITE ORDER and SINGLE ORDER.

Although there is no direct equivalent of the exclusive arc, there is the ability to annotate the model with additional constraints (shown in curly brackets, { }) and general notes.

There is no equivalent of the unique identification or primary key concepts. This is because within an object oriented system each object (an instance of an object class) is identified within the system by a system-generated identifier that is hidden from the user of the system.

Despite their popularity with IT professionals, UML class diagrams, like IDEF1X models, are often found to be difficult to understand by those not involved in data or object modelling.

Comparison of the notations

Figure A.7 shows for comparison the different relationship notations used in the Ellis–Barker, Information Engineering, IDEF1X and UML notations. Figure A.8 provides an overall comparison of the notations.

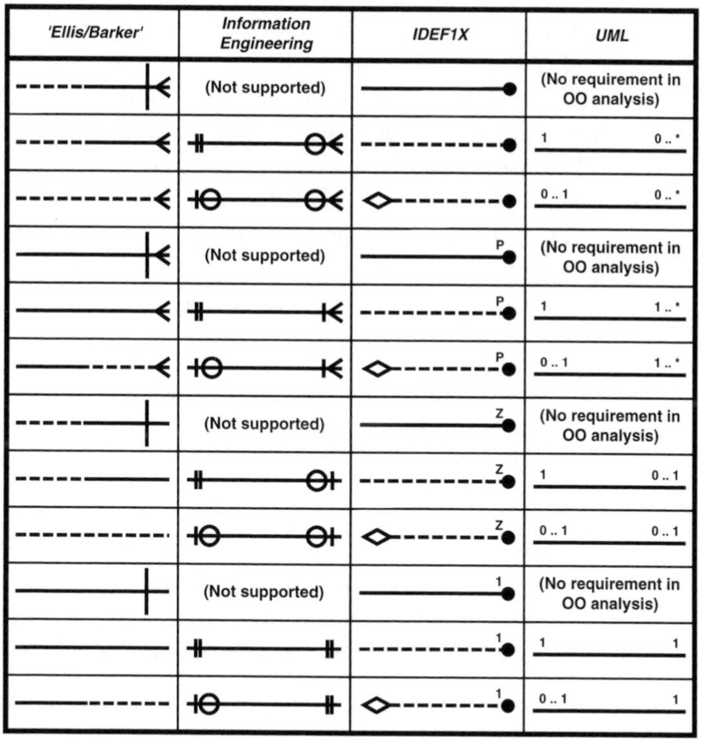

FIGURE A.7   *Comparison of the relationship notations*

	'Ellis/Barker'	Chen	Information Engineering	IDEF1X	UML
Dependent/independent entities	✗	✗	✗	✓	✗
Entity subtyping	✓	✗	✓	✓	✓
Multiple subtyping hierarchies	✗	✗	✓	✓	✓
Exclusive arcs	✓	✗	✓	✗	?
Identifying relationships	?	✗	✗	✓	✗
'n-ary' relationships	✗	✓	✗	✗	✗
'Many over time' relationships	✗	✗	✗	✗	✗

FIGURE A.8 *Comparison of the overall data model notations*

You will see that IDEF1X gets more ticks than any of the other notations in Figure A.8. One of those is because it provides the ability to use multiple subtyping hierarchies but this is a facility that I believe should not be available. Every time I have seen multiple subtyping hierarchies used I have seen confusion and errors. The discipline provided by the Ellis–Barker notation that there can only be a single subtyping hierarchy for any one entity is a sound discipline.

There are two question marks. Although UML does not have an explicit exclusive arc, the mutual exclusivity of relationships (associations) can be documented using the additional constraint concept. The Ellis–Barker notation can have relationships annotated to indicate that they are identifying relationships but most data modellers do not make use of this notation.

You will see that none of the notations distinguishes what I have called 'many over time' relationships. 'Many' relationships can cover three separate circumstances and it would be useful for the notations to distinguish between them. These three circumstances are:

- Many instances of the child entity are associated with the parent entity at the same time, but there is no implied sequence associated with those instances; for example, the personal computers installed in an open-plan office.

- Many instances of the child entity are associated with the parent entity at the same time, but there is a sequence associated with those instances; for example, the lines within an order (they are displayed in sequence down the page on a printed order) and the ticket coupons in an airline ticket (numbered in sequence from front to back).

- Only one instance of the child entity is associated with the parent entity at any one time, but there may be many instances of the child entity over time; for example, a person can only have one current British passport, but may have held many passports in the past and records need to be kept of those previous passports.

Hierarchical and Network Databases

For the majority of the discussions in this book we have been considering the relational model of data, first proposed by Edgar F. Codd (1970) when talking about the way that data is structured in databases. In the relational model, data is logically stored in relations, which are sets of tuples, with each tuple being a set of attribute–value pairs. In the physical embodiment of this model, with database management systems based on the SQL database language, the data is logically considered to be stored in tables.

Although it is the most common logical construct for storing data in databases, the table is not the only logical construct. Other models of data include:

- the hierarchical model;

- the network model;

- the multidimensional model;

- the object-oriented model.

Both the multidimensional model of data and the object-oriented model were discussed in Chapter 12. The hierarchical model of data and the network model of data are discussed in this appendix. Both these models predate the relational model of data, which was proposed by Edgar Codd to counter the shortcomings of these two models of data.

To provide a comparison, Figure B.1 shows a conceptual data model that will be developed into the hierarchical and network schemas and Figure B.2 shows some specimen data arranged as if it was stored in a relational database.

Hierarchical databases

The hierarchical model of data formed the basis for a number of early database management systems, the most prominent being IBM's Information Management System (IMS). IMS was first released in 1968 and is still in use today with many legacy mainframe-hosted applications used for accounting and inventory control.

Figure B.3 shows an example of a schema diagram for a hierarchical database. The schema in Figure B.3 has only one hierarchy, but there could be many hierarchies in a single database. Each hierarchy comprises a number of record types, with each record type comprising a number of field types. Each hierarchy has a root record type. In Figure B.3 the root is the **DEPARTMENT**

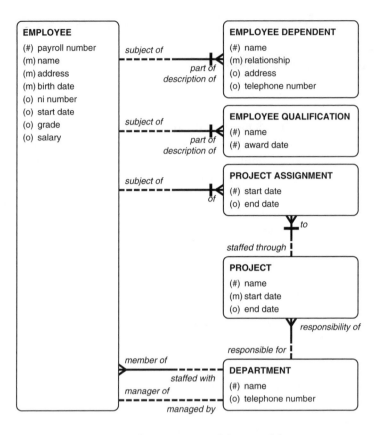

FIGURE B.1   *Conceptual data model*

employee

payroll_ number	name	address	birth_date	ni_number	start_date	grade	salary	department
AY334	Barbara Watson	3 Richmond ..	1952-12-06	XU996543B	1994-06-03	4	20340	Finance
AY478	John Wilson	55 Aberfan ..	1953-07-03	YA775421C	1972-12-05	5	13436	Production
BZ987	Joe Smith	The Manor ..	1964-02-24	ZR564439A	2003-09-01	1	35625	HQ
CA446	Phil Jones	37 Short ..	1974-05-05	BC906671A	1998-02-07	2	27750	Production
CX137	Jenny Rogers	37 Rushmore ..	1970-01-10	YC223456A	1995-01-03	2	27750	Finance
DJ777	Henry Phillips	33/2 Long ..	1974-05-05	SS677845D	1992-09-03	3	22570	Finance
EX115	Brian Thompson	29 Mayland ..	1979-06-11	JN905067C	1997-10-10	3	21785	Production
FJ678	Roger Harrison	9 Collier ..	1988-04-27	BH878754A	2004-11-05	4	14300	Finance
FL233	Jane Smith	99 Rushmore ..	1989-08-25	HL778923B	2006-12-08	5	12725	Production

employee_qualification

payroll_ number	name	award_date
CX137	Dip FM	1998-09
CX137	ACCA	2003-10-20
CX137	First Aid	2005-04-30

employee_dependent

payroll_ number	name	address	telephone_number
CX137	Mr John Rodgers	37 Rush ..	01377 376427
CX137	Miss A L Rogers	Flat 4 ..	01451 276810

department

name	telephone_number	managed_by
HQ	NULL	NULL
Finance	ext 452	CX137
Production	ext 664	CA446

project

name	start_date	end_date
Venus	2007-01-08	2007-03-23
Patriot	2007-01-29	NULL

project_assignment

of	to	start_date	end_date
AY478	Venus	2007-01-08	2007-03-23
EX115	Venus	2007-01-08	2007-01-26
EX115	Patriot	2007-01-29	2007-04-13
FL233	Patriot	2007-02-05	2007-04-13

FIGURE B.2   *Relational database occurrences*

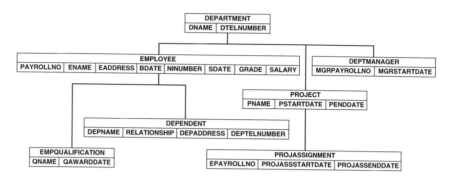

FIGURE B.3   *Hierarchical database schema*

record type, which has two field types, DNAME, the name of the department, and DTELNUMBER, the telephone number of the department.

Each hierarchy has a number of one-to-many parent–child relationship types. There may be zero, one or more child-record instances for each parent-record instance. In Figure B.3 these are (DEPARTMENT, EMPLOYEE), (DEPARTMENT, DEPTMANAGER), (DEPARTMENT, PROJECT), (EMPLOYEE, EMPQUALIFICATION), (EMPLOYEE, DEPENDENT) and (PROJECT, PROJASSIGNMENT). Instead of the relationships between a parent-record type and its child-record types being represented by the foreign key mechanism, as in a relational database, in a hierarchical database these relationships are represented by the parent–child links themselves. Despite this, you may note that there are some 'foreign keys' within the schema, for example, PAYROLLNO from EMPLOYEE appears as EPAYROLLNO in PROJASSIGNMENT and as MGRPAYROLLNO in DEPTMANAGER.

Figure B.4 provides an example of the data definition statements required to implement the schema from Figure B.3, with some of the more detailed syntax omitted. Note that the DEPARTMENT record type is specifically declared as being the root of the hierarchy. All the other record types are declared with the name of their parent-record type and with their sequence under the parent – EMPLOYEE is the first child of DEPARTMENT, DEPTMANAGER is the second child of DEPARTMENT, and so on. Also, most record types have an ORDER BY clause specifying how the records, the instances of the record type, are to be ordered. This ordering, both of the child-record types under their parent and of the individual records of a record type, is fundamental to the management of the data within a hierarchical database.

Figure B.5 shows how the data shown in Figure B.2 is stored as records within the hierarchical database declared using the statements in Figure B.4. In a hierarchical database, the records may be stored sequentially, reading the hierarchical trees from top-to-bottom and left-to-right. The resulting sequence is shown in Figure B.6.

Alternatively, the records may be linked using pointers, extra fields that contain data that identifies the location of the related record.

```
SCHEMA NAME = EMPLOYEEMANAGEMENT
RECORD
      NAME = DEPARTMENT
      TYPE = ROOT OF HIERARCHY
      DATA ITEMS =
            DNAME                      CHARACTER 25
            DTELNUMBER                 CHARACTER 15
      KEY = DNAME
      ORDER BY DNAME
RECORD
      NAME = EMPLOYEE
      PARENT = DEPARTMENT
      CHILD NUMBER = 1
      DATA ITEMS =
            PAYROLLNO                  CHARACTER 5
            ENAME                      CHARACTER 30
            EADDRESS                   CHARACTER 180
            BDATE                      CHARACTER 9
            NINUMBER                   CHARACTER 9
            SDATE                      CHARACTER 9
            GRADE                      CHARACTER 2
            SALARY                     INTEGER
      KEY = PAYROLLNO
      ORDER BY ENAME
RECORD
      NAME = PROJECT
      PARENT = DEPARTMENT
      CHILD NUMBER = 2
      DATA ITEMS =
            PNAME                      CHARACTER 25
            PSTARTDATE                 CHARACTER 9
            PENDDATE                   CHARACTER 9
      KEY = PNAME
      ORDER BY PSTARTDATE
RECORD
      NAME = DEPTMANAGER
      PARENT = DEPARTMENT
      CHILD NUMBER = 3
      DATA ITEMS =
            MGRPAYROLLNO               CHARACTER 5
            MGRSTARTDATE               CHARACTER 9
      KEY = MGRPAYROLLNO
      ORDER BY MGRSTARTDATE
RECORD
      NAME = EMPQUALIFICATION
      PARENT = EMPLOYEE
      CHILD NUMBER = 1
      DATA ITEMS =
            QNAME                      CHARACTER 25
            QAWARDDATE                 CHARACTER 9
      ORDER BY QAWARDDATE
RECORD
      NAME = DEPENDENT
      PARENT = EMPLOYEE
      CHILD NUMBER = 2
      DATA ITEMS =
            DEPNAME                    CHARACTER 30
            RELATIONSHIP               CHARACTER 12
            DEPADDRESS                 CHARACTER 180
            DEPTELNUMBER               CHARACTER 25
      ORDER BY RELATIONSHIP
RECORD
      NAME = PROJASSIGNMENT
      PARENT = PROJECT
      CHILD NUMBER = 1
      DATA ITEMS =
            EPAYROLLNO                 CHARACTER 5
            PROJASSSTARTDATE           CHARACTER 9
            PROJASSENDDATE             CHARACTER 9
```

FIGURE B.4   *Data definition statements for a hierarchical database*

Network databases

Like its predecessor, the hierarchical model of data, the network model of

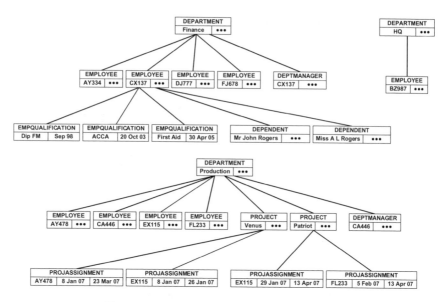

Figure B.5 *Hierarchical database occurrences*

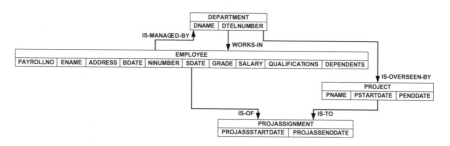

Figure B.6 *Hierarchical database records in sequence*

data formed the basis for a number of pre-relational database management systems. The model was based on the recommendations of the Conference on Data Systems Languages (CODASYL) Data Base Task Group, published in 1971. The most prominent product based on the network model was the Integrated Database Management System (IDMS) from Cullinet Software, Inc (now part of Computer Associates). Many IDMS implementations are still in use today.

Figure B.7 shows an example of a schema diagram for a network database. The main difference between the hierarchical model of data and the network model of data is that, in the network model, a record type can have more than one parent, whereas in the hierarchical model each record type is limited to only one parent. The 'links' between record types are known as sets. Each set has an owner record type (the parent, with only one occurrence allowed) and a member record type (the children, with zero, one or more occurrences). In Figure B.7, the **WORKS-IN** set has the **DEPARTMENT** record type as its owner and the **EMPLOYEE** record type as its member, whilst the **IS-MANAGED-BY** set has the **EMPLOYEE** record type as its owner and the

DEPARTMENT record type as its member. The arrow head is the equivalent of a crow's foot in an entity–relationship conceptual data model.

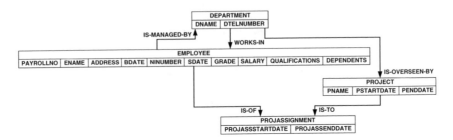

FIGURE B.7   *Network database schema*

There are two other points to note. Firstly, repeating groups, which in the relational model we remove in the move to first normal form, can be used in the network model, so the **EMPLOYEE** record type has two field types with plural names, **QUALIFICATIONS** and **DEPENDENTS**. Secondly, there are no foreign keys specified in the schema; the relationships between instances of the record types are specified in the sets. Foreign keys can, however, be specified in the network model if needed. One situation where they are probably needed is to implement a recursive relationship; most implementations of the network model do not support the concept of a set with both its owner and its member being of the same record type.

Figure B.8 shows the data definition statements required to implement the network schema shown in Figure B.7. Again, some of the more detailed syntax is omitted. The full network data definition statements include many that provide details of how the database is mapped to the physical storage.

There are definitions for both the records and the sets. The fields of the records are annotated with level numbers and the use of level numbers indicates repeating groups. The **QUALIFICATIONS** repeating group has two fields, **QNAME** and **QAWARDDATE**, and the **DEPENDENTS** repeating group has four fields, **DEPNAME**, **RELATIONSHIP**, **DEPADDRESS** and **DEPTELNUMBER**.

Figure B.9 shows how the example data is stored in a network database. The sets are maintained by a series of pointers. The **DEPARTMENT** record instance, the **FINANCE** record, which is the owner of one of the **WORKS-IN** sets has a pointer that points to the first member in the set, the **EMPLOYEE** record for the employee whose payroll number is AY334. This in turn points to the next **EMPLOYEE** record in the set, and so on. The last **EMPLOYEE** record in the set has a pointer that points back to the owner record, the finance department.

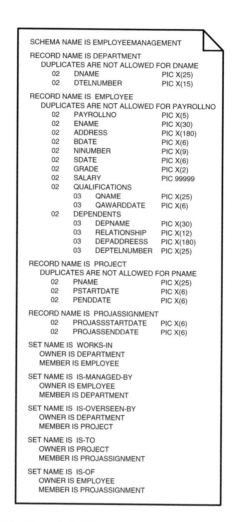

```
SCHEMA NAME IS EMPLOYEEMANAGEMENT

RECORD NAME IS DEPARTMENT
    DUPLICATES ARE NOT ALLOWED FOR DNAME
        02    DNAME              PIC X(25)
        02    DTELNUMBER         PIC X(15)

RECORD NAME IS  EMPLOYEE
    DUPLICATES ARE NOT ALLOWED FOR PAYROLLNO
        02    PAYROLLNO          PIC X(5)
        02    ENAME              PIC X(30)
        02    ADDRESS            PIC X(180)
        02    BDATE              PIC X(6)
        02    NINUMBER           PIC X(9)
        02    SDATE              PIC X(6)
        02    GRADE              PIC X(2)
        02    SALARY             PIC 99999
        02    QUALIFICATIONS
            03    QNAME          PIC X(25)
            03    QAWARDDATE     PIC X(6)
        02    DEPENDENTS
            03    DEPNAME        PIC X(30)
            03    RELATIONSHIP   PIC X(12)
            03    DEPADDREESS    PIC X(180)
            03    DEPTELNUMBER   PIC X(25)

RECORD NAME IS PROJECT
    DUPLICATES ARE NOT ALLOWED FOR PNAME
        02    PNAME              PIC X(25)
        02    PSTARTDATE         PIC X(6)
        02    PENDDATE           PIC X(6)

RECORD NAME IS  PROJASSIGNMENT
        02    PROJASSSTARTDATE   PIC X(6)
        02    PROJASSENDDATE     PIC X(6)

SET NAME IS  WORKS-IN
    OWNER IS DEPARTMENT
    MEMBER IS EMPLOYEE

SET NAME IS  IS-MANAGED-BY
    OWNER IS EMPLOYEE
    MEMBER IS DEPARTMENT

SET NAME IS  IS-OVERSEEN-BY
    OWNER IS DEPARTMENT
    MEMBER IS PROJECT

SET NAME IS  IS-TO
    OWNER IS PROJECT
    MEMBER IS PROJASSIGNMENT

SET NAME IS  IS-OF
    OWNER IS EMPLOYEE
    MEMBER IS PROJASSIGNMENT
```

FIGURE B.8   *Data definition statements for a network database*

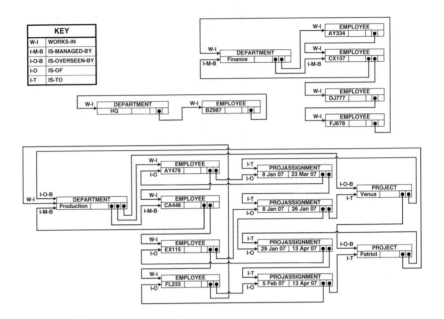

FIGURE B.9   *Network database occurrences*

Generic Data Models

What has become known as 'generic data modelling' is, to all intents and purposes, data modelling using all the conventional procedures and techniques of data modelling, but where the current business rules are not allowed to affect the shape of the model itself. Instead the model is adapted to treat such business rules as part of the subject matter being modelled. This provides longer-term stability to the model and to any databases whose design is informed by the model.

The main difference between 'traditional' data models and generic data models is that the latter are characterised by entities that are more abstract or generic than in a traditional data model. For example, in a model for a commercial business there could be a **PARTY** entity instead of separate **CUSTOMER**, **SUPPLIER** and **SUBCONTRACTOR** entities. Generic data models are also characterised by the inclusion of more 'type' entities. These are entities, such as **ASSOCIATION TYPE**, that allow for the recording in the database of the semantic definition of other data.

There are, however, other differences between traditional data models and generic data models, principally:

- There are generally a smaller number of entities in a generic data model than in a traditional data model, making it easier to understand (although its relevance to the business may be less obvious).

- Roles played by entity instances and associations between entities are represented in a generic data model by new entities (and associated relationships) and not by relationships alone.

- As a consequence of using abstract entities, for which 'real-world identifiers' are often not available, entity identifiers in a generic data model have to be artificial. These identifiers have to be managed to be unique. Such artificial identifiers are often called surrogate keys.

Generic data models can be developed for use at both the project and the corporate level. At the project level, the resulting database is more robust than if it had been developed from a 'traditional' data model, leading to the likelihood that the overall lifetime cost of the project is reduced. It is, however, at the corporate level that generic data models provide the greatest benefit. They enable different business viewpoints of data to be accommodated within the same data model. They also enable the easy accommodation of new business viewpoints as the business develops. Additionally, because they generally have fewer entities, they are more manageable and easier to understand.

Figure C.1 shows some of the stages on the continuum from generic to specific. The more generic the model, the more high level the names of the entities. The ultimate generic model has an entity called THING.

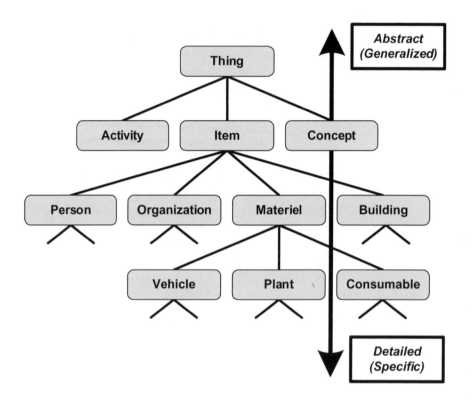

FIGURE C.1   *The generic to specific continuum*

The more abstract or generic the data model, the greater the stability and the wider the perspective of the model. This leads to a more stable database design, providing greater 'future-proofing'.

In their document *Developing High Quality Data Models*, the European Process Industry STEP Technical Liaison Executive (EPISTLE, 2003) have set out to describe how to develop data models that will:

- meet the data requirement;

- be clear and unambiguous to all (not just the authors);

- be stable in the face of changing data requirements;

- be flexible in the face of changing business practices;

- be reusable by others;

- be consistent with other models covering the same scope;

- be able to reconcile conflicting data models.

> *Aside*: The content of this EPISTLE publication is written by Matthew West who describes himself as the 'thought leader' for data management in Shell International Limited. He was developing these ideas at the same time that I was responsible for data management in the British Army. Unbeknown to each other, we were following an almost identical path in the development of our approach to data management. The EPISTLE work has been taken forward into an international standard – ISO 15926-2:2003 (Industrial automation systems and integration – Integration of life-cycle data for process plants including oil and gas production facilities – Part 2: Data model).

In this work, six principles that will lead to the development of high-quality data models have been identified. These are:

(1) Candidate attributes should be treated as representing relationships to other entity types.

(2) Entity types should have a local identifier within a database or exchange file. These should be artificial and managed to ensure uniqueness. Relationships should not be used as part of the local identifier.

(3) Activities, associations and event-effects should be represented by entity types (not relationships or attributes).

(4) Relationships (in the entity–relationship sense) should only be used to express the involvement of entity types with activities or associations.

(5) Entity types should represent, and be named after, the underlying nature of the object, not the role it plays in a particular context.

(6) Entity types should be part of a subtype–supertype hierarchy in order to define a universal context for the model.

> *Aside*: Note that EPISTLE are correctly using the term 'entity type' where we have used the shorthand 'entity' throughout this book.

What EPISTLE calls a 'high-quality data model' is a generic data model. They also use the term 'flexible design'. They have identified a number of advantages and disadvantages of developing data models such as this, which they have encapsulated in a diagram similar to Figure C.2.

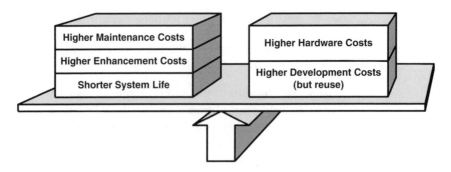

FIGURE C.2   *The cost-balance of flexible design*

All gains have to be paid for and the inherent flexibility gained by 'genericity' invokes a performance penalty.

Information systems that have their database design informed by generic data models have the following advantages:

- **Reduced maintenance costs.** Traditional designs tend to encapsulate the current business processes. As procedures change, information systems require maintenance to enable them to handle the revised procedures. Systems designed to be flexible from the outset do not incur this maintenance cost.

- **Reduced enhancement costs.** Similarly, the costs involved in adding additional functionality are reduced if the system is designed to be flexible.

- **Longer system life.** The maintenance and enhancement costs associated with traditional designs can become prohibitive, leading to a premature requirement to replace the system.

- **Design reuse.** Being designed to cover a wide scope and to be inherently flexible to change in business procedures, any single generic data model, its resulting database design and the software used to address that database design can be used in many different systems. This reduces, over time, the need for some data analysis and a considerable amount of database and software design.

> *Aside*: It is not the intention to claim that the use of a generic data model totally removes the need for data analysis. Any project reusing an existing generic data model should still analyse its data requirements to ensure that they can be met by the chosen generic data model.

On the other hand, information systems that have their database design informed by generic data models have the following disadvantages:

- **High development costs.** Initially, at least, the use of a generic data model as the basis of a database design for an information system leads to higher development costs than if a traditional data model is used. These higher development costs come about partly through the unfamiliarity of the developers with the concepts embodied in the model and partly from the fact that there is little tool support available for such development. These costs, however, are offset over time by the ability to reuse tested software components.

- **High hardware costs.** Flexible designs based on generic data models require more powerful hardware to achieve performance comparable to more traditional designs. These costs, over time, are offset by the continuing reduction in the cost of hardware.

An Example of a Data Naming Convention

This data naming convention is based on a convention developed for a recent client. A similar naming convention is described by Michael Brackett in his book Data Sharing: Using a Common Data Architecture, published by John Wiley & Sons in 1994.

Introduction

1. The purpose of applying a data naming standard to the naming of all data objects (entity types, attributes, domains and relationships in conceptual data models, and tables and columns in the logical schemas for SQL databases) is to ensure that all data objects have consistent, unique and meaningful names.

2. The parts of this data naming standard are:

   a. concepts used in naming (paragraphs 3 to 13);

   b. the naming of entity types in a conceptual data model (paragraphs 14 to 21);

   c. the naming of domains in a conceptual data model (paragraphs 22 to 25);

   d. the naming of attributes in a conceptual data model (paragraphs 26 to 30);

   e. the naming of relationships in a conceptual data model (paragraphs 31 to 33);

   f. the naming of tables in an SQL logical schema (paragraph 34);

   g. the naming of columns in an SQL logical schema (paragraphs 35 to 37);

   h. rules for abbreviations in data names (paragraphs 38 to 39);

   i. restricted terms (paragraph 40 and Tables D.1 to D.4);

   j. the naming of attributes – a formal description (paragraphs 41 to 46 and Table D.5).

Concepts used in naming

3. Each data object must have one, and only one, primary data name.

4. The primary data name for a conceptual data model data object must be the real-world name, fully spelled out, not codified or abbreviated. Such names must not be subject to any length restrictions.

5. The primary data name for an SQL database logical schema data object should be derived from an associated conceptual data model data object. Such names may be subject to length restrictions, and may, therefore, need to be abbreviated. Abbreviation of these names should be avoided wherever possible. Any abbreviation should follow the rules set out in paragraphs 38 and 39.

6. The primary data name for each data object (a conceptual data model data object or an SQL database logical schema data object) must uniquely identify that data object within the common data architecture.

7. The primary data name must provide consistency throughout the common data architecture. Restrictions are placed upon the use of some terms as described in paragraph 40.

8. The primary data name must unambiguously represent the underlying content and meaning of the data and not the way that the data is used or processed.

9. The primary data name must be meaningful to, and understood by, the business.

10. The primary data name must represent any variations in content or meaning of the data.

11. The primary data name must be complete, with the components of the name progressing from the general to the specific.

12. The primary data name must represent the conceptual or logical structure of data objects within the common data architecture.

13. All other names are secondary data names; each secondary data name must be cross referenced to the relevant primary data name.

The naming of entity types in a conceptual data model

14. Each entity type is named with a singular noun or noun phrase, with the name representing a single instance of the entity type.

Examples are:

VEHICLE

PURCHASE ORDER

15. Entity type names are normally shown in **BOLD SMALL CAPITALS** in textual descriptions.

16. Uniqueness of entity type names within the common data architecture is to be achieved as follows:

    a. Each entity type name is to be unique within the conceptual data model that includes the entity type.

    b. The concatenation of the name of the conceptual data model with the entity type name provides a unique name for each entity type within the common data architecture.

17. Abbreviations are not used in entity type names.

18. Entity subtypes can be named following one of two conventions. All subtypes of an immediate supertype are to be named using the same convention. The conventions are as follows:

    a. Entity subtype names comprise the immediate supertype entity name prefixed with an adjective to define the subtype.
        Examples are:

        VEHICLE OPERATION is a subtype of **OPERATION**

        VEHICLE MAINTENANCE OPERATION is a subtype of **VEHICLE OPERATION**

    b. Entity subtype names identify independent concepts.
        Examples are:

        FACILITY is a subtype of **RESOURCE**

        ORGANISATION is a subtype of **PARTY**

19. Entity types that 'characterise' another entity type are to have names that comprise the name of the entity type being characterised, now acting as an adjectival phrase, suffixed by a noun that represents the nature of the characterisation.
    Examples are:

    RESOURCE STATUS characterises **RESOURCE**

    EMPLOYEE QUALIFICATION characterises **EMPLOYEE**

20. Entity types that provide a categorisation or classification for instances of another entity type are to have names that comprise the name of the entity type whose instances are being categorised, now acting as an adjectival phrase, suffixed by one of the words CATEGORY, CLASS or TYPE as appropriate.

    Examples are:

    INDIVIDUAL SKILL CATEGORY categorises INDIVIDUAL SKILL

    EQUIPMENT TYPE categorises EQUIPMENT

    VEHICLE CLASS categorises VEHICLE

    [*Note*: A distinction can be drawn between the use of the suffix CATEGORY on the one hand and the use of the suffixes CLASS and TYPE on the other. CLASS and TYPE refer to 'business' categorisations where system users may need to add new classes or types as part of normal operations. CATEGORY refers to categorisations that are to be kept under strict control. These categorisations may have been modelled as domains for attribute values had it been possible to identify at the time of modelling a full and final set of values that would never change.]

21. Entity types that represent a relationship (or association) between two entity types can be named following one of two conventions, as follows:

    a. A name that represents the essence of the association formed from the rules above.
        Examples are:

        FACILITY VEHICLE CAPABILITY provides an association between FACILITY and VEHICLE

        ASSET STRUCTURE ELEMENT provides a recursive association on ASSET

    b. The names of the two entity types being associated are concatenated and suffixed by the word association. In the special case of a recursive association, the associated entity name is only used once.
        Examples are:

        OPERATION RESOURCE ASSOCIATION provides an association between OPERATION and RESOURCE

        PARTY ASSOCIATION provides a recursive association on PARTY

    The style of subparagraph a. above is preferred to that in subparagraph b. above. If the style of subparagraph b. is used, it is normally because this entity type represents a generic association and an additional categorisation entity type (for example, **PARTY ASSOCIATION CATEGORY**) is required.

The naming of domains in a conceptual data model

22. Each domain is named with singular noun or noun phrase, with the name representing the concept that the values of the domain collectively represent.

    Examples are:

    WEIGHT

    CONTROLLED NAME

23. Domain names are normally shown in **SMALL CAPITALS** in textual descriptions.

24. Uniqueness of domain names within the common data architecture is to be achieved as follows:

    a. For domains intended to be used across the common data architecture (i.e. where the same domain may be used within more than one conceptual data model), the domain name is to be unique.

    b. For domains to be used in a single conceptual data model, each domain is to be named with a name that is unique within that conceptual data model. The concatenation of the name of the conceptual data model with the domain name provides a unique name for that domain within the common data architecture.

25. Abbreviations are not used in domain names.

The naming of attributes in a conceptual data model

26. Each attribute is named with a singular noun or noun phrase, with the name representing the meaning of the value to be recorded. The name of the entity type of the attribute is not included in the name of the attribute, but is used with the attribute name when referring to the attribute conversationally.

Examples are:

designation (in EQUIPMENT TYPE, conversationally EQUIPMENT TYPE **designation**)

last service date (in EQUIPMENT, conversationally EQUIPMENT **last service date**)

international standard book number (in PUBLICATION, conversationally PUBLICATION**international standard book number**)

27. Attribute names are normally shown in **bold lower case** in textual descriptions.

28. Uniqueness of attribute names within the common data architecture is to be achieved as follows:

   a. Attribute names are to be unique within the entity type to which they belong. This is known as the 'short attribute name'.

   b. The concatenation of the name of the entity type to which the attribute belongs with the short attribute name provides a unique name for each attribute within the conceptual data model. This is known as the 'full attribute name'.

   c. The concatenation of the name of the conceptual data model with the full attribute name provides a unique name for each attribute within the common data architecture.

29. Abbreviations are not used in attribute names.

30. A more formal description of the naming of attributes is included at paragraphs 41 to 46.

The naming of relationships in a conceptual data model

31. Each relationship is named using two sentences of the following forms:

   Each VEHICLE <u>must be</u> *within* <u>one and only one</u> VEHICLE CLASS.

   Each VEHICLE CLASS <u>may be</u> *classification for* <u>one or more</u> VEHICLES.

   where:

   • in the first sentence:

      <u>must be</u> represents the fact that the entity type VEHICLE has mandatory participation with respect to this relationship, represented by a solid line on a conceptual data model diagram.

within is the link phrase associated with the entity type VEHICLE.

one and only one represents the fact that only one instance of the entity type VEHICLE CLASS can be associated with any one instance of the entity type VEHICLE through this relationship, represented by the absence of a crow's foot on a conceptual data model diagram.

- and in the second sentence:

may be represents the fact that the entity type VEHICLE CLASS has optional participation with respect to this relationship, represented by a dashed line on a conceptual data model diagram.

classification for is the link phrase associated with the entity type VEHICLE CLASS.

one or more represents the fact that many instances of the entity type VEHICLE can be associated with any one instance of the entity type VEHICLE CLASS through this relationship, represented by a crow's foot on a conceptual data model diagram.

32. Uniqueness of relationship names within the common data architecture is to be achieved as follows:

    a. Relationship names are to be unique within a conceptual data model.

    b. The concatenation of the name of the conceptual data model with the relationship name provides a unique name for each relationship within the common data architecture.

33. Abbreviations are not used in relationship names.

The naming of tables in an SQL logical schema

34. All tables are named with singular nouns or noun phrases in upper case, with the name representing a single instance of the concept recorded by a single row of the table; the underscore character is used as the separator in names consisting of a phrase of more than one word, for example:

```
VEHICLE
```

```
PURCHASE_ORDER
```

The naming of columns in an SQL logical schema

35. Except in the particular cases described in paragraphs 36 and 37, all columns are named with singular nouns or noun phrases in lower camel case, with the name representing the value recorded at the row–column intersection in the table. The name of the table is not included in the name of the column, but is used with the column name when referring to the column conversationally, for example:

    `designation` (in `EQUIPMENT_TYPE`, conversationally `EQUIPMENT_TYPE.designation`)

    `lastServiceDate` (in `EQUIPMENT`, conversationally `EQUIPMENT.lastServiceDate`)

    `isbn` (in `PUBLICATION`, conversationally `PUBLICATION.isbn`)

36. Columns declared as a single-column primary key of a table using the `IDENTITY` or `AUTONUMBER` datatype are named '`ID`'.

37. Columns declared as a foreign key are named with a composite name comprising seven elements. The first element is the opening square bracket character ([). The second element is a role name in lower camel case. This is generally derived from the associated link phrase of the conceptual relationship instantiated by the foreign key. The third element is the point (.) character. The fourth element is the name of the referenced table. The fifth element is the point (.) character. The sixth element is the name of the column in the referenced table referenced by this foreign key column. The seventh element is the closing square bracket character (]).
    Examples are:

    `[partOf.EQUIPMENT_TYPE.ID]`

    `[withinOrOtherwiseAssociatedWith.FACILITY.ID]`

Rules for abbreviations in data names

38. The abbreviation of data names is deprecated, but, if necessary, the names of SQL logical schema data objects (tables and columns) may be abbreviated. Names of conceptual data model data objects (entity types, domains, attributes and relationships) are not to be abbreviated.

39. The priority for selecting abbreviations is as follows:

a. standard abbreviations in use within the 'business' areas of XYZ plc;

b. abbreviations in common use within the United Kingdom;

c. abbreviations in common use internationally;

d. abbreviations contained in the Shorter Oxford English Dictionary, 5th Edition, published 26 September 2002, ISBN 0198605757;

e. abbreviations formed by the removal of all vowels from the word being abbreviated, except where the initial letter of the word is a vowel.

Restricted terms

40. To aid consistency in naming, a number of terms have restricted meanings. These are described in Tables D.1 to D.4.

TABLE D.1   *Restricted terms used in the naming of entity types*

Term	Restricted meaning
CATEGORY	This is used as a suffix in the name of a 'categorisation' entity type (ie, an entity type which provides a categorisation or classification for instances of another entity type) where the 'categorisation' entity type is included in the model principally for data management purposes (to allow a level of flexibility in a set of valid values for a business domain concept), as opposed to business purposes, and the instances of the 'categorisation' entity type need to be centrally managed.
CLASS	This is used as a suffix in the name of a 'categorisation' entity type (ie, an entity type which provides a categorisation or classification for instances of another entity type) where the 'categorisation' entity type is included in the model to represent a real-world business concept, such as providing a specification for a subset of the instances of the entity type being categorised, and the word 'class' is in common business use in this context, for example, **VEHICLE CLASS** categorising **VEHICLE**. In all other cases, the word **TYPE** is preferred for this role.
TYPE	This is used as a suffix in the name of a 'categorisation' entity type (ie, an entity type which provides a categorisation or classification for instances of another entity type) where the 'categorisation' entity type is included in the model to represent a real-world business concept, such as providing a specification for a subset of the instances of the entity type being categorised, for example, **EQUIPMENT TYPE** categorising **EQUIPMENT**.
DETAIL	This is used as a suffix in the name of a 'characterisation' entity type (ie, an entity type which provides further description or clarification for instances of another entity type) where the a 'characterisation' entity type provides information about a component part or an element of the entity type being characterised, for example, **SKILL SET DETAIL** characterising **SKILL SET**.

TABLE D.2   *Restricted terms used in the naming of domains*

Term	Restricted meaning
CODE	This is used to indicate that this domain is an enumerated domain that has three or more valid values.
INDICATOR	This is used to indicate that this domain is an enumerated domain that has exactly two valid values. These valid values are generally the Boolean values 'True' and 'False', but indicators are not restricted to the Boolean values.

TABLE D.3   *Restricted terms used in the naming of attributes*

Term	Restricted meaning
code	This is used to indicate that the attribute takes its values from an enumerated domain that has three or more valid values.
description	This is used to provide further clarification of the label or name of the entity type instance. Attributes with description in their name will almost invariably take values from GENERAL DESCRIPTIVE TEXT domain.
indicator	An indication that the attribute takes its values from an enumerated domain that has exactly two valid values. These valid values are generally the Boolean values 'True' and 'False', but indicators are not restricted to the Boolean values.
label	This is used to name a concept where it is felt necessary to maintain data management control over the values of the attribute. Attributes with label in their name will almost invariably take values from the CONTROLLED LABEL domain or from another domain that is a specialisation of the CONTROLLED LABEL domain.
name	This is used to name a concept where there is no requirement to control the values of the attribute. Attributes with name in their name will almost invariably take values from the BUSINESS NAME domain or from another domain that is a specialisation of the BUSINESS NAME domain.
number	This is used where it is necessary to provide some form of identification for some or all of the instances of the entity type. Real world examples are employee numbers and vehicle registration numbers. Despite their name, such 'numbers' generally include alphabetic and other non-numeric characters and it is meaningless to carry out arithmetic operations on the values (even if they are all numeric). Attributes with number in their name will have domains unique to themselves, such as the INTERNATIONAL STANDARD BOOK NUMBER domain.

TABLE D.4   *Restricted terms used in the naming of relationships*

Term	Restricted meaning
may be	This represents the fact that the referencing entity type has optional participation with respect to this relationship. (This is represented by a dashed line on a conceptual data model diagram.)
must be	This represents the fact that the referencing entity type has mandatory participation with respect to this relationship. (This is represented by a solid line on a conceptual data model diagram.)
one and only one	This represents the fact that only one instance of the referenced entity type can be associated with any one instance of the referencing entity type through this relationship. (This is represented by the absence of a 'crow's foot' on a conceptual data model diagram.)
one or more	This represents the fact that many instances of the referenced entity type can be associated with any one instance of the referencing entity type through this relationship. (This is represented by a 'crow's foot' on a conceptual data model diagram.)

The naming of attributes: a formal description

41. As described in paragraph 28b, a 'full attribute name' consists of the concatenation of the entity type name and the 'short attribute name', where the latter is the unique name of the attribute within the entity type.

42. There are a number of formal approaches to the naming of attributes, but most see a 'full attribute name' broken down into three components. These components can be given different names within different approaches to naming, but a common classification identifies these components as:

    - a **prime term**, which is mandatory;

    - a **modifier term**, which is optional;

    - a **class term**, which is mandatory.

43. The prime term identifies the context for the attribute, i.e. the set of things that this attribute can be used to describe. This is, effectively, the name of the entity type which includes the attribute.

44. The class term identifies the class (category or type) of the information that the attribute provides about the context.

45. The optional modifier term is used to discriminate between different attributes providing information of the same class for the same context or to provide some further specification or clarification to the attribute name.

46. Table D.5 below provides examples to illustrate the use of these concepts.

TABLE D.5 *Examples of formal attribute names*

	Terms		
Full Attribute Name	**Prime**	**Modifier**	**Class**
PERSON family name	PERSON	family	name
VEHICLE CATEGORY label	VEHICLE CATEGORY	(-)	label
STOCK HOLDING unit of measure	STOCK HOLDING	(-)	unit of measure
ASSIGNMENT start date	ASSIGNMENT	start	date
ASSIGNMENT end date	ASSIGNMENT	end	date

Metadata Models

Introduction

Data dictionaries and repositories are specialised information systems used by data managers and those involved in software development, as are the range of systems known as Computer Aided Software Engineering (CASE) tools. The use of these systems and tools is described in Chapter 10 but, like every other information system, they need a database to store their persistent data. The persistent data that is stored in these specialised information systems is metadata. The models specifying the design of these databases are often known as metadata models.

Metadata model to record conceptual data models

Figure E.1 shows a metadata model to support the concepts of conceptual data modelling. It has three major entity types – ENTITY, ATTRIBUTE and DOMAIN.

To handle the exclusive arc concept there are the RELATIONSHIP GROUP and RELATIONSHIP END entities in the model. A RELATIONSHIP GROUP links one or more RELATIONSHIP ENDS to their host ENTITY such that these RELATIONSHIP ENDS within the RELATIONSHIP GROUP are mutually exclusive. The two RELATIONSHIP ENDS at each end of a relationship are associated through the relationship where each RELATIONSHIP END must be *paired with* one and only one RELATIONSHIP END. Since exclusive arcs are rare, in most cases there is only one RELATIONSHIP END in a RELATIONSHIP GROUP.

In the conceptual data model snippet at Figure E.2, there are four RELATIONSHIP ENDS (labelled A, B, C and D) and three RELATIONSHIP GROUPS. The first of these RELATIONSHIP GROUPS is the combination of the RELATIONSHIP ENDS A and B; the second is the RELATIONSHIP END C on its own; and the third is the RELATIONSHIP END D on its own.

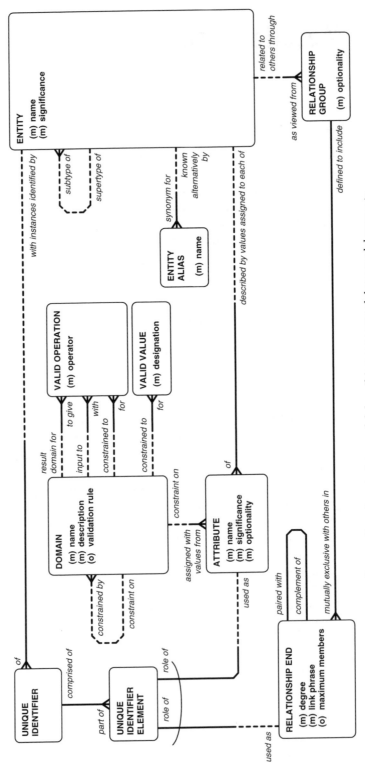

FIGURE E.1 A metadata model describing conceptual data model concepts

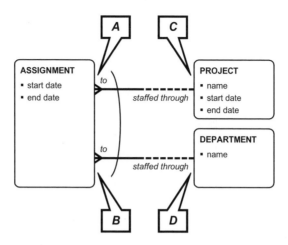

FIGURE E.2   *A conceptual data model snippet*

Unique identifiers are explicitly handled in this model. Each ENTITY may be *with instances identified by* one or more UNIQUE IDENTIFIERS. Furthermore, each UNIQUE IDENTIFIER must be *comprised of* one or more UNIQUE IDENTI-FIER ELEMENTS. Since the instances of an entity can be uniquely identified by the values of one or more attributes or by one or more related entity instances, the model shows that each UNIQUE IDENTIFIER ELEMENT must be *role of* one or more ATTRIBUTES or *role of* one or more RELATIONSHIP ENDS.

 The VALID VALUE and VALID OPERATION entities are included such that each VALID VALUE must be *for* one and only one DOMAIN and each VALID OPERATION must be *for* one and only one DOMAIN. Additionally, VALID OPERATION has two other relationships such that each VALID OPERATION must be *with* one and only one DOMAIN and each VALID OPERATION must be *to give* one and only one DOMAIN. For example, a VALID OPERATION may be defined for a 'Date' DOMAIN (the *for* DOMAIN) that adds (the operation held by the *operator* attribute) a number of days (the *with* DOMAIN is 'day time interval') to give a result which is another date (the *to give* DOMAIN is also 'Date').

Metadata model to record SQL logical schemas

Figure E.3 shows a metadata model covering the concepts involved in the logical schema for an SQL-based relational database. It enables the tables and columns in many different databases to be recorded. The uniqueness, referential and general constraints that may be declared for those tables and columns can also be recorded.

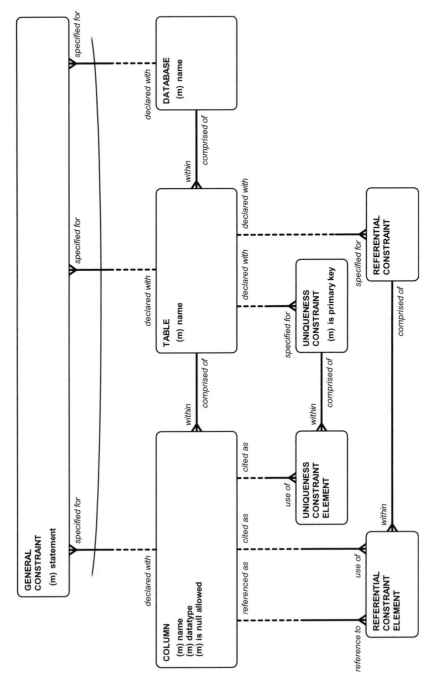

FIGURE E.3   *A metadata model describing physical SQL database concepts*

Metadata model to support the mapping of concepts

Figure E.4 shows how the two separate metadata models may be combined to provide the capability of recording how two or more conceptual data models relate to each other or how physical SQL implementations match the conceptual data models from which they are derived.

The mapping structure allows one or more elements of one conceptual data model to be mapped to one or more elements in another conceptual data model (for example, a many-to-many relationship in the first model is equivalent to two one-to-many relationships and an entity in the second model). One or more elements of an SQL schema can be mapped to one or more elements in its conceptual data model (for example, a supertype entity and its two subtype entities is implemented in one system by a single table with a number of constraints and in another system by three tables with two referential constraints and a general constraint to make those two referential constraints mutually exclusive at the 'supertype' end). The entities LOGICAL TO LOGICAL MAPPING and LOGICAL TO PHYSICAL MAPPING shown in Figure E.4 are high-level entities – the detail required to actually achieve the mapping is more complex.

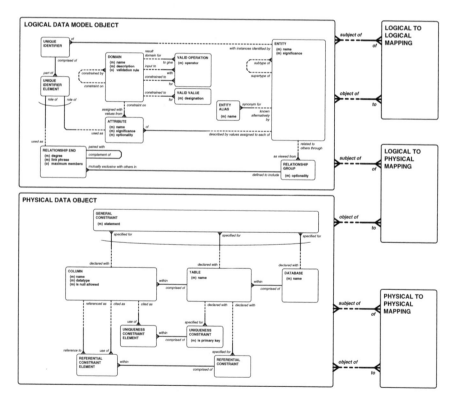

FIGURE E.4   *A metadata model showing mapping between elements*

The inclusion of processes

It is often useful to also map the logical and physical data structures to their equivalents associated with the processing of data – the process model, the programs and the modules in the applications. An early example of the application of this is the Data Dictionary System (DDS) developed by ICL Ltd (now Fujitsu Services Limited). This was originally released in 1976. It was the first commercially available data dictionary system to support both analysis of the business area and the design and development of the information system to support that business area. The structure of the DDS is shown in Figure E.5.

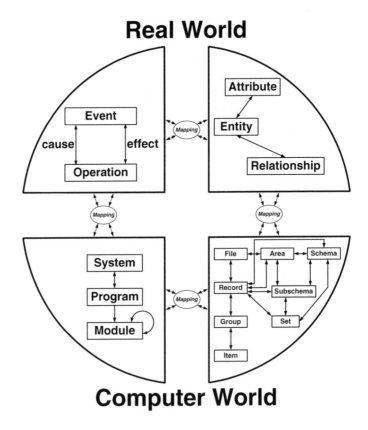

FIGURE E.5   *The ICL Data Dictionary System*

The left-hand side of the DDS provides for the documentation of the processes and applications; the right-hand side covered the data model and the database structure. The top half was labelled as the 'Real World' and covered the process and conceptual data models; the bottom half was labelled as the 'Computer World' and covered the applications and database structures.

A Data Mining Example

Introduction

This example uses just one statistical technique, the *a-priori algorithm*. This algorithm is used to find association rules in data. It uses data that appears more than a certain percentage of the time, the ' support threshold'.

The scenario

- A supermarket chain wishes to determine whether customers opt for either 'own-label' products or branded products.

- Raw data is available for each customer's purchases, recording the quantities of each product bought during each supermarket visit. The data from 500 such visits will be investigated.

- The support threshold is 15%.

Step 1

The raw data is scanned to determine the frequency of each product category bought during a visit. The results satisfying the support threshold are shown in Table F.1

TABLE F.1   *A-priori algorithm: Step 1 results*

Product Category	Count
Branded bread	286
Own-label bread	238
Own-label breakfast cereals	225
Branded breakfast cereals	192
Eggs	178
Potatoes	160

Step 2

The raw data is scanned again to determine the frequency of each pair of product categories bought during a visit. The results satisfying the support threshold are shown in Table F.2.

TABLE F.2   *A-priori algorithm: Step 2 results*

Product Category Pairs	Count
Branded breakfast cereals and branded bread	160
Own-label breakfast cereals and own-label bread	155
Eggs and branded bread	94
Eggs and own-label breakfast cereals	93
Potatoes and branded bread	83
Eggs and branded breakfast cereals	80
Eggs and own-label bread	78
Potatoes and own-label bread	77

Step 3

For each result in Step 2, the confidence level for the association rules for the pairs of product categories is calculated using the count figures from Steps 1 and 2. The results are shown in Table F.3.

TABLE F.3   *A-priori algorithm: Step 3 results*

Product Category Pairs	Association Rules	Confidence
Branded breakfast cereals and branded bread	If branded breakfast cereals are bought then branded bread is also bought	160/192 = 83%
	If branded bread is bought then branded breakfast cereals are also bought	160/286 = 56%
Own-label breakfast cereals and own-label bread	If own-label breakfast cereals are bought then own-label bread is also bought	155/225 = 69%
	If own-label bread is bought then own-label breakfast cereals are also bought	155/238 = 65%
Eggs and branded bread	If eggs are bought then branded bread is also bought	94/178 = 53%
	If branded bread is bought then eggs are also bought	94/286 = 33%
Eggs and own-label breakfast cereals	If eggs are bought then own-label breakfast cereals are also bought	93/178 = 52%
	If own-label breakfast cereals are bought then eggs are also bought	93/225 = 41%
Potatoes and branded bread	If potatoes are bought then branded bread is also bought	83/160 = 52%
	If branded bread is bought then potatoes are also bought	83/286 = 29%
Eggs and branded breakfast cereals	If eggs are bought then branded breakfast cereals are also bought	80/178 = 45%
	If branded breakfast cereals are bought then eggs are also bought	80/192 = 42%
Eggs and own-label bread	If eggs are bought then own-label bread is also bought	78/178 = 44%
	If own-label bread is bought then eggs are also bought	78/238 = 33%
Potatoes and own-label bread	If potatoes are bought then own-label bread is also bought	77/160 = 48%
	If own-label bread is bought then potatoes are also bought	77/238 = 32%

Step 4

The raw data is scanned again to determine the frequency of each triple of product categories bought during a visit. The results satisfying the support threshold are shown in Table F.4.

TABLE F.4   *A-priori algorithm: Step 4 results*

Product Category Triples	Count
Branded breakfast cereals, eggs and branded bread	80
Own-label breakfast cereals, eggs and own-label bread	78

Step 5

For each result in Step 4, the confidence level for the association rules for the triples of product categories is calculated using the count figures from Steps 1, 2 and 4. The results are shown in Table F.5.

TABLE F.5   *A-priori algorithm: Step 5 results*

Product Category Triples	Association Rules	Confidence
Branded breakfast cereals, eggs and branded bread	If branded breakfast cereals are bought then eggs and branded bread are also bought	80/192 = 42%
	If eggs are bought then branded breakfast cereals and branded bread are also bought	80/178 = 45%
	If branded bread is bought then eggs and branded breakfast cereals are also bought	80/286 = 28%
	If branded breakfast cereals and eggs are bought then branded bread is also bought	80/80 = 100%
	If branded breakfast cereals and branded bread are bought then eggs are also bought	80/160 = 50%
	If eggs and branded bread are bought then branded breakfast cereals are also bought	80/94 = 85%
Own-label breakfast cereals, eggs and own-label bread bought	If own-label breakfast cereals are bought then eggs and own-label bread are also bought	78/225 = 35%
	If eggs are bought then own-label breakfast cereals and own-label bread are also bought	78/178 = 44%
	If own-label bread is bought then own-label breakfast cereals and eggs are also bought	78/238 = 33%
	If own-label breakfast cereals and eggs are bought then own-label bread is also bought	78/93 = 84%
	If own-label breakfast cereals and own-label bread are bought then eggs are also bought	78/155 = 50%
	If eggs and own-label bread are bought then own-label breakfast cereals are also bought	78/78 = 100%

Step 6

The raw data is scanned again to determine the frequency of each quadruple of items bought during a visit. The results satisfying the support threshold are shown in Table F.6.

TABLE F.6 *A-priori algorithm: Step 6 results*

Product Category Quadruples	Count

Since there are no results that satisfy the support threshold, the process stops.

Conclusions

The following association rules are significant:

- If branded breakfast cereals are bought then branded bread is also bought (83%).

- If own-label breakfast cereals are bought then own-label bread is also bought (69%).

- If branded breakfast cereals and eggs are bought then branded bread is also bought (100%).

- If eggs and branded bread are bought then branded breakfast cereals are also bought (85%).

- If own-label breakfast cereals and eggs are bought then own-label bread is also bought (84%).

- If eggs and own-label bread are bought then own-label breakfast cereals are also bought (100%).

These significant association rules suggest that customers consistently purchase own-label or branded goods.

HTML and XML

Introduction

As described in Chapter 12, both HyperText Markup Language (HTML) and eXtensible Markup Language (XML) are derived from the Standard Generalised Markup Language (SGML). In SGML markup, extra information is provided by means of 'tags', enabling SGML documents to be read by both machines and humans.

HTML

The tags provided within an HTML document are purely concerned with the way that the information in the document is presented (rendered, to use the technical term), by a web browser. HTML tags can be used to achieve a number of effects. As well as enabling basic text formatting, HTML tags can specify links, known as hypertext links, to other information, both within the document and in other documents. They can also be used to call for the display of images stored externally to the HTML document. Program code created in a scripting language such as JavaScript or PHP can also be hosted within HTML documents, along with some limited features that allow data to be input to feed the scripting-language programs.

In an HTML document, the tags are enclosed in 'angle brackets' and in most cases are used in pairs, an opening tag and a complementary closing tag. The whole document is enclosed within a pair of tags that indicate that this is an HTML document; the opening tag is <html> and the closing tag </html>, the '/' being used in markup languages to indicate a closing tag. The document consists of two sections, a header, enclosed within the <head> and </head> tags, and a main body, enclosed within the <body> and </body> tags. The header provides information about the document to the browser whilst the body contains the information to be displayed.

Figure G.1 shows a document formatted using HTML and Figure G.2 shows the result of rendering this document using a web browser, Mozilla Firefox.

The header of the document in Figure G.1 contains two elements. The title element is mandatory and the text enclosed within the <title> and </title> tags is displayed in the title bar of the browser when the document is rendered, as can be seen in Figure G.2. The second element is an example of a metadata element. In this case the metadata element identifies me as the author of the document. Metadata elements are not displayed.

The body of the document contains six elements. These are four paragraphs, enclosed by <p> and </p> tags, and two headings. The first heading is at the highest heading level, enclosed by <h1> and </h1> tags, and the

```
<html>
  <head>
    <title> Display of Fig G.1 </title>
    <meta name="author" content="Keith Gordon">
  </head>
  <body>
    <p align="right"><a name=top></a>This is the top.
      <a href="#bottom">Click here</a> to move to the bottom.</p>
    <h1>  Principles of Data Management </h1>
    <h2>  Facilitating Information Sharing </h2>
    <p>This book is called <em>Principlesof Data Management</em> but it is
      really about having the policiesand procedures in place within an
      organization so that the various information systems that the
      organization uses to support its ativities can provide high quality
      information to their users, even ifthat information did not originate
      in the information system that theuser is currently using.<br><br>For
      this to happen the organization'sinformation systems must be able to
      share information.<br><br>This bob is aimed at three audiences:<ul>
      <li><strong>Data management practitioners</strong>, already committed
      to data management but need more information.<li><strong>IT/IS managers
      </strong>, who need to understandthe involvement required and the
      implications of implementing dat management.<li><strong>Business
      managers</strong>, who need to nderstand why data management is
      important to a business.</ul></p>
    <p>You can review a <a href="booksummary.htm">summary of each chapter of
      the book</a> or see <a href="datamdinformation.jpg">an example of a
      diagram from the book</a><br><b>This book is published by the
      <a href="http://www.bcs.org">British Computer Society</a>
      <object data="bcslogo.gif" type="image/gif" align="middle">The BCS Logo
      </object></p>
    <p align="right"><a name=botom></a>This is the bottom.
      <a href="#top">Click here</a> to move to the top.</p>
  </body>
</html>
```

FIGURE G.1   *An example of an HTML document*

other heading is at the second highest heading level, enclosed by <h2> and </h2> tags. HTML provides six levels of headings.

The main body of the text is contained in the first paragraph after the headings. The title of the book, Principles of Data Management, is enclosed by emphasis tags, the <em> and </em> tags. Most browsers render emphasis as italics; the same effect could be achieved by enclosing the title in <i> and </i> tags. Line breaks are forced in the paragraph by using <br> tags, for which there are no corresponding closing tags. This first paragraph ends with a list enclosed by <ul> and </ul> tags. This is an unordered list, so the items in the list are preceded by bullet points. If this had been an ordered list, using <ol> and </ol> tags, each item in the list would have been preceded by a number. The start of each list item is denoted by a <li> tag; there are no closing list item tags. The first few words of each list item are enclosed in <strong> and </strong> tags, which most browsers render as bold text; the same effect can be achieved by using <b> and </b> tags.

The next paragraph provides the user with hyperlinks to another document, an image and a website. Each of these hyperlinks is enclosed within <a> and </a> tags. The text between these tags is normally rendered in a different colour and underlined, the common representation for a hyperlink. Most regular users of web browsers understand that they need to click on this link with their mouse to move to the resource referenced by the link. The opening tag of each of these pairs of <a> and </a> tags has a single attribute that provides the hyperlink reference for the resource that the browser is to

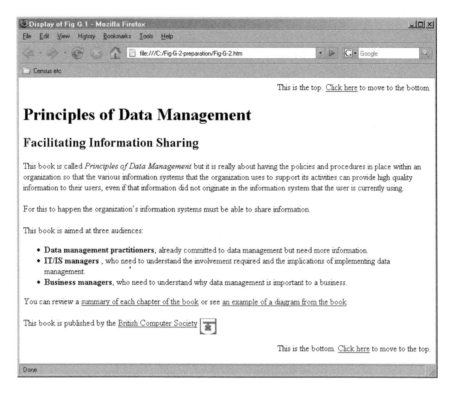

FIGURE G.2   *The HTML document rendered in Mozilla Firefox*

open if this link is selected. The first opening <a> tag has a reference attribute, href="booksummary.htm", that is the name of an HTML document that is co-located with the current document (no path information is provided, so it is assumed to be in the same location as the current document). The second opening <a> tag has a reference attribute, href="dataandinformation.jpg", that is the name of a JPEG image that is also co-located with the current document. This image is displayed as a complete page by the web browser. The third opening <a> tag has a reference attribute, href="http://www.bcs.org", that is the URI of the British Computer Society website. The next instruction in this paragraph is provided with <object> and </object> tags; this is an instruction to display the image contained in the "bcslogo.gif" file within the page.

The first and last paragraphs are similar to each other and are there to provide navigation within the document. They are both aligned to the right of the page, using the align attribute in the opening <p> tag and they both contain two sets of <a> and </a> tags to enable the in-document navigation. The first set of <a> and </a> tags in the first paragraph provide an anchor point in the document, called "top". The second set of <a> and </a> tags in the last paragraph contain the hyperlink reference, 'href="#top"', to enable navigation to that anchor point in the document. The other sets of <a> and </a> tags in these two paragraphs provide for navigation in the opposite direction to the bottom of the document. The example document is relatively short and these navigation anchor points and references are not really needed. They are included here to show how navigation may be provided within a large document.

HTML is purely concerned with the way that an information resource such as a document is presented by a web browser. It is not concerned with the meaning of the information contained in the document.

XML

XML is concerned with the definition and structure of the information in the document. XML has no tags to specify presentation.

```
<?xml version = "1.0"?>
<department>
  <department-name>Finance</department-name>
  <department-telephone>452</department-telephone>
  <department-manager>CX137</department-manager>
  <department-staff>
    <employee>
      <staff-no>AY334</staff-no>
      <first-name>Barbara</first-name>
      <last-name>Watson</last-name>
      <birth-date>12 June 1952</birth-date>
      <start-date>3 June 1994</start-date>
    </employee>
    <employee>
      <staff-no>CX137</staff-no>
      <first-name>Jenny</first-name>
      <last-name>Rogers</last-name>
      <birth-date>10 January 1970</birth-date>
      <start-date>3 January 1995</start-date>
      <qualifications>
        <qualification>
          <qualification-name>Dip FM</qualification-name>
          <qualification-award-date>September 1998</qualification-award-date>
        </qualification>
        <qualification>
          <qualification-name>ACCA</qualification-name>
          <qualification-award-date>2 October 2003</qualification-award-date>
        </qualification>
        <qualification>
          <qualification-name>First Aid</qualification-name>
          <qualification-award-date>30 April 2005</qualification-award-date>
          <qualification-expiry-date>29 April 2008</qualification-expiry-date>
        </qualification>
      </qualifications>
    </employee>
    <employee>
      <staff-no>DJ777</staff-no>
      <first-name>Henry</first-name>
      <last-name>Phillips</last-name>
      <birth-date>5 May 1974</birth-date>
      <start-date>3 September 1992</start-date>
    </employee>
    <employee>
      <staff-no>FL233</staff-no>
      <first-name>Jane</first-name>
      <last-name>Smith</last-name>
      <birth-date>25 August 1989</birth-date>
      <start-date>8 December 2006</start-date>
    </employee>
  </department-staff>
</department>
</xml>
```

FIGURE G.3   *An example of an XML document*

Figure G.3 shows an example of an XML document that provides details of the Finance department and its staff. Each item of data is known as an element and is enclosed within tags that describe the meaning of the data. For example, the element that is the name of a qualification is enclosed within <qualification-name> and </qualification-name> tags. Elements can be grouped. The name and award date of a qualification are both within a larger 'qualification' element, enclosed within <qualification> and </qualification> tags, and, in turn, a number of qualifications are listed within an even larger 'qualifications' element, enclosed within <qualifications> and </qualifications> tags.

XML documents have an inverted tree structure. At the top is a single root element, the 'department' element in this case. The tree structure for our document is shown in Figure G.4.

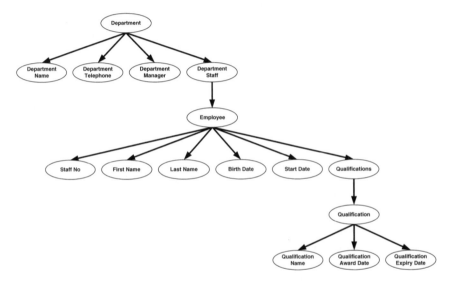

FIGURE G.4   *The tree structure of the XML document*

A valid XML document meets a number of technical criteria, the most important ones being:

- There is a single root element.

- Start tags and end tags match exactly.

- There are no overlapping elements; each node in the tree has only one parent.

An XML document can easily be read by a human being, especially if it is well laid out. The XML document shown in this appendix has each element on a new line and indentation is used to illustrate the nesting of elements. However, a valid XML document can be laid out in any way. At the extreme, there may be no new lines or spaces at all, although these documents are less easy for a human to read. An XML document is also machine-readable, providing the machine that is reading the document understands the tags.

In HTML, the tags are all standardised and included in a specification published by the World Wide Web Consortium (W3C); there is no equivalent standard for XML. The data enclosed by the <last-name> and </last-name> tags in our example could just as easily have been enclosed by <lastname> and </lastname> tags, <family-name> and </family-name> tags, or <surname> and </surname> tags (and no doubt you can think of other possible tags that could be used here). The number of possible tags that can be used in an XML document is, therefore, infinite; the definition of tags is uncontrolled.

The lack of standard tags for XML is a problem. XML provides a very effective way to transfer data but the XML structure to be used for that transfer of data has to be defined in the same way that a structure, or schema, has to be defined for a relational database. Both sending and receiving parties, be they machines or humans, have to use the same elements, with those elements specified with the same enclosing tags, and the meaning of the content of those elements being unambiguously defined. Without common element definitions data cannot be transferred. If XML is to be used within an enterprise or between enterprises there has to be the same commitment to data definition as would be needed for common database designs for the sharing of data between databases. The set of allowed elements needs to be defined and the structure, the way that elements can be nested within each other, also needs to be specified. For example, 'qualifications' can be within 'employee', 'qualification' can be within 'qualifications', and 'qualification-name' can be within 'qualification'. There have been a number of initiatives within particular industries to develop standard XML formats for the exchange of data between companies within that industry, but these initiatives are not co-ordinated. You can, therefore, end up with different formats for the same concept in different industries.

There are other problems with XML. First, it can generate documents that are very verbose to get over some quite simple data; this verbosity can inflate transmission and storage costs. Secondly, there are no datatypes in XML; everything is a character string. Thirdly, all XML structures are hierarchical in nature. This is a step backwards – hierarchical databases were replaced by network databases and then by relational databases because it is extremely difficult to represent the full complexity of data relationships using a hierarchical model alone. See Appendix B for an overview of hierarchical and network databases.

To document XML definitions and in an attempt to overcome some of these problems, the overall XML architecture includes a number of other components:

- Document Type Definition (DTD) is a specification of the rules a group of XML documents must follow to be valid; for example, the elements that are allowed within a document are specified. One problem with DTDs is that they are expressed in a language that is not XML.

- XML Schema Definition (XSD) is another way to specify the rules for a group of XML documents. An XSD is specified using an XML schema language and allows for more detailed constraints on a document's logical structure than can be achieved with a DTD.

- eXtensible Stylesheet Language (XSL) is the standard for describing presentation rules that apply to XML documents. The format of XML data can be converted into HTML so that it can be displayed using a web browser.

- XSL Transformations (XSLT) is a specification that describes how to transform XML documents from one format to another.

- XLink is a specification that describes how to define links between XML documents.

- XPointer is a specification that describes how to specify a particular element within a document as the target of a link.

- XPath makes it possible to refer to individual parts of an XML document to provide access to XML data from elsewhere.

- XQuery is a query language for XML. It is analogous to SQL in relational databases but it can only be used to read data, not to manipulate it. XQuery provides the ability to navigate, select, combine, transform, sort and aggregate XML data.

XML and Relational Databases

Introduction

As described in Chapter 12, the latest SQL standard includes a new part known as SQL/XML. This part introduces an **XML** datatype and facilities that provide for the composition of XML using data extracted from a relational database and, conversely, for the storage of data extracted from an XML document in a relational database. The **XML** datatype can be used in the same way as any other datatype, i.e. as a datatype for a column, as a variable or as a parameter for a function.

Representing data from a database as XML

The facilities that enable data to be extracted and then represented as XML offer a range of alternatives. The specimen data stored in the relational database tables shown in Figure H.1 are used to demonstrate these facilities.

department

name	telephone_number	managed_by
HQ	NULL	NULL
Finance	ext 452	CX137
Production	ext 664	CA446

employee

payroll_number	surname	forename	birth_date	start_date	department
AY334	Watson	Barbara	1952-12-06	1994-06-03	Finance
CX137	Rogers	Jenny	1970-01-10	1995-01-03	Finance
DJ777	Phillips	Henry	1974-05-05	1992-09-03	Finance
FJ678	Harrison	Roger	1988-04-27	2004-11-05	Finance

employee_qualification

payroll_number	name	award_date	expiry_date
CX137	Dip FM	1998-09	NULL
CX137	ACCA	2003-10-20	NULL
CX137	First Aid	2005-04-30	2008-04-29

FIGURE H.1   *Specimen data for XML representation examples*

One option is to output the complete contents of a table or a schema into a standard XML structure using a simple mapping. There are two possible approaches to this. The first of these approaches provides a structure that is a valid XML document. Figure H.2 shows the XML obtained when outputting the contents of the **employee** table using this approach.

```
<employee>
  <row>
     <payroll_ number>AY334</payroll_ number>
     <surname>Watson</surname>
     <forename>Barbara</forename>
     <birth_date>1952-12-06</birth_date>
     <start_date>1994-06-03</start_date>
     <department>Finance</department>
  </row>
  <row>
     <payroll_ number>CX137</payroll_ number>
     <surname>Rogers</surname>
     <forename>Jenny</forename>
     <birth_date>1970-01-10</birth_date>
     <start_date>1995-01-03</start_date>
     <department>Finance</department>
  </row>
  <row>
     <payroll_ number>DJ777</payroll_ number>
     <surname>Phillips</surname>
     <forename>Henry</forename>
     <birth_date>1974-05-05</birth_date>
     <start_date>1992-09-03</start_date>
     <department>Finance</department>
  </row>
  <row>
     <payroll_ number>FJ678</payroll_ number>
     <surname>Harrison</surname>
     <forename>Roger</forename>
     <birth_date>1988-04-27</birth_date>
     <start_date>2004-11-05</start_date>
     <department>Finance</department>
  </row>
</employee>
```

FIGURE H.2   *The employee table represented as a valid XML document*

The XML shown in Figure H.2 is a valid XML document because the XML is in the form of a true hierarchy, having a single root element. In this case the root element is called 'employee', the name being automatically derived from the name of table. There are a series of elements, called 'row', for each row in the table. Within each 'row' element there is an element for each column in the table, with the element name also being automatically derived from the column names.

The alternative approach provides XML elements without the root element. Figure H.3 shows the XML obtained when outputting the contents of the **employee** table using this alternative approach.

The XML shown in Figure H.3 has a series of elements, each named after the table name, with one element for each row of the table, but it lacks a root element. As before, within each row element there is an element for each column in the table, with the element name automatically derived from the column names. This output could be made into a valid XML document by simply adding a root element. This could be done automatically by the database management system.

It is also possible to create an XML document that contains data selected from one or more tables. This is achieved by using special SQL functions, known as XML publishing functions, within an SQL **SELECT** query. For example, the query shown in Figure H.4 can be used to produce the XML document similar to that shown in Figure H.5 (which is a copy of Figure G.3) from the data in Figure H.1.

```
<employee>
   <payroll_ number>AY334</payroll_ number>
   <surname>Watson</surname>
   <forename>Barbara</forename>
   <birth_date>1952-12-06</birth_date>
   <start_date>1994-06-03</start_date>
   <department>Finance</department>
</employee>
<employee>
   <payroll_ number>CX137</payroll_ number>
   <surname>Rogers</surname>
   <forename>Jenny</forename>
   <birth_date>1970-01-10</birth_date>
   <start_date>1995-01-03</start_date>
   <department>Finance</department>
</employee>
<employee>
   <payroll_ number>DJ777</payroll_ number>
   <surname>Phillips</surname>
   <forename>Henry</forename>
   <birth_date>1974-05-05</birth_date>
   <start_date>1992-09-03</start_date>
   <department>Finance</department>
</employee>
<employee>
   <payroll_ number>FJ678</payroll_ number>
   <surname>Harrison</surname>
   <forename>Roger</forename>
   <birth_date>1988-04-27</birth_date>
   <start_date>2004-11-05</start_date>
   <department>Finance</department>
</employee>
```

FIGURE H.3   *The employee table represented as XML without a root element*

```
SELECT
   XMLELEMENT(NAME department,
      XMLELEMENT(NAME department-name, d.name),
      XMLELEMENT(NAME department-telephone, d.telephone_number),
      XMLELEMENT(NAME department-manager, d.managed_by),
      XMLELEMENT(NAME department-staff,
         (SELECT
            XMLAGG(XMLELEMENT(NAME employee,
               XMLELEMENT(NAME staff-no, e.payroll_number),
               XMLELEMENT(NAME first-name, e.forename),
               XMLELEMENT(NAME last-name, e.surname),
               XMLELEMENT(NAME birth-date, e.birth_date),
               XMLELEMENT(NAME start-date, e.start_date),
               XMLELEMENT(NAME qualifications,
                  (SELECT
                     XMLAGG(XMLELEMENT(NAME qualification,
                        XMLFOREST(eq.name AS qualification-name,
                              eq.award_date AS qualification-award-date,
                              eq.expiry_date AS qualification-expiry-date)
                  FROM employee_qualification eq
                  WHERE e.payroll_number = eq.payroll_number)
         FROM employee e
         WHERE d.name = e.department))))))))
   AS department-details
FROM department d,
WHERE d.name = 'Finance';
```

FIGURE H.4   *An example SQL query to create an XML document*

The query uses the three publishing functions **XMLELEMENT**, **XMALGG** and **XMLFOREST**, all of which return XML structures of the **XML** datatype.

The **XMLELEMENT** function has two arguments. The first of these is the name that is to be given to the XML element that is produced and the second is the data that is to form that element. In Figure H.5 the first use of **XMLELEMENT**

```
<?xml version = "1.0"?>
<department>
  <department-name>Finance</department-name>
  <department-telephone>452</department-telephone>
  <department-manager>CX137</department-manager>
  <department-staff>
    <employee>
      <staff-no>AY334</staff-no>
      <first-name>Barbara</first-name>
      <last-name>Watson</last-name>
      <birth-date>12 June 1952</birth-date>
      <start-date>3 June 1994</start-date>
    </employee>
    <employee>
      <staff-no>CX137</staff-no>
      <first-name>Jenny</first-name>
      <last-name>Rogers</last-name>
      <birth-date>10 January 1970</birth-date>
      <start-date>3 January 1995</start-date>
      <qualifications>
        <qualification>
          <qualification-name>Dip FM</qualification-name>
          <qualification-award-date>September 1998</qualification-award-date>
        </qualification>
        <qualification>
          <qualification-name>ACCA</qualification-name>
          <qualification-award-date>2 October 2003</qualification-award-date>
        </qualification>
        <qualification>
          <qualification-name>First Aid</qualification-name>
          <qualification-award-date>30 April 2005</qualification-award-date>
          <qualification-expiry-date>29 April 2008</qualification-expiry-date>
        </qualification>
      </qualifications>
    </employee>
    <employee>
      <staff-no>DJ777</staff-no>
      <first-name>Henry</first-name>
      <last-name>Phillips</last-name>
      <birth-date>5 May 1974</birth-date>
      <start-date>3 September 1992</start-date>
    </employee>
    <employee>
      <staff-no>FL233</staff-no>
      <first-name>Jane</first-name>
      <last-name>Smith</last-name>
      <birth-date>25 August 1989</birth-date>
      <start-date>8 December 2006</start-date>
    </employee>
  </department-staff>
</department>
</xml>
```

FIGURE H.5   *An example of an XML document*

provides the department root element (the first argument is **NAME depart-ment**) and has as its second argument the specification of the hierarchy of elements that forms the rest of the document. The second use of **XMLELEMENT** provides the first element within the root element. This provides the name of the department (the first argument is **NAME department-name**) and has as its second argument the name of the column (**d.name**) from which the data is to be obtained. The second argument for the **XMLELEMENT** function can be any valid SQL expression, so it can even be an SQL **SELECT** sub-query. This is shown in the fifth use of the **XMLELEMENT** function.

The **XMALGG** function takes a single argument, the specification of an element, and returns XML that is a series of these elements. The 'department-staff' element is an aggregation of a number of 'employee' elements, where each employee has a 'staff-no', 'first-name', 'last-name', etc, and the 'quali-fications' element is an aggregation of a number of 'qualification' elements.

Each 'qualification' element is created using the **XMLFOREST** function. This function produces a 'forest' of elements (remember, an element is logic-ally a hierarchical 'tree' even if it only has one node) where each argu-ment specifies one of these elements. The 'qualification' element uses data from the **name** column, the **award_date** column and the **expiry_date** column of the **employee_qualification** table, but these are renamed as 'qualification-name', 'qualification-award-date' and 'qualification-expiry-date' respectively.

We have already seen that the XML values returned by the **XMLELEMENT**, **XMALGG** and **XMLFOREST** publishing functions are of the **XML** datatype. This is a datatype that is only known to the database management system. These val-ues can, however, be converted to character strings using another SQL/XML function, the **XMLSERIALISE** function.

Extracting relational data from an XML document

Just as there are a number of alternative approaches to the extraction of data from a relational database and publishing it as XML, there are also a number of approaches that can be used to take data from an XML document and place it in a relational database.

One approach is to use the concept of shredding, where the content of the XML document is decomposed and stored in tables created using the XML structure. For example, the XML document in Figure H.5 can be shredded back into the structure in Figure H.1 (although it yields only one row, the 'Finance' row, in the **department** table). Alternatively, an XML document can be shredded into a single table, known as an 'edge' table. Figure H.6 shows the edge table created from the document in Figure H.5. This edge table can then be used to populate other database tables.

There is also a function known as the **XMLTABLE** function. This function produces a virtual SQL table containing data derived from XML values. There are two arguments for this function. The first is the specification, expressed using XQuery, of the XML values that are used to provide the data for the virtual table. The second argument is a set of column definitions for the virtual table. The names of these columns may match the names of the relevant XML elements, in which case the column is automatically populated with data from that element. If the column names and the XML element names do not match then an XQuery expression has to be used to identify the source XML element for that column. Figure H.7 shows an example query using **XMLTABLE** and Figure H.8 shows the virtual table produced as a result of executing that query.

The data in this table can then be manipulated using SQL in the same way that the data in any other SQL table can be manipulated.

parent_id	child_id	node_name	content
null	1	department	null
1	2	department-name	Finance
1	3	department-telephone	452
1	4	department-manager	CX137
1	5	department-staff	null
5	6	employee	null
6	7	staff-no	AY334
6	8	first-name	Barbara
6	9	last-name	Watson
6	10	birth-date	12 June 1952
6	11	start-date	3 June 1994
5	12	employee	null
12	13	staff-no	CX137
12	14	first-name	Jenny
12	15	last-name	Rogers
12	16	birth-date	10 January 1970
12	17	start-date	3 January 1995
12	18	qualifications	null
18	19	qualification	null
19	20	qualification-name	Dip FM
19	21	qualification-award-date	September 1998
18	22	qualification	null
22	23	qualification-name	ACCA
22	24	qualification-award-date	2 October 2003
18	25	qualification	null
25	26	qualification-name	First Aid
25	27	qualification-award-date	30 April 2005
25	28	qualification-expiry-date	29 April 2008
5	29	employee	null
29	30	staff-no	DJ777
29	31	first-name	Henry
29	32	last-name	Phillips
29	33	birth-date	5 May 1974
29	34	start-date	3 September 1992
5	35	employee	null
35	36	staff-no	FL233
35	37	first-name	Jane
35	38	last-name	Smith
35	39	birth-date	25 August 1989
35	40	start-date	8 December 2006

FIGURE H.6   *An edge table created by shredding an XML document*

```
SELECT payroll_number, surname
FROM XMLTABLE (
   'doc("file:///C:/query/finance_department.xml")//department-staff'
   COLUMNS payroll_number CHAR(5) PATH 'employee/staff-no',
           surname VARCHAR(25) PATH 'employee/last-name',
           birth_date DATE PATH 'employee/birth-date')
WHERE birth_date < '1973-01-01';
```

FIGURE H.7   *A query on an XML document*

payroll_number	surname
AY334	Watson
CX137	Rogers

FIGURE H.8   *The result of the query on an XML document*

References

Barker, R. (1990) *CASE*METHOD: Entity Relationship Modelling.* Addison-Wesley, Reading, MA.

Butler Group (2004) *Data Quality and Integrity: Essential Steps for Exploiting Business Information.* Butler Direct Limited, Hull.

Central Computer and Telecommunications Agency (1994a) *Corporate Data Modelling.* HMSO, London.

Central Computer and Telecommunications Agency (1994b) *Data Management.* HMSO, London.

Chen, P.P.-S. (1976) The Entity–Relationship Model: Toward a Unified View of Data. *ACM Transactions on Database Systems*, 1:1, 9–36.

Codd, E.F. (1970) A Relational Model of Data for Large Shared Data Banks. *Communications of the ACM*, 13:6, 377–87.

Date, C.J. (2003) *An Introduction to Database Systems*, 8th Edition. Addison-Wesley, Reading, MA.

English, L.P. (2002) Total Quality data Management (TQdM) Methodology for Information Quality Improvement. In Piattini, M.G., Calero, C. and Genero, M.F. (eds), *Information and Database Quality*. Kluwer Academic Publishers, Boston, MA.

EPISTLE (European Process Industry STEP Technical Liaison Executive) (2003) *Developing High Quality Data Models* [online], www.matthew-west.org.uk/documents/princ03.pdf

Genero, M.F. and Piattini, M.G. (2002) Conceptual Model Quality. In Piattini, M.G., Calero, C. and Genero, M.F. (eds), *Information and Database Quality*. Kluwer Academic Publishers, Boston, MA.

Hay, D.C. (1996) *Data Model Patterns: Conventions of Thought.* Dorset House, New York, NY.

ISO/IEC 2382-1 (1993) *Information Technology – Vocabulary – Part 1: Fundamental terms.*

ISO/IEC 9075 (2003) *Information Technology – Database languages – SQL.*

ISO/IEC 13249-2 (2003) *Information Technology – Database languages – SQL Multimedia and application packages – Full-text.*

ISO/IEC 13249-3 (2003) *Information Technology – Database languages – SQL Multimedia and application packages – Spatial.*

ISO/IEC 13249-5 (2003) *Information Technology – Database languages – SQL Multimedia and application packages – Still image.*

Olson, J.E. (2003) *Data Quality: The Accuracy Dimension.* Morgan Kaufman, San Francisco, CA.

PricewaterhouseCoopers (2004) *Global Data Management Survey* [online], www.pwcglobal.com/images/gx/eng/about/svcs/grms/05-0187-A-Global-Data Mgmt-Survey.pdf

Reingruber, M. and Gregory, W.W. (1994) *The Data Modeling Handbook: A Best-Practice Approach to Building Quality Data Models.* Wiley-QED, New York, NY.

Further reading

The following books and publications provide useful further reading in addition to those listed in References:

Aiken, P., and Allen, M.D. (2004) *XML in Data Management*. Morgan Kaufman, San Francisco, CA.

Brackett, M.H. (1994) *Data Sharing Using a Common Data Architecture*. Wiley, New York, NY.

Cabinet Office e-Government Unit (2006) *e-Government Metadata Standard Version 3.1 29 August 2006* [online], www.govtalk.gov.uk/schemasstandards/metadata_document.asp?docnum=1017

Cabinet Office e-Government Unit Interoperability Framework (Continuing) *UK Government Data Standards Catalogue* [online], www.govtalk.gov.uk/gdsc/html/frames/default.htm

Cattell, R.G.C. and Barry, D.K.(eds), *The Object Data Standard: ODMG 3.3*. Morgan Kaufman, San Francisco, CA.

Central Computer and Telecommunications Agency (1995) *Data Management Standards*. HMSO, London.

Checkland, P. (1981) *Systems Thinking, Systems Practice*. John Wiley & Sons, Chichester.

Checkland, P. and Holwell, S. (1998) *Information, Systems and Information Systems: Making sense of the field*. John Wiley & Sons, Chichester.

Connelly, T.M. and Begg, C.E. (2004) *Database Systems: A Practical Approach to Design, Implementation and Management*, 4th edition. Addison Wesley, Harlow, England.

Date, C.J. (2001) *The Database Relational Model: A retrospective review and analysis*. Addison-Wesley, Reading, MA.

Date, C.J. (2005) *Database in Depth: Relational theory for practitioners*. O'Reilly, Sebastopol, CA.

Date, C.J. and Darwen, H (1997) *A Guide to the SQL Standard*, 4th edition. Addison-Wesley, Reading, MA.

Dick, K. (2000) *XML: A manager's guide*. Addison-Wesley, Reading, MA.

Hay, D.C. (2003) *Requirements Analysis: From business views to architecture*. Prentice Hall, Upper Saddle River, NJ.

ISO/IEC 9075 (2003) *Information Technology: Database languages*.

Melton, J. (2003) *Advanced SQL:1999: Understanding object-relational and other advanced features*. Morgan Kaufman, San Francisco, CA.

Melton, J. and Simon, A.R. (2002) *SQL:1999: Understanding relational language components*. Morgan Kaufman, San Francisco, CA.

Mullins, C.S. (2002) *Database Administration: The complete guide to practices and procedures*. Addison-Wesley, Boston, MA.

Simsion, G. and Witt, G. (2004) *Data Modeling Essentials*, 3rd edition. Morgan Kaufman, San Francisco, CA.

Sprague, R.A., Jnr. and McNurlin, B.C. (1993) *Information Systems Management and Practice*, 3rd edition. Prentice Hall, Eaglewood Cliffs, NJ.

Symons, C.R. and Tijsma, P. (1982) A Systematic and Practical Approach to the Definition of Data. *The Computer Journal*, 25:24.

Tozer, G. (1999) *Metadata Management for Information Control and Business Success*. Artech, Boston, MA.

Wilson, B. (1990) *Systems: Concepts, methodologies and applications*, 2nd Edition. John Wiley & Sons, Chichester.

Wilson, B. (2001) *Soft Systems Methodology: Conceptual model building and its contribution*. John Wiley & Sons, Chichester.

Index

The World Beyond Digital Rights Management
Jude Umeh

Digital content owners and commercial stakeholders face a constant battle to protect their intellectual property and commercial rights. Jude Umeh outlines the issues behind this battle, current solutions to the problem and looks to the future beyond digital rights management.

ISBN: 978-1-902505-87-9
Price: £34.95 Size: 246 x 172mm Paperback: 320pp
Published: Oct 2007 www.bcs.org/books/drm

IT Law An ISEB Foundation
Jon Fell (Editor)

IT professionals not only need to know the technology, they should be aware of how the law applies to the technology. This is a guide to the main aspects of law that an IT professional is most likely to come up against. A textbook for the 'ISEB Foundation Certificate in IT Law.'

ISBN: 978-1-902505-80-0
Price: £24.95 Size: 246 x 172mm Paperback: 320pp
Published: Oct 2007 www.bcs.org/books/isebITLaw

A Manager's Guide to IT Law
Jeremy Newton and Jeremy Holt (Editors)

This comprehensive guide to IT-related legal issues explains, in plain English, the most relevant legal frameworks, with examples from actual case law used to illustrate the most common problems. Including: IT contracts; systems procurement contracts; employment problems; instructing an IT consultant; intellectual property law; escrow; outsourcing; data protection.

ISBN: 978-1-902505-55-8
Price: £29.95 Size: 246 x 172mm Paperback: 180pp
Published: July 2004 www.bcs.org/books/itlaw

Data Protection & Compliance in Context
Stewart Room

This pragmatic guide provides practical advice on protecting data privacy under the Data Protection Act, human rights laws and freedom of information legislation; and gives a platform for building compliance strategies. Stewart Room, is the chair of the National Association of Data Protection and Freedom of Information Officers (NADPO).

ISBN: 978-1-902505-78-7
Price: £34.95 Size: 246 x 172mm Paperback: 304pp
Published: Oct 2006 www.bcs.org/books/dataprotection

Principles of Data Management
Facilitating Information Sharing
Keith Gordon

A practical guide to managing data – an increasingly valuble corporate asset in all organisations. Information is a key resource as important as equipment, assets, estate and capital. Invaluable for managing, marketing and IT directors and all business managers.

ISBN: 978-1-902505-84-8
Price: £29.95 Size 246 x 172 Paperback: 274pp
Published: Aug 2007 www.bcs.org/books/datamanagement

Practical Data Migration
John Morris

This guide contains techniques and strategies for ensuring data migration projects achieve maximum return on investment; ideas on rescuing ailing projects; and a model of best practice to be used for implementation of the methods. All blended with real life examples and clear definitions of commonly used jargon.

ISBN: 978-1-902505-71-8
Price: £29.95 Size: 246 x 172mm Paperback: 224pp
Published: May 2006 www.bcs.org/books/datamigration

World Class IT Service Delivery

Peter Wheatcroft

A manual on reaching and sustaining best practice in terms of performance, delivery and outlook in IT services to avoid customer dissatisfaction. Essential for IT service managers, IT directors, managers and procurement specialists.

ISBN: 978-1-902505-82-4
Price: £29.95 Size: 246 x 172 Paperback: 192pp
Published: May 2007 www.bcs.org/books/servicedelivery

Global Services
Moving to a Level Playing Field

Mark Kobayashi-Hillary and Dr Richard Sykes

Global Sourcing experts give an overview of how globalisation of the service industry is changing businesses and opening new opportunities to industries. A guide for managing, finance and IT directors and purchasing managers in all industries.

ISBN: 978-1-902505-83-1
Price: £29.95 Size: 246 x 172 Paperback: 192pp
Published: Apr 2007 www.bcs.org/books/globalservices

A Guide to Global Sourcing
Offshore outsourcing and other global delivery models

Elizabeth Anne Sparrow

The opportunities and obstacles associated with offshore outsourcing and other global delivery models. Country-by-country analysis of offshore services available.

ISBN: 978-1-902505-61-9
Price: £34.95 Size: 246 x 172mm Paperback: 196pp
Published: Nov 2004 www.bcs.org/books/globalsourcing

A Pragmatic Guide to
Business Process Modelling

Jon Holt

Explores all aspects of process modelling from process
analysis to process documentation by applying a standard
modelling notation, UML. Guidance for directors and
managers on business process modelling to improve
processes, productivity and profitability.

ISBN: 978-1-902505-66-4
Price: £29.95 Size: 246 x 172mm Paperback: 184pp
Published: Sept 2005 www.bcs.org/books/processmodelling

Business Process Management
A Rigorous Approach

Martyn A. Ould

A rigorous way of understanding the mass of concurrent,
collaborative activity that goes on within an organisation,
giving a solid basis for developing IT systems that
actually support a business' processes and improving
efficiency and profitability.

ISBN: 978-1-902505-60-2
Price: £34.95 Size: 246 x 172mm Paperback: 364pp
Published: Jan 2005 www.bcs.org/books/bpm

Business Analysis

Debra Paul and Donald Yeates (Editors)

A practical introductory guide for improving the effectiveness of IT
and its alignment with an organisation's business objectives.
Covers strategy analysis, modelling business systems/processes,
business case development, managing change, requirements
engineering and information resource management.

ISBN: 978-1-902505-70-1
Price: £29.95 Size: 246 x 172mm Paperback: 256pp
Published: Apr 2006 www.bcs.org/books/businessanalysis

Finance for IT Decision Makers
A practical handbook for buyers, sellers and managers (2nd Edition)

Michael Blackstaff

This covers aspects of finance relevant to professionals who make or influence decisions about IT. Written in plain language with practical examples, it explains: how to construct a financial case for IT projects; financing methods; current standards and legislation; cost/benefit analysis; investment evaluation methods; budgeting, costing and pricing; and more.

ISBN: 978-1-902505-73-2
Price: £34.95 Size: 246 x 172mm Paperback: 324pp
Published: July 2006 www.bcs.org/books/finance

Project Management in The Real World
Shortcuts to success

Elizabeth Harrin

This book provides a short cut to project management experience; it summarizes over 250 years of expertise from experienced project managers. It offers hints and tips on all aspects of project management including: managing project budgets; managing project scope; managing project teams; managing project plans; and managing yourself.

ISBN: 978-1-902505-81-7
Price: £24.95 Size: 246 x 172mm Paperback: 225pp
Published: Nov 2006 www.bcs.org/books/realworldPM

Project Management for IT-Related Projects
Textbook for the ISEB Foundation Certificate in IS Project Management

Bob Hughes (Editor)

The principles of IT-related project management, including project planning, monitoring and control, change management, risk management and communication between project stakeholders. Encompasses the entire syllabus of the 'ISEB Foundation Certificate in IS Project Management'.

ISBN: 978-1-902505-58-9
Price: £24.95 Size: 297 x 210mm Paperback: 148pp
Published: Aug 2004 www.bcs.org/books/projectmanagement

Software Testing An ISEB Foundation

Brian Hambling (Editor)

Providing a practical insight into the world of software testing, this book explains the basic steps of the testing process and how to perform effective tests. It supports the revised 'ISEB Foundation Certificate in Software Testing' and includes self-assessment exercises, worked examples and sample exam questions.

ISBN: 978-1-902505-79-4
Price: £24.95 Size: 246 x 172mm Paperback: 220pp
Published: Sept 2006 www.bcs.org/books/softwaretesting

Professional Issues in Information Technology

Frank Bott

This book explores the relationship between technological change, society and the law, and the powerful role that computers and computer professionals play in a technological society. Designed to accompany the BCS Professional Examination core Diploma module: 'Professional Issues in Information Systems Practice'.

ISBN: 978-1-902505-65-7
Price: £24.95 Size: 246 x 172mm Paperback: 248pp
Published: May 2005 www.bcs.org/books/professionalissues

Invisible Architecture
The benefits of aligning people, processes and technology

Jenny Ure & Gudrun Jaegersberg

The biggest problems faced in implementing computer systems, especially across different countries, are often not technical – they are 'socio-technical'. *Invisible Architecture* uses real examples to highlight the potential for harnessing 'soft' factors to competitive advantage.

ISBN: 978-1-902505-59-6
Price: £34.95 Size: 246 x 172mm Paperback: 104pp
Published: Mar 2005 www.bcs.org/books/invisiblearchitecture

BCS ORDER FORM

To order your book(s), please complete this form and send it to:
BCS Books, Turpin Distribution, Pegasus Drive, Stratton Business Park,
Biggleswade, Bedfordshire, SG18 8TQ, UK.
Fax: +44 (0)1767 601640 Tel: +44 (0)1767 604951
Enquiries to: Custserv@turpin-distribution.com
BCS Books are also available in all good bookshops.

	Price	Qty	BCS Member Price	Qty
The World Beyond Digital Rights Management	£34.95		£30	
IT Law: An ISEB Foundation	£24.95		£20	
A Manager's Guide to IT Law	£29.95		£20	
Data Protection and Compliance in Context	£34.95		£30	
Principles of Data Management	£29.95		£25	
Practical Data Migration	£29.95		£25	
World Class IT Service Delivery	£29.95		£20	
Global Services: Moving to a Level Playing Field	£29.95		£20	
A Guide To Global Sourcing	£34.95		£20	
A Pragmatic Guide to Business Process Modelling	£29.95		£25	
Business Process Management	£34.95		£30	
Business Analysis	£29.95		£20	
Finance for IT Decision Makers	£34.95		£25	
Project Management in the Real World	£24.95		£15	
Project Management for IT-Related Projects	£24.95		£15	
Software Testing	£24.95		£15	
Professional Issues in Information Technology	£24.95		£15	
Invisible Architecture	£34.95		£20	

P&P: UK £2.75 for the first book, plus 75p for any additional items.
Europe £5. Rest of world £12.

Postage: £ [   ]

Total: £ [   ]

Title: .... Initials: .... Surname: ....

Address: ....

BCS membership number (if applicable): ....

Telephone: .... Email: ....

I enclose a cheque ☐ made payable to 'The British Computer Society' or please charge my:

☐ Visa ☐ Mastercard ☐ Switch/Maestro ☐ American Express (please indicate)

Start date (Maestro/Switch only): .... Issue number (Maestro/Switch only): ....

Expiry date: .... Card number: ....

Name as it appears on card: ....

Signature: ....

*BooksUpdate service: please mark this box to receive occasional emails about new titles and
special offers on BCS publications (you can opt out from receiving these communications at any time).* ☐

Please note: Information is correct at the time of going to press. However it is subject to change without notice. MEM7-07